MORAY FIRTH
SHIPS AND TRADE

DURING THE NINETEENTH CENTURY

by

Ian Hustwick

SCOTTISH CULTURAL PRESS

This book is dedicated to my wife Patricia

First published 1994
Scottish Cultural Press
PO Box 106
Aberdeen AB9 8ZE
Tel/Fax: 0224 583777

Text © 1994 Ian Hustwick
Original line drawings © 1994 Sheena Bowman

British Library Cataloguing in Publication Data
A catalogue record for this book is available
from the British Library

ISBN: 1 898218 05 6

BaS3

Printed by BPC-AUP Aberdeen

CONTENTS

FIGURES

TABLES

FOREWORD

The Moray Firth forms a triangle with Inverness at its apex, and a base formed by a line running from Kinnaird Head to Duncansby Head. This area includes the rocky coasts of Caithness and Banffshire and the sandy beaches between Loch Fleet and the River Spey – a wide variety of coastline with unique features essential for the development of maritime trade in the Firth. The ports of Wick, Helmsdale and Fraserburgh have not been included in this volume because the trade of these ports was very largely confined to the processing and export of herring. The development of the herring trade and its markets on the Continent is complex and has been examined in other publications. It is mentioned in this volume only as it affected some of the Moray Firth ports.

During the seventeenth and eighteenth centuries ships were built in the Firth at Inverness, Garmouth, and Findhorn, but these were mainly small vessels up to 30-40 tons, and it was not until the Glenmore Company brought shipwrights up from England capable of constructing much larger vessels that ships of 300-500 tons were built. These shipwrights trained the local men in their skills, and as a result these men set up in business on their own account in Kingston and in other ports around the Firth. It is they who founded the shipbuilding industry which exists to this day. The ships which they built and manned were essential for trade within the boundaries of the Firth and for trading to and from Europe during that period. Speymouth is examined in detail because of its history and the number and size of ships launched in the 100 years of its existence as a shipbuilding centre. However, the situation there did not differ from any other shipbuilding centre, such as Inverness, Cullen or Findhorn, except in the numbers of ships built.

The men who owned the ships, either in whole or in part, were the inhabitants of the seaports and the majority were people with maritime interests. They were engaged in a variety of trades, although it is notable that these did not include the landowning classes who, because of its high loss rate, would not invest capital in what can only be described as a high risk venture. The men who manned the ships in whatever capacity were also local men, although not always from the port in which the vessel was registered. There was a large seafaring element amongst the inhabitants of the Firth and young men moved frequently between ships, gaining experience which would eventually lead to command.

The geography of the Firth has several unique features:

> . . . a set of major sand and shingle forelands, including substantial areas of raised beaches in the area between Loch Fleet and the westward side of the Spey . . . The area to the east of the Spey is also predominantly rocky in character with a series of small bays and coves. Each of the individual bay-head units is small and separated from its neighbour by headlands and relatively deep water. J S Smith (Proc.R.Soc.Edinburgh, 1986)

It was these features, together with the shelter afforded by the river mouths of the Ness, Findhorn, Spey, and Deveron, that provided natural harbours for the merchants of towns on the southern part of the Firth, enabling them, with their increasing merchant fleet, to develop trade with the rest of Britain and the Continent during the nineteenth century.

Much of this book is about ships and trade and, indeed, that was the initial objective. However, whilst investigating the type of ships and the voyages which they made to Russia, the Black Sea, Africa, China, America, and Australia, I became aware that it was not the ships but the shipbuilders and seamen to whom tribute should be paid. The men and their ships traded with Europe, and latterly with the rest of the world, achieving success with small ships and basic navigational aids in the face of great natural difficulties. Their trading activities, along with the ships that they built and manned, form part of the maritime heritage of Scotland and I trust that this volume will serve as a record of their achievements.

Ian Hustwick
Aberdeen
August 1994

ACKNOWLEDGEMENTS

In 1990. deciding to fill in some gaps in the family tree. I needed to ascertain which of my ancestors were shipmasters, what ships they sailed on and the trade undertaken by these ships. The answers to these questions lay in many diverse places such as the Scottish Record Office, the National Maritime Museum, Elgin Public Library, and the Aberdeen Maritime Museum. The search provided an excellent reason for visiting all the harbours of the Moray Firth.

The truth of the old Scots saying 'If ye danna spier ye'll nivir fin oot' was well proven in my search and I wish to thank the many people who were 'spiered at' and who so willingly provided me with the information I sought. I trust that if they read this book they will consider their efforts to have been justified.

I particularly wish to acknowledge the help given by the following:- Mr Lawrence Brander and Mr George Innes, for providing access to the Ledgers of the *Highlander* and the *Orient*; Mr Peter Fitzgerald, Science Museum London, for advice and access to the Geddie collection of ship plans; to the staff of the Scottish Record Office, in particular Mrs Margaret McBryde and Miss Jane Brown, for their courteous attention to my many requests for access to the archives in their care; Mr James Henderson for filling in so many gaps in my knowledge of nineteenth century sailing ships; Mr Edwards, curator of Aberdeen Maritime Museum, for access to museum records; Dr John Smith, Department of Geography, University of Aberdeen, for supplying many sources of information; Mr James Skelton, Garmouth, who provided details of Speymouth ships and information on Kingston; Mr Harry S M Taylor, Edinburgh, for providing a considerable amount of information on Moray Firth ships; Miss Hilary Lamont, Elgin, for providing access to the Ledgers of the *Express* and the *Caledonia*; Mr David Alston, Curator. Cromarty Court House, for access to his manuscript 'The Burgh of Cromarty'; Mr William More, Harbour Master, Burghead, for providing access to the harbour registers for 1861-1893.

Special tribute must be paid to the services provided by two libraries: the Queen Mother Library of Aberdeen University and the Local Studies section of Elgin Public Library – I spent many happy hours delving into their records. The quality and range of information available was magnificent, and my many requests for information were met with courtesy and efficiency. I wish to acknowledge particularly the assistance given by Mrs J Beavan, of the Queen Mother Library, and Mr Mike Seton and Mr Graeme Wilson of Elgin Public Library.

A considerable amount of information and assistance was provided by Dr Iredale, District Archivist, and Mr Barret, Assistant Archivist, Moray District Council; Mrs Cluer, Archivist, Grampian Regional Council; Miss Isabella Deans of the Local Studies Section of Aberdeen Central Libraries; and the late Mr James Wood, whose many articles on the maritime history of Speymouth were a valuable source of information.

I wish to pay tribute to Mrs Sheena Bowman for her excellent work on the cover of this book and for providing various illustrations, including the rigs of ships; and I am also very grateful to Mr George Bain, Mr George Innes and Mr Ian Rennie who read the entire text, making many suggestions.

My apologies and thanks to Miss Fiona Bain who had the task of translating my handwriting into a very presentable manuscript in record time.

Thanks are also due to the following:- Mrs Barbara Geddes, Elgin; Mrs Patricia Bingham, Garmouth; Mr Ellen, Curator at Nairn Fishery Museum; Mr Ronald Gordon, Nairn; Mr Mathew Shand, Nairn; Mr James Slater, Portsoy; Mr J McWilliam, Portsoy; Mr and Mrs C Hood, London; Mr Feggans, Customs and Excise, Inverness; Mr Anderson, Customs and Excise, Aberdeen; Mr R Clunas, Inverness; Mr James Bell, Dornoch;

In closing, I wish to acknowledge the information and inspiration provided by my father, the late Mr William Hustwick, which led to this book being written. His detailed work on the family tree and his notes on Kingston and Garmouth which were written for his grandson (my son) many years ago formed the basis for my research.

I am also grateful for the financial assistance towards publication provided by Moray District Council and Aberdeenshire Educational Trust.

The author acknowledges assistance from a Glenfiddich Living Scotland Award towards his research.

MORAY FIRTH
SHIPS AND TRADE

DURING THE NINETEENTH CENTURY

1 SHIPBUILDING

Introduction

When one visits the villages of Kingston and Garmouth in the parish of Speymouth, it is hard to envisage that for a considerable part of the nineteenth century these were busy ports and a major centre for shipbuilding. The shipyards produced more tonnage than the rest of the Moray Firth ports, and their merchants traded with China, Africa and Australia as well the Mediterranean and the Baltic. The ships they launched may have been smaller than those being built in Aberdeen, but the quality of the seamen who sailed in them and the men who owned and managed them was as good as any in Scotland.

The mouth of the Spey was not an ideal place to construct a shipyard 200 years ago. The river was subject to severe floods and frequently changed its course, making it difficult to choose a suitable site for building and launching ships. In addition, there was no skilled labour available locally and shipwrights and other tradesmen had to be brought in and provided with housing. The Spey, however, regardless of its faults, was one of the reasons why a shipbuilding industry developed at the mouth of the river. Roads and the means of moving heavy baulks of timber were non-existent in these early days; the river was, and had been for a considerable time, the only effective means of transporting felled tree trunks to Garmouth.

The forests of upper Strathspey comprised mainly of Scots Pine of very large girth and the timber they produced was of a quality and size which was eminently suitable for the building of ships – in addition it was both plentiful and cheap. At that time Britain was a major industrial power with considerable overseas possessions, requiring a large merchant fleet to transport goods to and from its colonies, and a navy to protect its lines of communications. These conditions meant that there was a considerable demand for ships and the timbers required to build them. Garmouth had long been noted as a port that supplied timber and, when the demand for ships increased, it was a natural choice as a site for a shipyard because of this resource. If there were difficulties due to the river and the lack of skilled labour, these would be overcome.

The shipyards constructed and built many large ships, so local men trained as shipwrights and eventually became established as shipbuilders. Supplies of large trees from Strathspey soon became exhausted, but the shipyards remained because they were effective in meeting the needs of local merchants engaged in maritime trade. By the early part of the nineteenth century the shortage of local timber was not a problem, as adequate supplies of good quality timber were available from the Baltic and North America.

The Speymouth shipyards developed because they had a plentiful and cheap source of raw material – wood. They died because, in the latter part of the century, it was more economical to operate ships built of iron – a material not available in the north of Scotland – which were larger than the ships which could be built in local yards. During their 100 years of existence the yards produced more than 600 ships, some of which were in operation well into this century. They deserve a place in the ship building annals of this country.

KINGSTON AND GARMOUTH

Apart from one claim in the *Banffshire Journal* that ships for the Scottish Navy were built at the mouth of the Spey, there is no mention in any of the books dealing with the history of the parish of Speymouth in the eighteenth century of ship building being carried out there prior to 1786. The only evidence to support the view that vessels were constructed prior to that date are the graves in Essil Churchyard of:–

Alex Winster, Ship Carpenter at Spey.	died 1676
Richard Winster, Ship Carpenter, Garmouth.	died 1696
Wm. Terras, Ship Carpenter.	died 1805 aged 75

The area at the mouth of the Spey was well suited for building ships as there was sheltered water, adequate ground for laying keels, and a plentiful supply of suitable timber. The maps of the eighteenth century show the existence of a sawmill in Garmouth where timber was converted for building as well as for export. It is likely that ships were built in the area by shipbuilders from the south of Scotland and England, bringing in skilled men who left when the ship had been completed. The first record of ships being built at the mouth of the Spey was by Dodsworth and Osbourne, who formed the Glenmore Company or The Hull Company as it was sometimes called. This information is taken from the Old Statistical Account (OSA) which also lists the names of 19 ships built between 1786 and 1789:

I am informed that, subsequent to 1793, they built twenty-four vessels, two of which were upwards of 750 tons register burthen; two of nearly 600 tons; the rest from 50 to 500 tons. Several other shipbuilders have during that time built 16 vessels, measuring from 29 to 200 tons; of these Mr W Geddie built 43, and he still carries on the business successfully. All these vessels were built of highland natural grown fir timber, and have been found to last as long as many vessels built of oak; and are insured at Lloyds and by the other sea insurance companies on equal terms with vessels built of oak. The four large vessels above mentioned were long employed by government in transport service; and two of them were afterwards engaged by the East India Company in the India and China trade.

When Ralph Dodsworth and William Osbourne – timber merchants in Hull – purchased Glenmore Forest from the Duke of Gordon and commenced building ships in 1786, they brought about two significant changes. The first was in the scale of the timber operations and the second was the introduction of shipwrights capable of building large ships. There had been timber extraction by the York Building Company in the 1730s. However the scale of the timber felling from 1786 onwards by the Glenmore Company was considerable, and must have been one of the first major timber felling operations in northern Scotland. The extraction of timber from the forests of upper Speyside had been a developed industry during the eighteenth century, long before Dodsworth and Osbourne set up their operations in Kingston. Felling of the massive trees and their transportation to the banks of the Spey must have been a very difficult business, given the nature of the ground. Once the trees were on the river bank, the task of floating them down river was undertaken by men known as 'floaters', who had been doing this work for generations. It was dangerous work, and the old Parish Record of Speymouth for 1732 records the deaths of two men who were swept out to sea whilst floating timber down the River Spey. The best description of how these men transported the timber is given by the Rev George Birnie:-

When sawmills were constructed at Kingston most of the wood was floated, in the earlier days, in single logs and spars sometimes to the number of 20,000 at a time when there was a big spate, while men to the number of from fifty to eighty on either side of the river, with long poles, pushed out the logs when they threatened to stick on the banks. These men received 1s 2d a day, together with what was termed 'a competent allowance of spirituous liquor.' But despite the fact that men were stationed at the mouth of the river to hook the timber into calm water as it arrived, much of it drifted to sea and was lost, so this method was abandoned and the logs built into rafts, each of which were steered by two floaters, who received 30s per raft.

Not only had the floater to have in mind a perfect chart of all hidden rocks and shoals, but also, when logs were floating singly, he required great presence of mind and deftness in the use of the pole with its hook arrangement, by which he could push or pull an unruly log when it stuck on the bank and formed an obstruction that would speedily cause an inextricable accumulation of the timber that followed. Against dry weather the lochs far up in the forest were dammed by high embankments with large sluices that could be unlocked in the night so that the flood was timed to reach the logs along the banks of the stream in the early morning when the floaters were ready to attend to them . . . As soon as the logs reached the Spey they were taken in hand by the Spey floaters and formed into rafts. This was done by boring a hole in each end of the log and driving in iron plugs with eyes through which strong withes or wattles were passed, thus binding together the requisite number of logs. On the top of the raft a platform of deals was built which formed a flooring for the floaters to stand upon. Two roughly made oars or gears as they were called completed the equipment of the raft. When the raft was set afloat, the two steersmen took their posts at either end, each armed with a gear which he inserted between two stout pegs in rowlock fashion. The two gears gave great steering power to the floaters by acting in concert as helms fore and aft. Expert floatsmen believed in making the current as far as possible do the steering by keeping the raft in deep water. There was a temptation to make a too vigorous use of these improvised helms especially at the sharp bends where the current in most cases kept the raft in position. When it consisted of masts fifty or sixty feet long there was a risk of turning them lengthways across the stream with serious results. *Proc.London Moray Club, 1932*

Timber was also transported overland but, as the only bridge was at Fochabers, the horses and carts had a considerable journey over poor quality roads before reaching Kingston. It became obvious that if a bridge were built at Craigellachie, the timber would have a much shorter distance to travel to the coast and the Commission for Highland Roads and Bridges agreed to fund part of the cost if the local lairds would make up the balance. Needless to say the lairds were not eager to make a contribution to a project which gave them no profit, and the Government eventually agreed to pay the difference. Governments are never very eager to spend money which in their opinion should come from private sources, but there was a very good reason why the purse strings should have been loosened. In 1810 Napoleon, as a result of his successful campaigns on the Continent, restricted the supply of timber suitable for shipbuilding from the Baltic. The Royal Navy at this time was scouring the world for supplies of timber for masts and spars, and the timber resources of Speyside were of considerable value due to the quality of timber and its availability. The new bridge was designed and built in Wales from cast iron, constructed in pieces suitable for transport by sea, and was erected in 1814. Apparently the Glenmore Company was responsible for transporting individual parts of the bridge from Kingston to its present site.

Rothiemurchus Forest was composed of Scots Pine, or Fir as it was known at that time – a timber of the same genus as Baltic Redwood. As the climate in the north of Scotland was the same as many of the Baltic countries, the timber displayed the same characteristics – hard and resinous. Fir was particularly suitable for use as masts and spars because of its high resin content – it had the essential quality of supple resilience.

Timber was a major export from Garmouth, as it was used by the naval yards at Woolwich and Deptford and by shipyards in Hull. One of the merchants for importing Spey timber would have been William Osbourne. In the 1780s there was a considerable demand for timber for both naval and merchant ship construction and every available source of suitable timber both at home and abroad was used. The cost of building ships increased considerably, and this would have made the Englishmen consider investing in a forest with which they were familiar and which produced timber at low cost.

The second change brought about by the Glenmore Company was achieved by bringing up from England shipwrights capable of constructing large ships. The Scots shipwrights may well have been able to build small ships of 30-40 tons, but different techniques were required in order to construct ships of 300-500 tons, and the incomers had the necessary skills to do this. It was these craftsmen who built the larger ships, and in so doing taught the Scots so that they, in turn, would be able to construct ships not only in Speymouth but elsewhere in the Firth.

The original shipyard was built by Dunfermline House on land close by the Spey, but the river had one of her periodic spates and shifted her bed eastward, causing a problem of how to get ships launched. Not to be outdone, the company built a canal from the shipyard to the river, launched the ships into that and floated them down to the river. It was this attitude to the problems of building ships that ensured the standing of the English company in the eyes of the native Scots. The Glenmore Company spent £10,000 in purchasing the forest of Glenmore – a very large sum in those days – initiated large scale timber extraction, and improved the method of transporting timber down the Spey to Kingston by clearing the river bed. They were also instrumental in getting the Craigellachie Bridge built in order that timber could be brought to Speymouth by an overland route. According to newspapers the company had a reputation for fair dealing and reimbursing suppliers without delay. In addition they built larger ships than had ever been seen on the Moray Firth, many of which were capable of sailing round the world.

Osbourne was a timber merchant and ship owner and did not have the necessary skills to build ships. He did however have a cousin, Thomas Hustwick, who was a shipwright working in Dover. According to newspaper reports he was appointed Marine Superintendent, although it is doubtful if such a term was in use in those early days. Thomas, together with his wife, came North in 1786 and was soon building the first shipyard beside Dunfermline House, then a single story stone structure in what is now Kingston. What his wife, who came from London, must have thought of coming to live in a converted salmon store, during a Scottish winter and spring, amongst people whose speech would have been totally different to that spoken in her native city can only be speculated upon. She survived very well, however, and bore her husband four children. Thomas became well acclimatised and is on record as enjoying the local whisky on the festive occasion following the launch of a ship. A community grew up round Dunfermline House, as more shipbuilders and sawyers came to work in the new shipyard and in the other yards which were built nearby, and the community was called Kingston after Thomas Hustwick's birthplace (Kingston upon Hull). A newspaper report of a ship launch is given below:-

GARMOUTH, April 21, 1795: Notwithſtanding the aſſertion of a celebrated author ſome years ago, that no trees grow in Scotland, is muſt give pleaſure to every real friend and lover of his country to hear, that there are trees, even in this north country, fit for building ſhips of very conſiderable burthen. Yeſterday, a very fine veſſel of 700 tons was launched at Kingſton Port, on the mouth of Spey, in the neighourhood of this place, conſtructed wholly of Fir Wood from the Duke of Gordon's Foreſt, by the Engliſh Glenmore Company; who, for ſome years paſt, have built ſeveral exceeding fine veſſels of the ſame wood, both for their own uſe and for ſale, which have given the greateſt ſatisfaction. This being the largeſt ſhip that ever was built here, or perhaps any where in Scotland to the northward of Leith, the owners had agreed that it ſhould be called THE DUKE; But on its being launched, and the ceremony of naming it juſt about to be performed, the Duke of Gordon, who was preſent, begged he might be allowed to change the name to that of THE PRINCESS OF WALES; this was inſtantly complied with, amidſt the approbation of a great concourſe of ſpectators, who gave his Grace much credit for the propoſal – and it was the general wiſh that, as this was probably the firſt veſſel that had the honour of being a Name-daughter to the Princeſs of Wales, it might prove auſpicious; that her Royal Highneſs might become the Protectreſs of commerce, and, during the courſe of a long and happy life, might ſee it promoted by numerous ſucceſſion of ſuch name daughters. (*Aberdeen Journal* 28 April 1795)

With the exception of vessels built for Osbourne and other English owners, the ships built at Speymouth were small, because the cargoes they were required to carry were minute by present day standards, and it was not until the Industrial Revolution in the latter part of the eighteenth century that there was large scale production of commercial goods. Coal, timber and herring were the bulk cargoes, but their transport was limited as the loading and discharging of these cargoes was carried out by manual labour, when the ship was lying on her side on a beach in a position which made the task very difficult. As the demand for goods of all types increased, so did the size of vessels and the pressure for harbours to be constructed. Work of this nature was costly and was provided initially by local landowners, Town Councils and, in some instances, the Commission for Highland Roads and Bridges.

The second period in ship building at Speymouth began with the closure of the Glenmore Yard and a slump following the end of the very costly Napoleonic War. The closure did not mean that ship building ceased in Speymouth. The Company had trained many shipwrights, and the period up to the end of the 1840s saw twelve yards in operation at different times and between them they produced some 120 ships. They were not large ships, mainly between 50-100 tons, a size which was common at that time in European waters and eminently suitable for the growing coastal and Baltic trade. Their hull design had been used for at least 80 years and the only development was the general acceptance of the schooner rig.

Reflecting the demand for ships to carry goods and raw materials to and from Britain and her overseas possessions, and also the considerable traffic around the country's coastline, 193 ships were recorded as being built by the Speymouth yards in the period 1816-50 (see Table 1.3b). Without an adequate road system, Britain was dependant upon a large number of ships to transport goods. The extent of the trade can be determined by the record of ship movements in 1844. In that year 123,557 ships, with a total tonnage of 9,619,829 cleared out of British ports. These movements, taken from Lloyds Register of Shipping for that year, would only be a record of ships clearing from major ports, and would not take account of ships leaving from smaller ports and the many beaches which were used to load and discharge cargoes.

	1831-40	1841-50	1851-60	1861-70
Total Tonnage	4,395	6,427	10,542	17,528
Number of Ships	59	77	95	103
Average Tonnage	74	83	111	170

Table 1.1: Average tonnage of ships constructed in Speymouth 1831-70

The third and most productive period of ship building started in the 1850s and continued for the next 25 years. About 280 ships were built during this period, many of which were in excess of 200 tons. Records of shipbuilders Alexander Hall & Sons (Aberdeen) show that during the 1850s and 1860s many of these vessels were larger (500-800 tons) than those constructed at Speymouth. It is noteworthy, however, that Halls were also building vessels of 150, 200 and 300 tons showing that there was still a demand for smaller ships at that time.

The trend towards constructing larger vessels by local owners had been evident for some time, and this is shown in Table 1.1. These were built for local ship owners in order to meet the requirements of trade in British coastal waters and the Baltic. The average size of vessel being constructed in yards to the south of the Firth was much larger, because ship owners required vessels capable of taking bulk cargoes as far afield as Australia, China and Africa. These owners could also obtain the capital required to build these large and therefore more expensive ships.

These large vessels required better methods of construction and the use of stronger timbers – capable of withstanding stress – such as pitch pine, oak, and elm. Much of the timber had to be imported from North America and the Baltic. However, Lloyds Survey records of ships under construction show that local timber was still used.

Local timber merchants would have had to maintain large stocks of these timbers, tying up large amounts of capital in order to meet the requirements of local builders. Demand for timber must have been considerable at certain times. The *Banffshire Journal* (1856) records that the number of vessels on the stocks of various builders were as follows:-

Duncan	5
Young	2
Hay	1
Geddie	4
Badenoch & Young	2

An exceptional period perhaps, but records show that between 1852 and 1870, yards were each building on average two ships a year.

From 1850 to 1880 the number of yards did not vary much, with some builders ceasing production and others taking their place. Four firms, however, continued to build ships for 30 years, albeit with sons succeeding fathers during that period.

The decade which commenced in 1880 saw the demand for larger ships built of iron, and later steel, increase because of their lower cost and greater cargo-carrying capacity. This resulted in the Speymouth yards experiencing a marked decline in orders, a position that was not confined to the Moray Firth. The remaining shipbuilders were Geddie, Duncan and Kinloch who built some ships as speculative ventures, and newspaper records show that the first two had vessels lying in the stocks for two years before they were sold. Eighteen ships were built during this period with the last Findhorn-owned ship, the *Janet Storm*, being built in 1890. She was a 113 ton schooner and in a way it was fitting that the last vessel to be build in Kingston was engaged in the coasting trade, like so many of her predecessors. She sank off the Bell Rock in 1892 with the loss of all her crew.

As the demand for ships fell, the younger shipwrights, carpenters and other skilled tradesmen in Garmouth and Kingston moved to other ship building centres, both in Britain and abroad. Garmouth and Kingston's only connection with the sea was with shipmasters and seamen, who formed a significant portion of the population of the two villages.

	IRON & STEEL		TIMBER	
	1881	**1888**	**1881**	**1888**
Tonn. of ships launched	483,882	366,600	18,159	8,762
Number of ships	388	262	273	170
Average tonnage	1,247	1399	67	52

Table 1.2: Decline in the use of wood for shipbuilding, 1881 & 1888
(source: Lloyds Register)

THE SPEY

Garmouth's position as a trading port and Kingston's as a shipbuilding centre were considerably affected by the behaviour of the Spey at its mouth. This was mainly due to the rapid fall in the river over the last few miles of its course.

The mouth of the Spey alters more rapidly from year to year than almost any other section of the coastline of Britain. The steep lower course of the river, below Fochabers, runs over a gravel fan which is bounded on either side by a number of shingle ridges extending west from Portgordon. The older ridges were probably formed when the sea stood higher than now; the latest ones nearer the sea are lower, and the most recent extends from Tugnet across the mouth of the river and deflects its flow towards Kingston . . . Except for the growth of sand-dunes opposite Lossiemouth this western end of Spey Bay has altered little in living memory, but the position of the mouth of the Spey has fluctuated violently throughout the last two centuries . . . Vessels of 350 tons burden were able to enter the Spey at the end of the eighteenth century, and ships were built at Garmouth and Kingston until about 1875. But the shifting waterway was a constant source of trouble and expense. Much money was spent in stopping up a mouth which threatened to carry off the houses at Tugnet and a few years later in 1815 attempts to protect the bank at Kingston cost about £300. At this time the mouth of the river was little more than twenty yards wide. Then, in August 1829, the river came down in spate: the water rose 13 feet 9 inches above the ordinary level at Kingston, and a breach 400 yards wide, was made in the shingle at the mouth of the river. Six years later an admiralty survey was made which shows the river channel in more or less its present position. In the interval, the shingle spit at the mouth has run through three circles of evolution. A T Grove, *Scottish Geographical Magazine* 71 (1955)

Maps of the mouth of the Spey for 1725, 1835, 1857, 1870 and 1903, (Fig 1.2), show where the changes have been and, since the article was written, the river has endeavoured to change its course more than once. The movement of gravel down the river, and the westerly drift of sand and gravel along the firth, created a bar at the river mouth, limiting the movement of ships.

The sites of the early Kingston yards would have altered as the river moved in a northerly and then a north-westerly direction. No doubt when the site of the first shipyard was built by Dunfermline House, it had been close to the river bank.

Fig 1.1: Shipbuilder's yard, Prince Edward Island, Canada
(Mr James Henderson, Aberdeen)

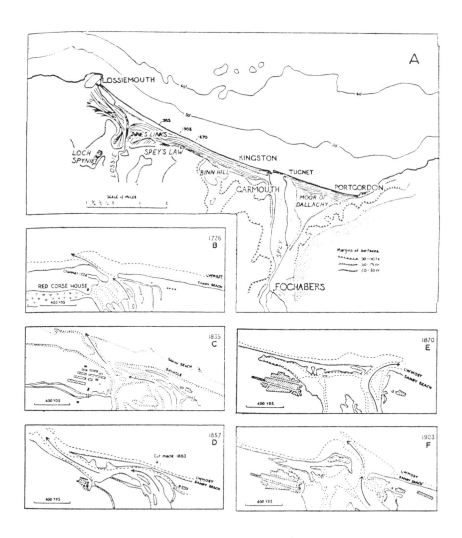

Fig. 1.2: Spey Bay and the mouth of the River Spey - insets B-F indicate positions of the river outlet from 1726 to 1903 *(Scottish Geog.Mag. 1955 (17)*

SHIPBUILDERS

Using the information extracted from the shipping registers for Banff, Inverness, Peterhead, Hull, Lloyds Register, local directories and census records, a list of shipbuilders has been compiled which shows the periods in which they operated (Table 1.3a) and the numbers of ships which they built (Table 1.3b). As will be seen from the records of ships built in Speymouth (Appendix B), the number of ships ascribed to individual builders for the period up to 1850 could be increased considerably, as only 72 percent of ships on the list show the name of the builder. Lloyds Register did not show the names of builders until the 1860s, and the only sources for information on the names of shipbuilders prior to that year are the Customs Register of Shipping and local newspapers of the period. It is reasonable to assume that the Speymouth yards built ships before 1860 which were registered in other ports, for local vessels traded round coastal Britain and their qualities would have been well known.

The record of shipbuilders in the eighteenth century is also incomplete as there are references in the *Aberdeen Journal* of the period to builders launching unnamed ships. As they were small ships and perhaps of poor quality they may not have been considered worthy of inclusion in Lloyds register by the owner.

The entries in Russels and Blacks directories for Garmouth and Kingston give the names of three shipbuilders whose names do not appear in either Lloyds or the shipping registers. These builders are Anderson & Young, Badenoch & Stewart, and Geddie & Young. One possible reason for these omissions may be that one person in each of these partnerships was merely providing capital, and the ships that they built would have been recorded against the name of the builder: Geddie, Young, or Stewart.

LOCATION OF SHIPYARDS

The first known shipyard in Speymouth was that of the Glenmore Company which was situated, according to a 1788 map, immediately to the east of Dunfermline House, and in the period up to 1815 yards occupied by Leslie, Winchester and Geddie were also situated in that vicinity.

The Spey rose 17 feet during the 'Muckle Spate' of 1829, causing considerable loss of livestock and damage to farmland and bridges. It was a disaster for Kingston as a spit of land on which a dozen houses were built to the south east of Dunfermline House was swept away and the river mouth was considerably widened, with the result that the old harbour at Garmouth became unsafe for ships. The river altered its course in later years but its unpredictability made any question of investment in port development an unrealistic proposition. Sir Dick Lauder's account of the Moray Flood describes the impact on Garmouth and Kingston and mentions that the *Barbara & Ann*, a Kingston-owned vessel, was swept from her moorings together with two other ships and driven on to the beach.

The course of the Spey was changed. It now flowed to the north of Kingston and yards were resited in order to launch ships in the most convenient position. Yards in those days consisted solely of a hard base for the keel, and ships were constructed in the open without shelter from the elements. The early shipwrights drew lines for the ribs on the sand or earth.

Builder	Estimated Period as Shipbuilders	Recorded Number of Ships Built
Dodsworth & Osbourne/Glenmore Coy	1785-1815	47
Wm Geddie (G♦), Jas Geddie (G), Wm Geddie (K♦), Jas Geddie (K), Alex Geddie, John Geddie	1802-1890	147
John Duncan, James Duncan & Joseph Duncan	1837-1884	91
Wm Kinloch	1865-1888	40
Alex Spence	1866-1878	17
Alex Young	1842-1866	14
Alex Hay	1839-1871	13
A Leslie	1786-1844	26
Winchester	1804-1830	10
Proctor	1819-1828	6
Anderson	1817-1835	3
Badenoch & Young	1836-1855	3
Logie	1802-1816	2
Simpson & Geddie	1802-1813	3
Falconer	1803	1
Robertson	1803	2
Palmer	1838	1
Hustwick	1841	1
Young Bros	1841	1
Stewart	1861	3
Lee	1872-1877	4
Anderson	1883-1889	3
Demster	1802-1814	3
Skelton	1810	1

(♦ G: Garmouth; K: Kingston)

Table 1.3a Shipbuilders in Speymouth 1785-1890

1785-1815	1816-1850	1851-1860	1861-1870	1871-1880	1881-1890
Glenmore Co	–	–	–	–	–
Simpson/ Geddie	Geddie (K)	Geddie (K)	Geddie (K)	Geddie (K)	–
Leslie	Leslie	–	–	–	–
Winchester	Winchester	–	–	–	–
Falconer	–	–	–	–	–
Logie	Proctor	–	–	–	–
Robertson	Anderson	–	–	–	–
Geddie	Geddie (G)	Geddie (G)	Geddie (G)	Geddie (G)	Geddie (G)
Demster	Hay	Hay	Hay	Hay	–
Skelton	Duncan	Duncan	Duncan	Duncan	Duncan
	A Young	A Young	A Young	Lee	–
	Young Bros		–	–	–
	Hustwick	–	Stewart		Anderson
	Palmer	–	Spence	Spence	–
	Badenoch	Badenoch	Kinloch	Kinloch	Kinloch
	& Young	& Young			
Ships built **119**	**192**	**93**	**103**	**87**	**19**

Table 1.3b: Number of ships built (according to builder) in Speymouth 1785-1890

Later maps show the existence of sheds which were used by the shipwright for drawing the actual lines of the ship from the plans, the carpenter's shop, and store, and from these records and the statements made by George Anderson in his book *Kingston-on-Spey* it is possible to give the location of later builders' yards. Anderson places the site of the Glenmore yard to the west of the village, but the site of this yard has been marked in a different place on earlier maps and it is this reference that has been used. Duncan's yard was built on the Glenmore Company's site.

The Ordnance Survey map of Kingston (Figure 1.3), based on a 1870 survey, gives the location of the following yards: William Kinloch [1], Alex Spence [2], Geddie (Kingston) [3], John and James Duncan [4], William Anderson [5], and Geddie (Garmouth) [6]. Other yards would have been situated to the west and east of the Kinloch yard when the river mouth was west of the village.

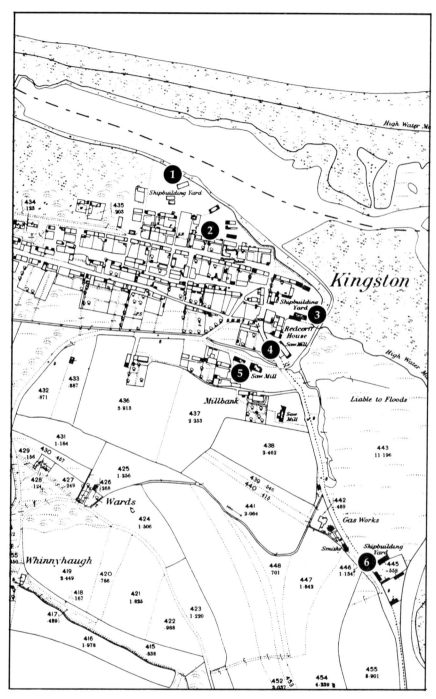

Fig 1.3: Extract from Ordnance Survey map of Kingston 1871
(reproduced from Ordnance Survey Mapping)
1: Kinloch; 2: Spence; 3: Geddie (K); 4: Duncan; 5: Anderson; 6: Geddie (G)

	1791	1841	1851	1861	1881
Shipbuilders	–	6	5	5	4
Shipwrights	–	64	9	7	4
Ship Carpenters	32	–	21	72	40
Squarewrights	–	2	9	1	–
Sawyers	20	23	8	10	2
Sawmillers	8	–	2	6	1
Mill Wrights	–	7	3	5	1
Boat Builders	–	2	2	2	1
Blacksmith	5	13	9	15	4
Foundryman	–	–	2	1	2
Engineer					
Iron Merchant	–	2	–	2	–
Rope & Sail Maker	–	4	4	4	2
Block Maker	–	5	3	4	2
Pilots	–	–	2	2	–
Coopers	–	2	1	3	–
Painters	–	–	–	1	1
Seamen	30	–	–	–	–
Ships launched in year of Census	Not Known	14	6	9	2

Table 1.4: Analysis of men employed in maritime trades, Speymouth 1791-1881
(Source: Speymouth OSA and Census records)

ASSOCIATED TRADES 1790-1890

The number of Speymouth men engaged in trades associated with shipbuilding are shown in Table 1.4. Records are not available for the period between 1790 and 1841; however, it is reasonable to assume that there would have been a steady growth in employment of skilled men. As Speymouth became established as a shipbuilding centre, there was an increased demand for specialists such as millwrights, rope makers, sail makers, and timber merchants and the figures reflect this.

The number of men employed shows a marked reduction in 1851, caused by a fall in the demand for new ships due to an over supply in the latter part of the 1840s. The number of shipbuilders remained stable however, although they would have had to draw in their belts for a short time. The relief came with the discovery of guano off the coast of Peru, and the temporary repeal of the navigation laws as a result of the Irish famine. These and other factors brought about an increased demand for ships from 1853 which continued for the next 25 years. The number of shipbuilders did not increase as each yard simply produced more ships. The size of ships had been steadily increasing, and the amount of working capital required to acquire timber and employ labour whilst the ship was built and sold precluded new men coming into the industry unless they had financial backing.

The 1841-57 census records list the number of men employed as shipwrights and ship carpenters and also the names of their apprentices. The 1861 Census did not make a distinction between carpenters and apprentices so they have been included in a single classification. There is an apparent discrepancy in the number of shipwrights in 1841 and the number in 1861. It is assumed that men were describing themselves as shipwrights in 1841 because they were building ships, even though they had not served the normal seven year apprenticeship required for this trade. The men described as ships' carpenters in 1861 could well have been men working in the shipyards and capable of building ships but who were not indentured to a master shipwright.

The census records give the number of ship masters, master mariners and seamen. These are not given in the table, as Garmouth and Kingston were noted as villages which had more men at sea than at home so the census figures do not give the true position of numbers employed in marine trades. The number of men employed by 1881 reflected the reduction in the demand for Speymouth ships, and numbers steadily declined until 1890, when Geddie launched the last ship, the *Janet Storm*.

SAWS AND SAWMILLERS

The OSA for the Parish of Speymouth deals at some length with timber felling in Strathspey and the conversion of it into planks, deals, and masts by sawmills prior to the timber being floated down the Spey. The Glenmore Company had two large sawmills at Kingston, one operated by wind and the other by water, the first with 36-40 saws and the other 30-36 saws.

These sawmills would most likely have used gang or vertically operated saws, which were effective but slow. They were essential to the operation of a large shipyard which required a considerable amount of timber. Until the invention of the bandsaw it was not possible for sawmillers to produce timber with the curved shapes required for ships' ribs; this could only be done by men operating pit saws, a method of cutting timber which had been in operation since Roman times. Pictures of medieval shipyards show sawyers working in these pits around the ship.

Pit Saw

The pit saw, whilst simple in concept, had to be operated by experienced men as they were dealing with very heavy pieces of timber. The trunk needed to be well positioned and supported, the lines drawn by the shipwright clearly marked, with a good secure foothold essential for the man on the top. The pit man, down among the sawdust with the light obscured by the mass of timber above, had to follow the pace, alternately pulling the saw down and lifting, periodically applying an oil rag on the end of a stick from a pot he kept on a recess in the wall of the pit. When the light was bad, as in winter, his only light would be a candle stuck on a piece of wood.

The saws were seven feet in length tapering from a width of 10 inches to 3 inches, with different handles at either end. The one at the top was a T-shaped upright of iron, 21 inches long, called a tiller, with a slight curvature that set the user just that much back from his work. The pit man's handle was called a box, which was removable so that the saw could be withdrawn at the end of the cut. All the planks cut were made in a row then the trunk was levered forward to enable the process to be resumed. The teeth of the saw were inclined one way and the saw cut only on the down stroke. The function of the topman was to draw the saw following the line marked on the timber with the pitman acting as the donkey pushing the saw along so that the sawdust fell in front of him and not in his eyes. The topman was paid at a higher rate than the pitman as he was more highly skilled. The timber when cut was assembled by the shipwright and then shaped by the adze. The Glenmore Company employed sawyers, as the census records show, in addition to the sawmillers. Figure 1.4 shows pit sawyers at work.

Fig 1.4: Pit sawyers at work

TIME TAKEN TO CONSTRUCT A SHIP

It is not possible to determine how long it took to complete a ship for much would have depended upon whether the vessel was being built in a large or small yard, for a customer, or as a speculative venture. Lloyds Survey records are the only source of information and from them it is only possible to give approximate times that ships were on the stocks. The times taken to build three Kingston ships are given below:-

	Tons	Framing	Beams Installed	Ship Completed
Glenmore	254	April 1858	May 1858	Aug 1858
Spinnaway	437	December 1874	April 1875	Aug 1875
Dispatch	109	Oct/Dec 1883	Jan/Nov 1884	Aug 1888

If it is assumed that the initial work on the hull and the frames took two months the *Glenmore* would have been completed in seven months. The *Spinnaway*, as it was a larger vessel, took ten months to complete.

The construction of the *Dispatch* was a very different story. Started in the autumn of 1883, work progressed very slowly until November 1884, then it ceased altogether until August 1887, when work commenced again for a three month period. Completion did not take place for a further year. It must be assumed that this was a speculative venture, at a time when demand for ships was decreasing as ship building records show, and Geddie must have been a happy man to see her sailing out of Speymouth. The *Dispatch* did not stay long in Scottish ownership and she was sold to a Gloucester ship owner, where she was employed on the Newfoundland trade. Her five years on the stocks did not harm her for she lasted for 47 years, ending up as a hulk in Avonmouth.

TIMBERS USED IN SHIP BUILDING

Surveys carried out by Lloyds on four Speymouth ships are of considerable interest in that they show the methods of construction, the materials used and the time taken to build the ship. The large sailing ships built in the later part of the century in Aberdeen and the Clyde were built to detailed written specifications, but it is unlikely that these were prepared for the Moray ships as they would have been constructed to recognised local standards. The only details necessary would have been tonnage, rig, and whether the hull would require to be copper sheathed.

Details of the timbers used in the construction of four ships are given below and these illustrate the increasing use of imported timbers over a 45-year period. A description of the terms used is given in the Glossary.

A copy of the Survey carried out on the schooner *Lass o' Down* is given in Fig 1.5a and Fig 1.5b. This ship has practically the same dimensions and was built in the same year and by the same builder as *Orient* – a vessel whose voyages and costs are dealt with in Chapter 4.

Lloyds Registers, in describing Spey-built vessels in the early part of the century, always used the term 'fir' instead of pine and no doubt ships prior to 1815 were built of this timber throughout. Timber was also obtainable from the Baltic, but when Napoleon restricted supplies to the British this would have made the supply of Spey timber much sought after by shipbuilders. After the Napoleonic war, when supplies from other countries became available again, the Baltic became the major supplier, together with North America which supplied timber suitable for ship building, such as pitch pine.

	Jessie	*Glenmore*	*Spinnaway*	*Dispatch*
Launched	1843	1858	1875	1888
Tonnage	107	254	437	109
Keelson	Baltic Fir	Baltic Red Pine	Greenheart	Pitch Pine
Deck Beams	Larch	Larch	Baltic Oak	Larch Fir
			Pitch Pine	
Planking	Larch	Spey Fir	Baltic Red Pine	Fir
				Pitch Pine
Wales	Baltic Oak	American Oak	Pitch Pine	Baltic Oak
Deck	Fir	Yellow Pine	Yellow Pine	Yellow Pine

Table 1.5: Details of timber used in the construction of four ships

1	FLYING JIB
2	OUTER JIB
3	INNER JIB
4	TOPSAIL
5	SQUARESAIL
6	MAIN GAFF TOPSAIL
7	MAINSAIL

SLOOP

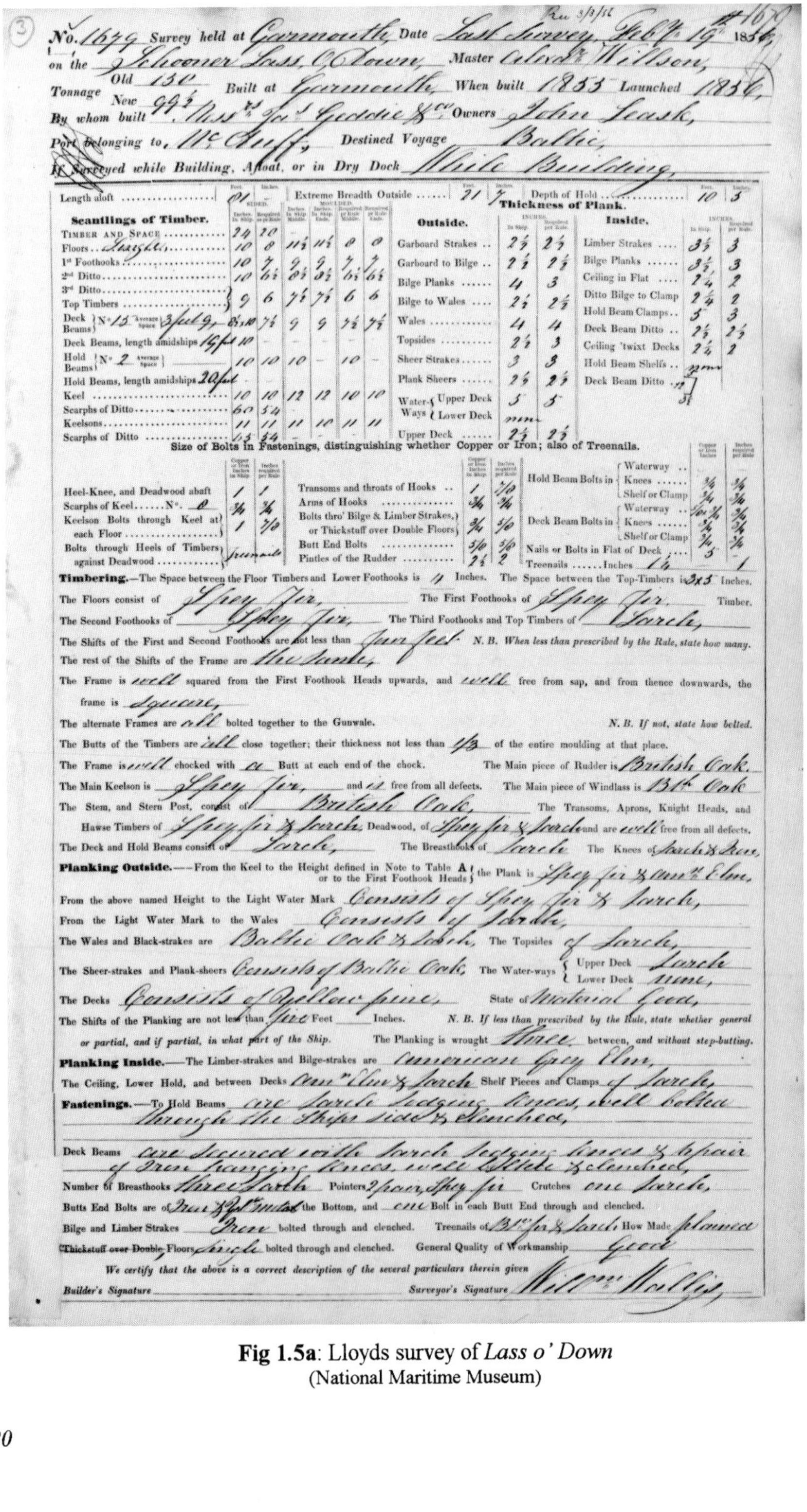

No. 1679 Survey held at Garmouth Date Last Survey Feb'y 19th 1856
on the Schooner Lass O'Down Master Alexd'r Willson
Tonnage Old 130 New 99½ Built at Garmouth When built 1855 Launched 1856
By whom built Mess'rs Ja's Geddie & Co. Owners John Leask
Port belonging to, McDuff, Destined Voyage Baltic
If Surveyed while Building, Afloat, or in Dry Dock While Building

Length aloft 81 ft. | Extreme Breadth Outside 21 ft. 7 in. | Depth of Hold 10 ft. 5 in.

Scantlings of Timber.	Sided: Inches in Ship	Sided: Required as per Rule	Moulded: Inches in Ship, Middle	Moulded: Inches in Ship, Ends	Moulded: Required per Rule, Middle	Moulded: Required per Rule, Ends
Timber and Space	24	20				
Floors .. Single	10	8	11½	11½	8	8
1st Foothooks	10	7	9	9	7	7
2nd Ditto	10	6½	8½	8½	6½	6½
3rd Ditto / Top Timbers	9	6	7½	7½	6	6
Deck Beams No. 15 Average Space 3 ft 9 in	8x10	7½	9	9	7½	7½
Deck Beams, length amidships 19 ft	10	–		–		
Hold Beams No. 2 Average Space	10	10	10	–	10	–
Hold Beams, length amidships 20 ft						
Keel	10	10	12	12	10	10
Scarphs of Ditto	60	54				
Keelsons	11	11	11	10	11	11
Scarphs of Ditto	65	54				

Thickness of Plank.

Outside.	Inches in Ship	Required per Rule
Garboard Strakes	2½	2½
Garboard to Bilge	2½	2½
Bilge Planks	4	3
Bilge to Wales	2½	2½
Wales	4	4
Topsides	2½	3
Sheer Strakes	3	3
Plank Sheers	2½	2½
Water-Ways Upper Deck	5	5
Water-Ways Lower Deck	none	
Upper Deck	2½	2½

Inside.	Inches in Ship	Required per Rule
Limber Strakes	3½	3
Bilge Planks	3½	3
Ceiling in Flat	2¼	2
Ditto Bilge to Clamp	2¼	2
Hold Beam Clamps	5	3
Deck Beam Ditto	2½	2½
Ceiling 'twixt Decks	2¼	2
Hold Beam Shelfs	none	
Deck Beam Ditto		

Size of Bolts in Fastenings, distinguishing whether Copper or Iron; also of Treenails.

	Copper or Iron Inches in Ship	Inches required per Rule
Heel-Knee, and Deadwood abaft	1	1
Scarphs of Keel ...... No. 8	¾	¾
Keelson Bolts through Keel at each Floor	1	7/8
Bolts through Heels of Timbers against Deadwood	treenails	
Transoms and throats of Hooks	1	7/8
Arms of Hooks	¾	¾
Bolts thro' Bilge & Limber Strakes, or Thickstuff over Double Floors	¾	5/8
Butt End Bolts	5/8	5/8
Pintles of the Rudder	2½	2
Hold Beam Bolts in Waterway / Knees / Shelf or Clamp	¾	¾
Deck Beam Bolts in Waterway / Knees / Shelf or Clamp	¾	¾
Nails or Bolts in Flat of Deck	5	
Treenails ...... Inches 1¼		1

Timbering.—The Space between the Floor Timbers and Lower Foothooks is 4 Inches. The Space between the Top-Timbers is 3x5 Inches.
The Floors consist of Spey Fir, The First Foothooks of Spey Fir, Timber.
The Second Foothooks of Spey Fir, The Third Foothooks and Top Timbers of Larch,
The Shifts of the First and Second Foothooks are not less than Four feet N. B. When less than prescribed by the Rule, state how many.
The rest of the Shifts of the Frame are the same,
The Frame is well squared from the First Foothook Heads upwards, and well free from sap, and from thence downwards, the frame is square,
The alternate Frames are all bolted together to the Gunwale. N. B. If not, state how bolted.
The Butts of the Timbers are all close together; their thickness not less than 1/3 of the entire moulding at that place.
The Frame is well chocked with a Butt at each end of the chock. The Main piece of Rudder is British Oak.
The Main Keelson is Spey fir, and is free from all defects. The Main piece of Windlass is Bt'h Oak
The Stem, and Stern Post, consist of British Oak, The Transoms, Aprons, Knight Heads, and Hawse Timbers of Spey fir & larch, Deadwood, of Spey fir & larch and are well free from all defects.
The Deck and Hold Beams consist of Larch, The Breasthooks of Larch The Knees of Larch & Iron,

Planking Outside.—From the Keel to the Height defined in Note to Table A or to the First Foothook Heads the Plank is Spey fir & Am'n Elm,
From the above named Height to the Light Water Mark Consists of Spey fir & Larch,
From the Light Water Mark to the Wales Consists of Larch,
The Wales and Black-strakes are Baltic Oak & Larch, The Topsides of Larch,
The Sheer-strakes and Plank-sheers Consists of Baltic Oak, The Water-ways Upper Deck Larch Lower Deck none,
The Decks Consists of Yellow pine, State of Material Good,
The Shifts of the Planking are not less than Five Feet Inches. N. B. If less than prescribed by the Rule, state whether general or partial, and if partial, in what part of the Ship. The Planking is wrought Three between, and without step-butting.

Planking Inside.—The Limber-strakes and Bilge-strakes are American Grey Elm,
The Ceiling, Lower Hold, and between Decks Am'n Elm & Larch Shelf Pieces and Clamps of Larch,

Fastenings.—To Hold Beams are Larch Lodging Knees, well bolted through the Ship side & clenched,
Deck Beams are secured with Larch lodging knees & 1 pair of Iron hanging knees, well bolted & clenched,
Number of Breasthooks three Larch Pointers 2 pair, Spey fir Crutches one Larch,
Butts End Bolts are of Iron & Y'l metal the Bottom, and one Bolt in each Butt End through and clenched.
Bilge and Limber Strakes Iron bolted through and clenched. Treenails of Bt'c fir & Larch How Made planed
~~Thickstuff over Double~~ Floors, Single bolted through and clenched. General Quality of Workmanship Good

We certify that the above is a correct description of the several particulars therein given
Builder's Signature Surveyor's Signature Will'm Wallis

Fig 1.5a: Lloyds survey of *Lass o' Down*
(National Maritime Museum)

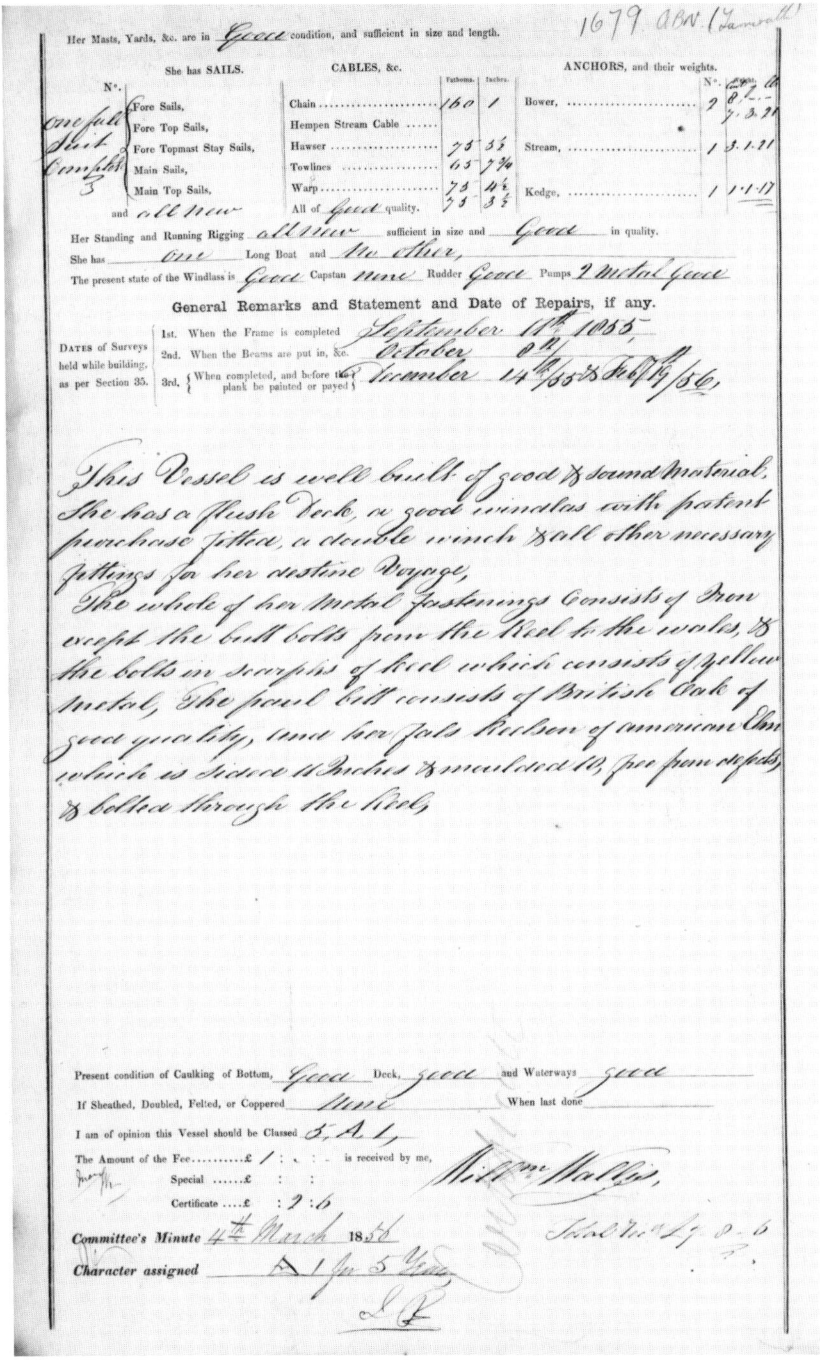
1679. ABN. (Tamworth)

Her Masts, Yards, &c. are in Good condition, and sufficient in size and length.

She has SAILS.	CABLES, &c.	Fathoms.	Inches.	ANCHORS, and their weights.	N°.	Weight.
Fore Sails,	Chain	160	1	Bower,	2	8.2.– / 7.3.21
Fore Top Sails,	Hempen Stream Cable					
Fore Topmast Stay Sails,	Hawser	75	3½	Stream,	1	3.1.21
Main Sails,	Towlines	65	7¾			
Main Top Sails,	Warp	75 / 75	4½ / 3½	Kedge,	1	1.1.17

N°. one full Suit Complete 3, and all new. All of Good quality.

Her Standing and Running Rigging all new sufficient in size and Good in quality.

She has One Long Boat and No other,

The present state of the Windlass is Good Capstan none Rudder Good Pumps 2 metal Good

General Remarks and Statement and Date of Repairs, if any.

DATES of Surveys held while building, as per Section 35.
1st. When the Frame is completed September 18th 1855,
2nd. When the Beams are put in, &c. October 8th
3rd. When completed, and before the plank be painted or payed November 14th/55 & Feb 19th/56,

This Vessel is well built of good & sound Material, She has a flush Deck, a good windlas with patent purchase fitted, a double winch & all other necessary fittings for her destine Voyage,
The whole of her Metal fastenings Consists of Iron except the butt bolts from the Keel to the wales, & the bolts in scarphs of keel which consists of yellow metal, The fowl bill consists of British Oak of good quality, and her fals Keelson of american Elm which is sided 11 Inches & moulded 10, free from defects & bolted through the keel,

Present condition of Caulking of Bottom, Good Deck, good and Waterways good

If Sheathed, Doubled, Felted, or Coppered None When last done

I am of opinion this Vessel should be Classed 5 A 1,

The Amount of the Fee.........£ 1 : – : – is received by me,
Special ......£ : :
Certificate ....£ : 2 : 6

Willm. Wallis,

Total £1 : 2 : 6

Committee's Minute 4th March 1856

Character assigned A 1 for 5 Years

Fig 1.5b: Lloyds survey of *Lass o' Down*
(National Maritime Museum)

THE BANK AGENT

One man who played a very important part in the development of the ship building industry was the Bank Agent. There was only one bank in Garmouth – the Caledonian Banking Company – whose head office was in Inverness. The agent listed in Blacks Directory for 1844, 1852 and 1863 was Hugh Rose Thomson, who married a daughter of William Hustwick and who then became related by marriage to two ship building families and several ship masters. He stayed in the Bank House in Garmouth and would have been very well placed to assess the state of maritime trade and ship building, especially when it came to lending money to the local individuals who were involved in these activities.

Shipbuilders had to wait, on occasion for considerable lengths of time, before they received payment from prospective owners; timber merchants – and Hugh Thomson was a timber merchant as well as bank agent – also needed to be paid, as would the men. No ledgers are known to exist that show payments made by shipbuilders, so it is not possible to state whether they received payment from prospective purchasers whilst the vessel was being constructed, or had to wait until the ship was launched. They certainly could not have received payment if the vessel was built as a speculative venture, as many of them were according to newspaper reports.

Working capital would have been essential and both timber merchants and builder would be likely to have had loans to bridge the period before payment was due. Hugh Thomson would have been in a good position to assess the risk involved, and both he and his son, who succeeded him as Agent, must have exercised sound judgement, for the names of several ship-building firms appear in both the 1850 and 1880 census records.

In addition to providing finance for the building of ships, banks were frequently involved in lending money to people purchasing shares in ships, and there again the bank agent's judgement would have been invaluable in assessing the financial standing of a person wishing to obtain a loan. These loans were recorded in shipping registers, although the entry was normally limited to a statement that the loan was at an agreed rate of interest. When on rare occassions a rate was quoted it was five percent.

Shipwright's Adze

2 TRADING PORTS

Introduction

The Moray Firth ports whose trading and shipbuilding activities are described in this chapter varied widely in the amount of trade carried out and also in the numbers of ships built. Six of the ports had trading interests outwith the Firth and in addition their ships acted as carriers for the smaller ports. Three of the ports – Garmouth, Inverness and Banff – were large shipbuilding centres constructing ships in excess of their own requirements. The rest of the ports built a small number of ships which enabled them to meet the needs of the community and their hinterland.

A number of small ports are not listed because the trade carried out by them was small and they built very few ships. At one time these ports – such as Fortrose and Rosemarkie – were busy centres but, as ships became larger, trade was directed to other ports and their importance declined.

Brora and Helmsdale would have traded with ports on the southern shores of the Firth such as Banff, Portsoy and Inverness. Both ports were established as early as the seventeenth century, and it is reasonable to assume that they would have needed products from these areas. Shipping movements taken from Burghead Harbour records, the *Inverness Courier* and the *Banffshire Journal,* however, show only a very limited number of exports and imports between the two areas. Helmsdale developed as a major fish processing centre during the nineteenth century and exported herring to the Baltic. In view of this, Helmsdale may well have had the resources to obtain goods from other areas of Scotland.

MACDUFF

The village of Macduff had a harbour as early as 1783 and additions were made in 1822 and 1877. According to the NSA, Macduff merchants exported cattle, grain, and fish and imported lime, coal, salt and wood.

Macduff had at least four shipyards in the period 1800-30 when 23 of the 30 ships recorded as being built in the port were constructed. Two locally built ships, the *Macduff* and the *Alpha* are recorded in the 1829 Collector of Customs Quarterly Accounts as taking cargoes of herring to Hamburg and a third, the *Jean*, returning from Gothenburg with a cargo of iron and timber. It is not possible to state if these ships were owned by residents of Macduff or Banff.

There are no official records available to show the extent to which residents of this port owned ships capable of undertaking deep sea voyages. However, one record which does exist shows that, whilst the port was not as active as, say, Banff, some of its citizens were willing and capable of investing in shipowning. The following inhabitants of Macduff, Portsoy and Banff were shareholders in the *Lufra*, a vessel of 704 tons, built by Hall of Aberdeen in 1870. This represented a considerable investment by these men at that time, as the cost of the vessel was £10,000 according to Hall's records.

Wm Anderson	Merchant	Macduff
James Moir	Bank Agent	Portsoy
John Cruickshank	Druggist	Macduff
John Anderson	Builder	Macduff
David Storm	Merchant	Macduff
James Hodge	Master Mariner	Macduff
Alexander George	Solicitor	Macduff
James Smith	Merchant	Banff

(source: James Henderson, Aberdeen)

During 1840-60, Macduff was a regular port of call for steamers on the Inverness–Aberdeen–Leith service.

BANFF

The Royal Burgh of Banff's trading links with the Baltic and the Continent extend as far back as the fifteenth century, well before the present harbour was built in 1775. The burgh obviously had a prosperous and active merchant class residing within its boundaries and because of its importance as a centre of trade, was the obvious site for the office of the Collector of Customs for Banff , who was responsible for recording the movement of goods in ports between Pennan and the mouth of the Spey.

The OSA and the NSA (1795-97; 1835-36) record the imports of iron and timber from Sweden, hemp from Russia, and flax from Holland. Exports were herring for the Baltic States, livestock and grain for England. The NSA also states that very few foreign vessels landed cargoes at Banff because there was not a great deal of water in either the inner or outer harbours, and many of the cargoes recorded by Customs were landed along the Banff and Moray coastline. There are no records to show how many ships actually used the harbour for loading and discharging cargoes, but Customs records show a considerable amount of trade during the period 1805-30. This trade would in the main have been controlled by the merchants of Banff and Portsoy, the two main trading ports in the area at that time.

Another indication of trading activity was the number of ships owned and built in a port. The earliest record of ships being built in Banff is 1786, with fifteen ships built there during the eighteenth century. The *Aberdeen Journal* records the entry into Aberdeen Harbour of eight Banff-registered vessels between 1750 and 1752. Other records show that there were nine shipmasters residing in the town at that time, evidence of significant maritime resources. Unfortunately, details of ships registered in Banff during 1780-1830 are unavailable, although records show that 63 ships, ranging in size from 21-153 tons, were built there during that period. The number of ships registered could well have been much larger, as merchants often purchased ships that had been constructed elsewhere in Britain. The NSA shows that in 1836 Banff merchants possessed the following ships – one brig (155 tons); 18 schooners (1567 tons); 48 sloops (2579 tons); of these vessels, ten schooners and eleven sloops belonged to Banff, with the rest belonging to the ports of Fraserburgh, Gamrie, Macduff, Portsoy, Portgordon, and Garmouth.

A record of Banff trading activities, obtained from the shipping intelligence columns of the *Banffshire Journal* for the period 1850-80 (Customs records were not available after 1830), shows that the harbour was in regular use, although it may not have been engaged in as much foreign trade as other Banffshire ports. This was possibly due to the silting up of the harbour, which limited the size of ship using the port. However, Banff had a considerable trade with London. According to Barclay (1906), in 1836 ten to twelve ships with a total tonnage of 1200 made an average of nine voyages per year carrying in total 11,000 tons of merchandise. The cargoes consisted of grain, herring, salmon, cattle, and cured pork.

It is not possible to record how many ships were owned by residents of Banff in later years, but it must be assumed that there were a considerable number, as 138 ships were constructed there during the nineteenth century. A number of these ships would have been built for owners in other ports. The majority of these ships were, according to Lloyds Register, shown to have Banff as their home port. The destination and the voyages of these ships record that the merchants had trading contacts as extensive as any in Scotland – Ireland, Norway, Spain, Newfoundland, Sweden, and Russia. However, if the larger ships had remained in local ownership they, like the Garmouth ships, would have traded from other British ports and the Continent where there were better facilities and opportunities for obtaining cargoes.

An example of the trading activity for one year of a Banff-owned ship the *Konigsberg* is given below. She must have been well managed in order to obtain so many cargoes in a nine-month period. It is assumed that she was laid up during the winter in Aberdeen, as facilities would have been inadequate for this purpose along the Banffshire coast.

The Konigsberg belonged to a more modern day. She was built in 1877 for Mr John Merson; latterly she belonged to Captain Reid. She was built in Spey by Mr Duncan, and was lost a few years ago off Fraserburgh in a succession of gales that wrought much loss on Moray Firth shipping. Captain Malcolm's eye kindles as he recites some of the doings of this very fast ship. He recalls, for instance, a season when she was commanded by Captain Cowie, and he was himself mate. The ship left Inverness in ballast to the Firth of Forth, and went to Konigsberg with coals. She returned with a cargo of barley to Islay, went from that in ballast to Troon, and loaded coals there for St Petersburg. Thence she came to Kirkcaldy with a cargo of oilcake, and loaded up at Charleston with coals for St Petersburg. From the Russian capital she went with a cargo to Maryport in Cumberland. Thence she went in ballast to Westonpoint, and loaded salt, again for St Petersburg, where she loaded crushed bones for Aberdeen. The ship was laid up at Aberdeen on 29th November, having started from Inverness in the beginning of March, and in the interval gone once to Konigsberg and three times to St Petersburg. Never, says Captain Malcolm, did a sailing ship do better. (W Barclay. *A Lost Industry*).

PORTSOY

The first harbour was built by Sir Patrick Ogilvie before 1701 and was still in use in 1724. The Earl of Seafield constructed a new harbour between 1825 and 1828, but the outer pier was demolished by storms in 1839 leaving only the old harbour in use. There are no records in existence to show the extent of trade carried out by the merchants of this port during the eighteenth century, apart from reports in the *Aberdeen Journal* of 1750 and 1752 which records the entry of five Portsoy ships into Aberdeen Harbour. Pigot's Directory for 1837 describes Portsoy as 'a thriving port with a safe harbour which has been greatly improved and can take vessels up to 200 tons burden. The export trade consists of herring, grain, and stone, with coal being the main import. Industries consist of fish curing, flax dressing, woollen manufacturing and distilling.' The existing structure was rebuilt in 1884. As the town celebrated its tercentenary in 1993 – a notable achievement – it was a safe haven for ships long before the construction of its first harbour.

The customs records for Banff, which included cargoes landed at Portsoy, gives details of cargoes carried by Portsoy-owned ships from Rotterdam and Porsgrunn, a port near Oslo. The port may have been small but, like Findhorn and Garmouth, it possessed a group of merchants who built a harbour and warehouses, acquired ships and traded across the North Sea in vessels of less than 50 tons. In addition to these merchants there must have been a number of good ship masters, for the NSA for 1842 states that Portsoy merchants owned eight ships with a combined tonnage of 556 tons, and that there were eight to ten Baltic traders visiting annually, bringing in bones and taking back herring. Another export was marble for the English pottery industry – apparently it was superior to the local product.

Nineteen ships were built in Portsoy – two in 1792-99 – with the majority being built between 1850 and 1870.

SANDEND

The port does not get more than a brief mention in historical records; however it was a good location for building, for between 1786 and 1872 eighteen smacks, sloops and schooners were launched. Shipbuilding and repair work was still being carried out in Sandend as late as 1993.

CULLEN

Cullen, which had the status of Royal Burgh in the twelfth century, was engaged in seaborne trade, and some harbour facilities did exist in the seventeenth century. These were in poor condition and some limited improvements were made in the early part of the eighteenth century. However the entry in the OSA (1794) for Cullen states that a harbour did not exist and one was required for the importation of coal.

A small substantial harbour was built by the Earl of Seafield in 1817 and then enlarged in 1834 by an additional quay, this providing what the NSA described as one of the best harbours in the Moray Firth, giving a depth at the pier head of 8½-12 feet.

Boat and ship building was carried out in Cullen because an ample supply of suitable timber was available. Three master shipbuilders employed around 22 men, and between 1806 and 1844, 69 vessels of 15-40 tons were built, in addition to a large number of fishing boats. There were also four ships of 40-100 tons burden with a total tonnage of 270 belonging to the port (NSA).

The main imports were coal, salt, stones, and barley. Exports consisted of herring, dried fish, timber, oats, and potatoes.

BUCKIE

There was a fishery settlement in Buckie from the middle of the seventeenth century, and by the end of the next century there were 14 boats and a yawl fishing from the village. In addition there were six sloops of 18-60 tons owned by local merchants. The first harbour was built in 1843 and extended in 1852 to include a harbour of refuge. Boat and ship building was carried out at the end of the eighteenth century but it was not until 1860 that trading vessels of any size were built. According to the NSA (1842), Buckie at that time was a busy port with 117 large and 28 small fishing vessels.

PORTGORDON

When Portgordon harbour was built in 1797, with capital provided by the Duke of Gordon, it provided a much needed facility in that part of Banffshire. It was a very busy port in the first half of the nineteenth century, serving the town of Keith and a large hinterland. Principal imports were salt, coal and fertiliser; exports consisted of grain and herring.

The harbour was enlarged in 1870 to accommodate the increasing number of fishing boats, although Portgordon's importance as a trading port had started to decline by this time. In the early part of the century the average tonnage of ships was low – 40-50 tons – and the harbour was more than adequate for vessels of that size. As the size of ships increased, it became less easy for them to enter the port, and because Buckie could easily accommodate ships with a deeper draught, trade gradually moved away. Even though the importance of its harbour declined, Portgordon retained strong maritime connections, with a large number of its population continuing to hold Masters Certificates – Buckie merchants provided capital to build ships whilst Portgordon provided the seamen.

The harbour has one unique feature – a hole in the west wall which was used by horses and carts to enter the harbour at low tide in order to load or off-load ships. Apparently the opening was not intended for that purpose – it was built so that tidal currents could be admitted to clear silt from the harbour.

Shipbuilding was never a major industry in Portgordon; only seven ships were built there, six of them betwen 1853 and 1860.

GARMOUTH

Because of its position beside a river which gave shelter to ships, Garmouth was the port for Elgin and the surrounding area from as early as the fourteenth century, and eighteenth century maps of Speymouth show ships anchored at the mouth of the river opposite Garmouth and Tugnet. The port did not have any quays, and vessels would have loaded and unloaded their cargoes by means of lighters. Up to the beginning of the nineteenth century this was the normal method of dealing with cargoes where there were no flat beaches available. To overcome this problem, and to provide shelter for ships and fishing boats, land owners and the Commission for Highland Roads and Bridges spent considerable sums on the provision of harbour facilities. Because of the difficulty in controlling the Spey, very little was spent in providing facilities – such as wharves – in Garmouth, so trade in the latter part of the century would have been limited.

Regardless of these difficulties, there was considerable trade through the port during the eighteenth century as shown by this extract (OSA 1791-92):-

Vessels sailing from Spey with timber for various places	82
Touched at Spey and having taken salmon to London after also taken salmon from other ports	24
Yarn, oats and meal	3
	109

Arrived in Spey	
With boats	11
With empty kits, stores and roofs	5
With salt, iron and goods	7
	23

The NSA also gave details of trade carried out in Spey and this shows a considerable increase in trade since the first records were taken:-

Navigation

Notwithstanding the disadvantages connected with the harbour of Garmouth, it is gratifying to know that, compared with what it was in 1792, the trade and shipping of the port (of Speymouth) has greatly increased. I have no means of ascertaining the number of vessels which entered here during any year from 1792 till 1816. From 1st January 1816 till 31st December 1825, a period of ten years, 1863 vessels besides boats sailed, three-fourths of which at least were loaded with timber and grain. This gives an average of 186 yearly.

The following is the number of vessels which arrived and sailed for the seven years from 5th January 1826 to 5th January 1833, as per Custom-house books:

	1826	1827	1828	1829	1830	1831	1832-3
General arrivals	191	155	123	111	98	130	138
General sailings	201	164	127	113	96	125	140
Imports - coal	64	61	67	46	43	41	57
Exports - timber & grain	97	82	76	85	61	56	86

During the ten years from 1st January 1816 to 31st December 1825, the greatest number of vessels entering the harbour was 257 in 1818, and the least 154 in 1822.

From the pilotage book kept here, the number of vessels which sailed during 1834 appears to have been 204, fifty of which were loaded with grain, chiefly oats and wheat, and carried at least 18,000 quarters to various English ports, and chief towns in the south of Scotland. A large proportion of the remainder were loaded with timber. The rest sailed in ballast. During last year, forty cargoes of Scotch coals, equal to 3,000 tons, were delivered here for various lime-burners and distillers. Twenty cargoes of English coals were imported from Sunderland during the same period, containing 18,000 imperial barrels, and sold at from 1s. 9d. to 2s. per barrel. Since the division of the moor of Garmouth nearly forty years ago, till then common to all the feuars, and supplying many of the inhabitants with turf for fuel, coals and wood are universally used for fire. Indeed, in many houses a peat or turf fire was never seen.. There are twelve vessels belonging to the port, of from 29 to 84 tons registered burthen, whose total tonnage is 685 tons; and they are manned by 55 seamen. All the masters, with two exceptions, and nearly all the men, are natives of Garmouth and Kingston; and besides these, several masters, seamen and ship-carpenters, originally belonging to this place, go to sea from other ports. With two exceptions, all the masters of the above twelve vessels are part or sole owners of the vessels they command.

Although they never enter the harbour, the Spey Fishing Company's salmon smacks should be included in the Garmouth shipping. From 8 to 12 of these are annually employed in conveying salmon to the London market. From the best information I can obtain, 73 cargoes of salmon were last year shipped in whole or in part in the bay; 52 of these were sent direct to London, the rest were sent to Aberdeen, and there re-shipped for London. Each cargo contains on an average 280 boxes, containing 1 cwt. of fish, and may be estimated as worth £5 each box, taking the average prices of the whole season.

Details of the amount of trade passing through Garmouth from 1830-50 are not obtainable from official records; newspaper reports state some 30 to 40 vessels used the port annually. It is reasonable to assume that the nature of the trade carried out did not alter substantially. Exports would have consisted of yarn, oats, meal, salmon; with imports of fertiliser and timber from the Baltic. As well as loading or discharging cargoes, ships would also have used the port to have repairs carried out by the shipyards.

Blacks Directory gives the names of ships owned by residents of Kingston and Garmouth for 1850 (16) and 1863 (27), with an increase in the tonnage from 57 to 119 tons. Many of these vessels traded outwith the Firth, and the *Orient*, whose trading record is analysed in Chapter 4, made many voyages outwith British coastal waters and only rarely loaded or discharged cargoes in her home port.

LOSSIEMOUTH

In 1683, on the advice of a German engineer called Peter Brauss, the Town Council of Elgin, apparently concerned about the growing importance of the port of Findhorn, decided to build a harbour at Elgine Head. This harbour became choked with sand and a new harbour was constructed at Stotfield in 1839. A few years later the inner harbour basin was increased in size and the North Quay was extended. These developments made Lossiemouth the major port for the area, as Findhorn's ability to deal with vessels over a certain size was restricted because of a bar. The investment in harbour facilities was justified because of the increased use of the harbour by trading vessels and fishing boats, the latter increasing so considerably that by 1863 there were 117 boats belonging to the port. Eleven fish curers dealt with the processed catches and exported to Stettin, Danzig and Hamburg.

During the 1850s three shipbuilders were in operation – Jake Geddie, William Geddie, and a Mr Jack – and, by 1873, 31 ships had been constructed when, according to the shipping register, building ceased. Boat building was carried out during and after that period, however, because of the rise in the importance of herring and white fishing.

In 1863 there were 14 trading vessels belonging to the port, ranging from 20-134 tons and capable of dealing with the coastal and Baltic trade carried out from the port. Two steamers, the *Dundalk* and the *Britannia*, called in at Lossiemouth on their weekly voyages to and from Leith.

BURGHEAD

The old fishery village of Burghead, or Brochheid as it was then, was demolished in 1793 to make way for a new town, and in 1809 a harbour was built together with warehouses which still flank the quay side. The harbour was enlarged to its present size in 1858 by the landowner, William Young, who had spent considerable sums of money in carrying out other improvements to the harbour prior to this date.

According to the NSA (1836-37), Burghead had a considerable trade of exports of salmon, herring, oats, and meal, with imports of lime, coal, bone dust, and timber, with 400 ships entering the port annually. Twelve ships belonged to town merchants and there was regular trading with Aberdeen, Leith, London and Liverpool. From the 1840s Burghead was a regular port of call for steamers operating the weekly run between Inverness, Aberdeen and Leith.

Bradshaw (1861) gives details of the thrice weekly service between Littleferry and Burghead by the paddle steamer *Heather Bell* belonging to the Sutherland Steam Packet Company. This vessel was replaced by the SS *Icantho* and then by the *Edith*; the service ceased in 1866. A packet sailed from Burghead to Sutherland (Helmsdale) as early as 1809 and these sailings connected with the North of Scotland Steamship Company's run to and from Aberdeen. In the 1870s this trade bypassed Burghead and ships sailed direct from Littleferry and Helmsdale to Leith.

Fig 2.1: Burghead Harbour c1900 (Moray District Council)

31

Burghead merchants owned ten ships in 1844, but by 1863 this had fallen to two. However, about 250 ships entered the port during this period, so that at the time it was still a busy port, although not as active as Lossiemouth. The Burghead Harbour Order of 1858 lists a wide range of goods on which harbour dues would be charged, giving a good indication of the extensive trade carried out by the port (see Appendix 1). Port records for the period 1863-92 show that there was a considerable amount of trade with Scottish, English, Baltic and Continental ports. The annual tonnage of vessels entering the port increased from 18,550 in 1863 to 37,735 tons in 1892, fully justifying the 1858 decision to further develop the port facilities.

The *Maggy Jappy* is the earliest recorded ship built at Burghead (1792 shipping register) although, according to records from the Clyde shipbuilding firm Stephen of Linthouse, shipbuilding was apparently well established there by 1750. Various members of the Stephen family worked in the Burghead yard and continued to work there after William Stephen moved to Aberdeen in 1793. His son Alexander later moved to Arbroath and Dundee, and then to the Clyde.

Shipbuilding was not a major industry in Burghead, with only 22 ships being built between 1800 and 1850. They varied considerably in size from a boat of 17 tons to a barque of 128 tons in 1841.

Burghead still attracts a fair amount of traffic, exporting cattle feed, malted barley and stones to the Continent and importing malting barley. There is also continued use of the harbour by fishing boats.

FINDHORN

Because of its sheltered anchorage, Findhorn – or Findorn, the name recorded on early maps – and Garmouth were the only two natural ports on the shore of the Firth during the seventeenth and eighteenth centuries. Both were active ports, Findhorn serving Forres, and Garmouth (and latterly Lossiemouth) acting as ports for Elgin and the surrounding areas. Due to the westerly shift of sand along the coast, both Findhorn and Garmouth's ability to deal with large vessels was limited at times by bars at the mouth of both rivers.

In 1778 an Act was passed to enable Hector Munro Esquire to maintain a harbour and pier at the town of Findhorn, and from the list of harbour dues given in the Act it would appear that, despite the bar, the merchants of Findhorn were confident that trade between the Continent, the Baltic and England would continue.

Findhorn-owned ships are recorded as having paid dues to the Danish authorities at Elsinore to pass through the Sound between Denmark and Sweden in order to reach the Baltic, and Aberdeen harbour records for the seventeenth century state that there was a regular trade between the two ports.

The port continued to be active, because Lossiemouth's harbour could take only small ships. It was also the outlet for a large and prosperous agricultural area. The range of goods on which shore dues were charged in 1852 is a good indicator of the level of activity of the port at that time. Principal exports were wheat, barley, oats, flour, timber, timber sawn pit props, stones, herring, and potatoes; and the main imports consisted of coal, iron, salt, rubble, stones, hewn timber, and general goods. According to the North Sea Pilot, Findhorn was still an active port in 1914, with vessels of 12 feet draught able to use the small harbour.

Exchequer records for the seventeenth century show the movement of two Findhorn vessels, the *Lodovick & William* and the *James & Isobel*. Court of Session records for 1706 give the names of two ships' carpenters – John Nicoll and Robert Watson – so it can be assumed that shipbuilding was being carried out in Findhorn at that time. According to Blacks Directory local merchants owned fourteen ships in 1852, with Lossiemouth and Burghead owning thirteen and six respectively. The number of ships owned by the three ports was ten, twelve, and two by 1863. If the population is taken into account, it is obvious that Findhorn – with a population of 890 – had a high proportion of ship owners compared to Lossiemouth (pop. 2496) and Burghead (pop. 1099). The tonnage of the Findhorn ships in 1863 ranged from 61-160 tons, with the larger vessels capable of trading with Baltic and Mediterranean ports. The Shipping Registers show that 45 ships were built in Findhorn: twelve between 1793 and 1816, 22 between 1821 and 1850 with only ten being launched between 1855 and 1873.

NAIRN

Thomas Telford altered the course of the River Nairn and built a quay along the western bank of the new river channel in 1826. As this development brought about increased use of the harbour by fishermen and sailing vessels, an additional quay was built on the opposite bank in 1830. According to the NSA there were also considerable exports of herring and white fish.

Shipbuilding was spasmodic with five of the ten ships built being constructed between 1850 and 1856. Along with most other ports on the southern shore of the Moray Firth, Nairn was a regular port of call for the steamers on the Inverness, Aberdeen, Leith service.

INVERNESS

The records of the Collector of Customs for Inverness for the period 1805-30 show that the town had considerable trade with Russia, and the range of goods which were imported is given in Appendix 2. Inverness' trade differed from that of Banff both in the nature of the goods imported and in volume. Inverness, as a linen producer, imported flax and hemp whilst Banff, with a developing boat and shipbuilding industry, mainly imported timber. The following table illustrates the difference in volume of trade (NSA 1827):-

	IMPORTS				EXPORTS			
	British		Foreign		British		Foreign	
	Ships	Tons	Ships	Tons	Ships	Tons	Ships	Tons
Banff	9	445	21	1,634	19	1,267	15	1,110
Inverness	10	1,219	---	---	2	130	---	---

The port had six vessels regularly trading with the Continent and was the centre of the Custom House District from the mouth of the Spey to the Dornoch Firth. Annual imports consisted of 400-600 tons of hemp and three to four cargoes of timber and Archangel tar. In 1835, 75 ships (with a combined tonnage of 4800 tons) were registered as belonging to Inverness. Many of these ships were quite small – 30-40 tons – and would have been engaged in the coastal trade for the western end of the Firth.

Pigots Directory for 1837 recorded the ships engaged on coastal traffic as follows:-

Inverness - London	1 steamship	4 sailing vessels
Inverness-Leith	1 steamship	3 sailing vessels
Inverness-Aberdeen	-	2 sailing vessels
Inverness-Glasgow	4 steamships	-

The movement of ships during 1850, 1860 and 1870 shows a marked decline in maritime activity and this is surprising in view of the town's geographical position and size. The record of ship movement, compiled from the *Inverness Courier*, does not take account of the cargoes which must have been carried by the paddle steamers which operated regular weekly services during the 1840s-60s between Inverness and Leith. More than one company was engaged in this trade so it must have been considerable. The railways which served Inverness from both Perth and Aberdeen were capable of carrying a large amount of goods, and newspaper records of the time show that in 1860-70 the railway carried considerable amounts of cattle and timber. This included livestock which moved through Inverness from 1840-80 and it can be assessed by the extent and range of its maritime and rail facilities serving the town.

Although Inverness did not apparently have an extensive maritime trade, there were a considerable number of ships built in the port between 1830-76, with 123 ships launched. Most of the ships built in the early part of the period were small, necessary for work within the Firth and it was not until 1860-70 that larger vessels capable of undertaking foreign trade were built. The Customs Register of Ships for Inverness shows that many ships were purchased from other parts of Britain, so that the merchant fleet at that time would have been much larger than the number actually built in the town.

Fig 2.2: Inverness Harbour 1889 (Bob Charnley Collection)

Fig 2.3: Nairn Harbour 1895 (The Nairn Fisheries Museum)

LITTLEFERRY AND BURGHEAD
STEAM COMMUNICATION.

SUTHERLAND STEAM PACKET COMPANY (*Limited*).
The Splendid New and very Fast STEAMER,

"HEATHER BELL."
R. H. HUDSON, Master.

Built expressly for the Trade, will, after 1st APRIL, until further Notice, Sail as
under, unless prevented by any unforeseen circumstance :—

FROM LITTLEFERRY FOR BURGHEAD
(Stopping off Portmahomack, weather, &c., permitting),

MONDAY and WEDNESDAY, not before 7.30 A.M., and FRIDAY (without
stopping off Portmahomack), not before 6 A.M., meeting the Edinburgh
Steamers at Burghead.

FROM BURGHEAD FOR LITTLEFERRY
(Stopping off Portmahomack) on MONDAY, WEDNESDAY, and FRIDAY, on
the Arrival of the 'Bus from ALVES STATION, but not before 1.30 P.M.

FREIGHTS ON GOODS AND STOCK VERY MODERATE.

Passage Fares —1st Cabin, 5s. ; 2d Cabin, 3s.

First-rate accommodation for Carriages, Horses, and every description of Live Stock, on
deck. An Omnibus runs from the Hotel at Golspie to and from Littleferry, in connection
with the Steamer. An Omnibus also runs between Burghead Pier and the Alves Station of
the Inverness and Aberdeen Junction Railway, conveying Passengers to and from the
Steamer. According to present arrangements, Passengers arriving at Alves Station by the
11.45 up, and 12.30 down trains are in time for the Steamer ; and Passengers by the
Steamer from Sutherland are (weather, &c. permitting) landed in time to proceed by the
same Trains east and west. These arrangements, as to 'Bus and Trains are stated merely
for the information of Passengers, but the Company do not undertake to forward Passengers
by Omnibus ; nor do they undertake to ship or land at Portmahomack unless a Boat is off
waiting for the Steamer, so as to prevent detention.

Passengers, Goods, and Stock, can be forwarded from Burghead for Edinburgh and
London by Steamer every Friday Morning, and for London direct every alternate Tuesday.
Application for further information may be made to
Mr. HILL, Innkeeper, Golspie.
Mr. GUNN, Innkeeper, Dornoch.
The COMPANY'S OFFICE at Littleferry ;
Or here to P. CHRISTALL, Agent and Manager.

Fig 2.4: Advertisement for Littleferry-Burghead Steamer
(reproduced from the *Northern Times*)

AVOCH

Avoch, which had limited harbour facilities, served a prosperous hinterland and was a serious competitor to Cromarty as its flat beaches enabled ships to be loaded and off loaded in safety. The exports for the area were grain, cattle, herring and stones with imports of coal, iron, salt, hemp and whisky.

CROMARTY

During the sixteenth and seventeenth centuries there was a significant amount of trade between Cromarty and northern Europe, including Russia, and this was due in part to its position within the Cromarty Firth. The town developed as an industrial centre and port in the latter part of the eighteenth century, when the laird of Cromarty, George Ross, built a brewery, factories for the production of rope, nails and spades and developed pig rearing, supplying the English pork and bacon market. These developments were successful for a time and, coupled with the return of the herring, Cromarty became a centre for trade for the northern part of the Firth.

There were shipwrights employed in the port during the eighteenth century but no record exists of any ships built. The *Aberdeen Journal* in 1748 and 1751 records the entry of two Cromarty-owned ships into Aberdeen Harbour. The town had four shipbuilders in the early part of the nineteenth century who built fourteen ships between 1811 and 1850, as well as small fishing craft. These were, however, small vessels suitable only for coastal trading reflecting the decline of Cromarty as a trading and industrial centre in the 1830s and 1840s.

Whilst Cromarty's position as an active port declined, there is evidence that, because of its sheltered position, large ships anchored offshore and unloaded their cargoes into smaller vessels for shipment to other Moray Firth ports.

DINGWALL

Unlike other towns in the Cromarty Firth, Dingwall had neither a harbour nor good sandy beaches on which vessels could load or unload cargoes, and the town's trade suffered as a consequence. Cargoes had to be loaded and discharged on the mud flats to the east of the town. This was a slow, cumbersome process.

A small harbour was built during the eighteenth century which was ineffective because of mud brought down by the River Peffery, so the Town Council decided to develop the existing harbour and build a canal to the Firth. This was completed by 1817. Neither the harbour nor the canal was a commercial success because of silting caused by insufficient flow of water in the river; to overcome this problem, by 1870 the canal had been improved and deepened. However the harbour was never able to provide sufficient income to maintain it, and the canal gradually deteriorated, its effectiveness being further reduced when the railway company built a bridge across the river. As the railway provided the most effective method of transporting goods and people, the canal and harbour fell into disuse in 1884.

INVERGORDON

Invergordon was a busy trading centre during the late eighteenth and early nineteenth centuries because it afforded shelter to vessels, which were able to land their goods on the beach. A pier was built in 1817 and extended in 1828 because of the volume of trade. The Moray Firth steamers on the Inverness-Leith service always called at Invergordon on both the outward and inward journey because it served a large agricultural hinterland.

PORTMAHOMACK

The harbour at Portmahomack was built by Lord Tarbet in 1698 together with a meal girnal, but it fell into disrepair. The Commission for Highland Roads and Bridges built a new harbour in 1815. The NSA records that in 1839-40, 112 vessels with a total tonnage of 6896 tons entered the port. Grain was the main export with the principal ports being London, Leith and Liverpool.

The harbour was rebuilt in 1857, with the main imports being coal and salt. The main export was herring, which was shipped to Memel (Russia) and Stettin (Germany).

DORNOCH FIRTH, BONAR BRIDGE and MEIKLE FERRY

Apart from Portmahomack there were no harbours in the Firth which served its eastern end; ships loaded and discharged cargoes on Tain and Dornoch beaches as they were sufficiently hard to allow the passage of horses and carts at low tide. There was a small pier at Meikle Ferry which could take vessels of 300 tons. A wooden pier was built during the 1830s at Bonar Bridge by a local landowner, and there is a notice in Tain museum detailing the charges for goods being loaded and discharged. The list covers lime, coal, oats, barley, potatoes, deals, pit props, slates, herring, salt, and wool. This shows that, what is now a quiet corner of the Firth, had been a thriving centre for trade. A stone pier was built in 1877 and the harbour order lists charges for a variety of goods including bacon, hemp, hoops, spirits, turpentine, pitch, and turnips. According to the North Sea Pilot for 1914, the pier at Bonar was at that time capable of being used by vessels with a draught up to ten feet. Exports were wool, barley, pit props, railway sleepers, and peats.

The upper part of the Firth became silted up due, apparently, to the extensive timber felling to the west of Bonar Bridge, and with the advent of the railway the pier at Bonar Bridge became obsolete. The pier at Meikle Ferry is still, however, in use by mussel fishermen.

LITTLEFERRY

Shipping intelligence columns frequently recorded cargoes being loaded and discharged at Littleferry, a small port at the mouth of Loch Fleet. The volume of shipping movements is surprising because there was a bar at the mouth of the loch which effectively limited the size of the ships which could enter the port. There was a good depth of water in the loch itself – 16-18 feet at Littleferry – but, according to the OSA, only ships of 5-10 tons could cross the bar, which was caused by the action of wind and tide, and varied in height during the eighteenth and nineteenth centuries; this occasionally allowed larger ships to use the port. Due to the movement of the sand banks, entrance to Littleferry was never easy and ships always required the assistance of a pilot. The Commission for Highland Roads and Bridges considered developing Littleferry as a harbour by improving access, and plans were prepared, but the scheme never came to fruition.

There was a regular service between Littleferry and Burghead up to the 1860s (see Fig 2.4), and the volume of trade – mainly cattle – was such that steamer services were operated between Littleferry and Leith during the 1870s. The reasons for the development of this steam service were twofold – the cost of tolls on the turnpikes leading to markets in the south, and the reduction in value of livestock as a result of the long overland journey. The saddest cargoes must have been the emigrants who left the land in their thousands hoping for a better life in Canada and Australia.

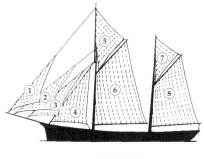

1	Flying Jib
2	Outer Jib
3	Inner Jib
4	Fore Stayssil
5	Main Gaff Topsail
6	Mainsail
7	Mizzen Jackyard Topsail
8	Mizzen

KETCH

Fig 2.5: The schooner *Dispatch* 1888 (National Maritime Museum, London)

SMALL PORTS

Small ships were built round the coast of the Firth on various sites, since all that was required was a firm base beside the sea, a plentiful supply of timber, shipwrights and sawyers. Ships in the early part of the century were built to a standard design which required no plans, as the 'eye' of the shipbuilder was all that was required. If the builder was successful and timber could be purchased at the right price, more ships were built, but usually lack of capital on the part of prospective purchasers and the builder made men move on to seek employment elsewhere, and the site reverted to just being part of the beach.

The list of ships built in the Moray Firth given in Appendix B includes a section on ships built in various small ports; in some parts of the coast which did not possess a harbour such as Beauly, Munlochy, Fowles; and in Fochabers which is not even on the coast.

Summary of ships built 1781-1895

Table 2.1, showing the number of ships built 1781-1895 under different tonnages, illustrates the significant difference between those constructed in Speymouth and elsewhere in the Firth. If Banff is excluded from the total, it will be seen that 60 percent of the ships constructed in ports other than Speymouth did not exceed 50 tons, reflecting the demand for ships capable of using the small harbours and where necessary the beaches round the Firth. These small ships, which in the early part of the century were rigged as sloops and latterly as schooners, were mainly engaged in the considerable coasting traffic within the Firth. Some of the small ports built a few vessels of 100-200 tons, all of which were capable of undertaking deep sea voyages, but most would have been engaged in coastal traffic in order to meet the needs of their home port.

The major difference between Speymouth and the other Moray Firth ports lay in the number of vessels built and their size. Practically half of the ships built in the Firth during the nineteenth century were built in Kingston and Garmouth, as were 80 percent of the ships of 100 tons or more.

The reasons why Speymouth predominated as a shipbuilding centre were:-

1. A ready supply of timber from Speyside forests of the right quality. Thus the price per ton and therefore production costs were kept at a reasonable level.
2. Long experience in building large ships so the yards were able to design and construct ships at a price owners could afford.
3. A group of ship owners capable of owning and managing ships using locally built vessels in the Coastal, Baltic, African and Australian trade.

TONS	Less than 29	30 to 49	50 to 99	100 to 149	150 to 199	200 to 249	250 to 299	300 to 349	350 to 399	400 to 500	
					No. of Ships						
Banff	7	11	95	33	11	4	1	–	–	–	162
Buckie	25	2	5	–	2	–	–	–	–	–	34
Burghead	7	5	11	2	–	–	–	–	–	–	25
Clachnaharry	10	3	5	–	–	–	–	–	–	–	18
Cromarty	5	4	3	1	1	–	–	–	–	–	14
Cullen	59	7	3	–	–	–	–	–	–	–	69
Findhorn	6	12	20	6	2	2	–	–	–	–	48
Inverness	40	26	44	12	2	6	1		–	–	131
Lossiemouth	6	7	13	1	2	3	–	–	–	–	32
Macduff	5	5	15	5	–	–	–	–	–	–	30
Nairn	4	–	4	1	1	–	–	–	–	–	10
Portsoy	–	3	15	2	2	–	–	–	–	–	22
Rosehearty	9	1	2	–	–	–	–	–	–	–	12
Sandend	6	4	7	–	1	–	–	–	–	–	18
Sundry Ports	42	3	20	1	–	–	–	–	–	–	66
Total	231	93	262	64	24	15	2	–	–	–	691
Speymouth	16	48	275	116	52	29	28	32	8	9	613
TOTAL	248	140	530	178	76	44	30	32	8	9	1295

Table 2.1: Tonnage of ships built in the Moray Firth 1782-1895

	1785 to 1800	1801 to 1810	1811 to 1820	1821 to 1830	1831 to 1840	1841 to 1850	1851 to 1860	1861 to 1870	1871 to 1880	1881 to 1895	Total
Speymouth	62	38	39	36	59	77	93	103	87	19	613
Other Yards	41	80	59	126	81	94	74	78	46	12	691
Total	103	118	98	162	140	171	167	181	133	31	1304

Table 2.2: Number of ships built in the Moray Firth 1782-1895

Ownership of vessels by Moray Firth residents, 1881

In the early part of the nineteenth century, multiple ownership of vessels was rare. Local directories for Moray ports show that ships were owned by people who resided in the ship's home port. The majority of the ports at that time were small, and only capable of taking schooners of 100 tons or less. By the latter part of the century, however, the position had changed; ships on average were much larger, more expensive to build, and there were fewer vessels which were owned and commanded by one man.

An analysis of the ownership of vessels in the Moray Firth in 1881 is given in Table 2.4, showing that the average tonnage (if Garmouth and Kingston ships are excluded) was between 80-160 tons. The larger vessels could not use the smaller ports and the greater majority of the ships belonged to either Banff or Inverness.

The position of Garmouth and Kingston shipowners was markedly different from those in other parts of the Firth. The number of vessels owned and the average size of the ships was twice as large as the majority of Firth vessels. Ships with tonnages in excess of 300 tons were capable of travelling as far afield as Australia and China. This size of ship was too small, however, to be capable of operating profitably on these routes on a regular basis because of their relatively low cargo capacity and high crew costs. This was the period when large sailing vessels in excess of 1000 tons were being operated in large numbers from British ports. The small ships had to confine themselves to shorter voyages in order to operate profitably. Records show that these ships traded with North and South America, Africa and the Mediterranean ports on a regular basis. All the Garmouth- and Kingston-owned ships had Banff as their home port. It is doubtful, however, if these ships ever returned to Banff because of its limited facilities.

Fig 2.6: Wick Harbour 1890 and the schooner *Elba*
(The Johnston Collection, The Wick Society)

A list of Garmouth and Kingston shipowners, and the number of ships owned by them is given in Table 2.3. It is noteworthy that six out of the ten owners were shipbuilders. Ships required a considerable amount of maintenance during each voyage, and repairs were carried out each winter when the vessel was laid up. It would be reasonable to assume that the ships owned by these shipbuilders would return to Speymouth to have their annual overhaul at the owner's yard. There would thus be a considerable saving in repair costs to these owners.

The ownership of these ships required a considerable capital outlay by these owners and business acumen in managing (it is assumed profitably) vessels which were trading in many overseas ports. Shipowning was a high risk business.

Owner	No of ships	Total tonnage	Av. tonnage
J Duncan Jnr & Co	5	1481	296
W Kinloch	6	2151	359
James Geddie	2	776	388
James Geddie Jr	1	249	-
Alex. Marr	1	235	-
J Mill	3	810	270
J Winchester/G Swanson	1	187	-
A MacDonald	2	839	419
James Duncan	1	312	-
Wm Geddie	1	312	-

Table 2.3: Ownership of vessels (Garmouth and Kingston residents) 1881

Residence of Owners	No. of ships	Total tonnage	Average tonnage	Registered Port
Garmouth & Kingston	23	7352	320	Banff
Inverness (I)	22	3199	145	Inverness
Banff (B)	16	1811	113	Banff
Lossiemouth	13	2596	200	1 Ln; 1 B; 2 L; 9 I
Macduff	9	776	86	8 B; 1 Leith
Portsoy	9	1195	133	7 B; 2 P
Portgordon	9	1289	143	Banff
Nairn	6	570	95	Inverness
Burghead	4	542	136	Inverness
Invergordon	3	467	156	G; Lp; A
Buckie	3	277	92	Banff
Cullen	2	285	143	Banff
Tain	2	162	81	Tain
Portessie	2	163	82	Banff
Beauly	1	90	90	Inverness
Fortrose	1	96	96	Fortrose
125				

I: Inverness; B: Banff; L: Lossiemouth; Ln: London; P: Portsoy; G: Glasgow;
Lp: Liverpool; A: Aberdeen

Table 2.4: Ownership of vessels (ports and towns in the Moray Firth) 1881

3 TRADE

Introduction

The earliest record of trade being carried out in the Moray Firth is a Charter granted in 1393 by Thomas of Dunbar, Earl of Murray:-

Be it knawyn tyl al men thrw yis present lettres Vs Thomayse of Dunbarr . Eryl of Murreffe, for tyl have grauntyt and gyfin tyl ye aldirman . ye baylis . of wre Burgh of Elgyne . and to ye burges . of y^t ilke al ye wol . ye clathe and al vthir thyngis . y^t gais be schipe owte of wre hafine of Spee .

No doubt other Royal Burghs on the Firth would also have received similar charters although the Elgin charter is the only one in existence. This document, which is in excellent condition, can be examined in the Moray District Archives in Forres.

According to the annals of the Royal Burgh of Forres a trading union called a 'Hanse' was formed and received recognition from King David I in the first half of the twelfth century. The ports which formed this Hanse were Aberdeen, Inverness, Elgin, Forres and Nairn. The next record of trade is found in the account books of the Burgh of Elgin for the period 1585-1620, where references are made to arrests of 'unfreemen' arriving in 'ye port of Spey' with salt and 'tymmer fra Norway.'

Trade with the Continent and the Baltic was not substantial compared to that carried out by ports on Scotland's east coast such as Leith, Dundee, and Aberdeen and was limited to the export of grain and salmon. By the seventeenth century, however, the Firth was exporting timber, malt, corn, and salmon to the Continent and these trade links continued to grow as production of these goods increased. Another important factor was the emigration of Scots to Holland, Sweden, Poland, Russia and Germany. By the eighteenth and nineteenth centuries there were well established merchants in these countries, acting as agents for their fellow Scots for the movement of goods to and from Scottish and English ports.

Banff, Spey and Findhorn merchants owned ships in the seventeenth and eighteenth centuries because of the established markets for bulk grain and timber. During this period there was also trade between the Firth and the rest of Scotland and England, imports consisting mainly of coal from Northumberland and Fife, and exports of timber and fish. In addition there was a long-established, regular trade in salmon with London.

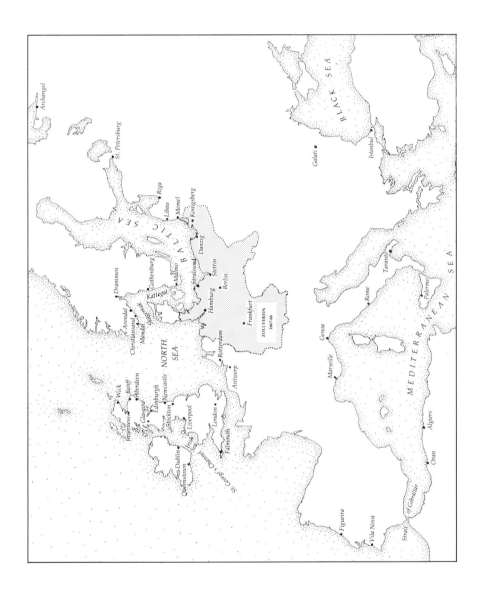

Fig 3.1: Principal European ports trading with the Moray Firth

When the Glenmore Company built their shipyard at Kingston, the necessary skills were brought to the area to enable larger ships to be constructed, and many of the shipwrights they trained set up yards in other ports in the Firth. Ships at that time were not large, 60-70 tons, and the ability to construct such a vessel was well within the capabilities of a trained shipwright. The development of the shipbuilding industry took some 25 years and growth in building was accompanied by the availability of trained seamen and masters and a merchant class willing to develop trade.

The records of trade were maintained by the Scottish Board of Customs from 1741-1831, after which the function was transferred to London. These records for the period up to 1830, which are held in the Scottish Record Office, provide a very detailed account of all goods imported, together with the name of the vessel, its master, where it was built, the name of the merchant importing the goods and where the goods were obtained. This record is not available for the period after 1830 and the only source of information on goods imported and exported is the shipping intelligences provided by the *Banffshire Journal* and the *Inverness Courier*. Early copies of these newspapers contain little information on shipping movements, thus the record of trade listed starts in 1850 and continues at 10-year intervals until 1880. After 1880 there was a significant fall in ship movements recorded by these newspapers. The railways were moving the goods which at one time were carried by coasters; in addition, goods were being moved in larger quantities by steamships which were more reliable so that fewer ship movements were required. Sailing ships were still owned and operated by local owners but their trading activities were mainly between British and foreign ports.

Trade records therefore fall into two distinct groups – 1805-1830 and 1850-1880 – with the first analysis being completed from the detailed record compiled from Customs records, and the second from information obtained from the shipping intelligence section of two major newspapers. The newspapers merely record the main cargo – timber, bone dust or in some cases 'goods'– so it is only possible to provide an analysis based on these broad descriptions for the later part of the period.

TRADE 1805-1830

The majority of goods imported into the Firth during this period came from Norway, Germany and Russia, and the variety and volume of the traffic shows that there was in existence an effective network of traders on both sides of the North Sea capable of purchasing, transporting and paying for a considerable range of goods. Historians who have published studies of early trade between Scotland and the Baltic (Smout; Jackson), have remarked on the number of Scots who settled in various Baltic ports and, because they were so successful, became prominent citizens in their adopted country.

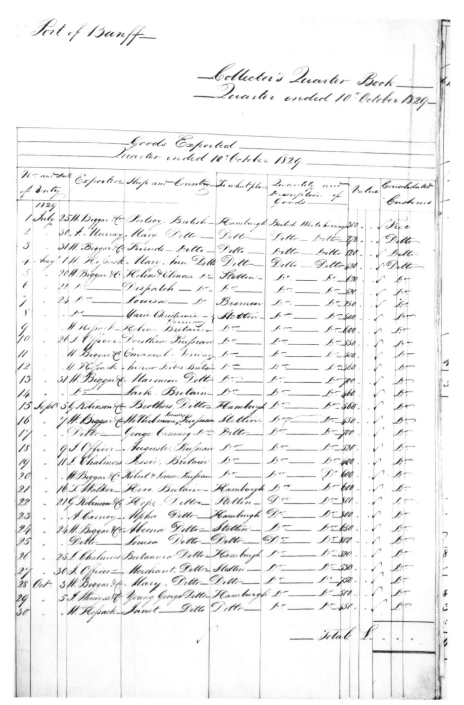

Fig 3.2: Record of Herring exported from Banff in the quarter ended October 1829

The existence of these Scots traders in the major European ports facilitated the movement of goods and must have had a significant effect on the development of trade. Researchers have identified Scots from Montrose, Arbroath and Aberdeen who settled in the Baltic ports, but it is likely that merchants from Inverness, Findhorn, Burghead, Portsoy, or Banff would also have sent members of their families to ports where there was considerable trade, such as Danzig, which was a major importer of herring.

Herring was exported in considerable quantities to Germany during this period, and this was done in spite of significant competition from the Dutch and Norwegians. This trade expanded markedly after 1830, keeping large numbers of people in employment. An extract from the Custom Register giving a list of the ships exporting herring for the quarter ending October 1829 is given in Fig 3.2. The value of the cargoes was considerable and shows the extent of the trade between the Firth and the Baltic. There was considerable risk attached to these ventures and there appears to have been no system in existence whereby an owner could obtain insurance.

Appendix 2 analyses the trade between Moray Firth ports and Scottish, English and foreign ports, together with a breakdown of ship movements between the Inverness-Banff Custom areas. The Customs register for these towns did not relate specifically to these ports; Inverness was responsible for the area from Helmsdale to Garmouth, including the busy ports of Nairn, Findhorn and Burghead; Banff was the centre of Customs operations from the Spey to Pennan. The volume of trade was very large for this area. There were differences, too, in the pattern of trade carried out between these two areas. Inverness traded mainly with Russia in order to obtain hemp, flax, timber, masts and spars. Banff imported timber, masts and spars mainly from Norway, except for the period during Napoleon's continental blockade. Flax was a major import destined for the linen mills which at that time operated in Huntly, Keith and Inverness. The trade in flax through Banffshire decreased, however, as the price of this commodity increased and larger and more efficiently run mills in Aberdeen and Dundee captured the trade.

The imports of timber would have been principally for the construction of ships as stocks of very large trees in upper Speyside were considerably reduced by 1815. Large stocks of timber were still available but, as the trees were comparatively small their use for shipbuilding was limited, and builders had to go elsewhere for timber of the required size and quality. In addition to shipbuilding there would have been a demand for timber for house building, as more and better quality houses were being built, and this made it necessary to purchase Baltic and North American timber, which was more suitable than the home grown timber for this purpose. Baltic countries produced a range of timber which met the demand of shipbuilders – size and quality – with Norway, Russia and Germany supplying oak, beech, and fir. Another major import was birch, which was used as staves for herring barrels and in the construction of harrows.

Considerable quantities of masts and spars were imported, and this trade continued for most of the century as Britain lacked the long cold winters and warm summers necessary for the production of good quality pine timber. This timber has a high resin content which makes it supple, an essential requirement for masts, and Baltic pine was ideal for this purpose. Riga supplied the timber for main masts and yards, and Norway the timber for the lighter spars. Strathspey, until stocks were exhausted, would also have been a supplier of masts and spars, for its climate was also suitable for the production of timber with a high resin content. Most of the exports from Kingston during the eighteenth and nineteenth centuries would have also been for this purpose.

The Customs records for Banff and Inverness show in meticulous detail all items of cargo taken in by individual ships. These records, which must have taken a large number of people to monitor, check and record, were summarised and reported annually to Parliament showing the level of exports and imports and countries issuing and receiving the goods. Figure 3.3 shows the wide range of goods taken into the Banff Customs area for the period 15-21 September 1826: timber and spars for shipbuilders, flax for the mills, oak bark for tanning sails, birch for coopers, clover seeds for farmers; the Rhenish wine and Dutch cheese would probably be for the local gentry with Cologne water for their ladies. Of the six ships listed, two were British, two Norwegian and two Russian, indicating the extent of this trade.

EXPORTS 1850-1880

Appendix 3 analyses exports and imports under port of destination and origin, using information extracted from local newspapers of the period. The statistics are divided between exports and imports from individual ports and name the principal cargoes – grain, timber, goods – and record the growth of movements in principal cargoes rather than a detailed and complete list of their movement. A large number of cargoes were mixed with no one item predominating and so were described as 'goods'.

The Moray Firth was primarily an agricultural area with strong fishing and timber industries, and over the period these industries were developed in order to meet a growing demand for their products in the South and West of Scotland and the northeast of England.

Trade with the Continent was not large in relation to the imports from that area. The statistics are to some extent misleading in that they record ship movements from Moray Firth ports and do not include exports from Fraserburgh, Peterhead, Helmsdale and Wick. The reason for the small number of exports of herring is that although the fish were caught by experienced and well-equipped fishermen from various parts of the Firth, the majority of catches were landed at the larger fishing ports because of their better facilities.

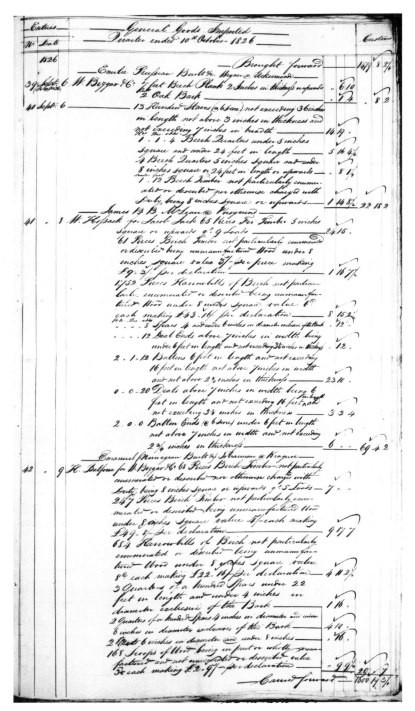

Fig 3.3a: Extract from Banff Customs Register quarter ending October 1829

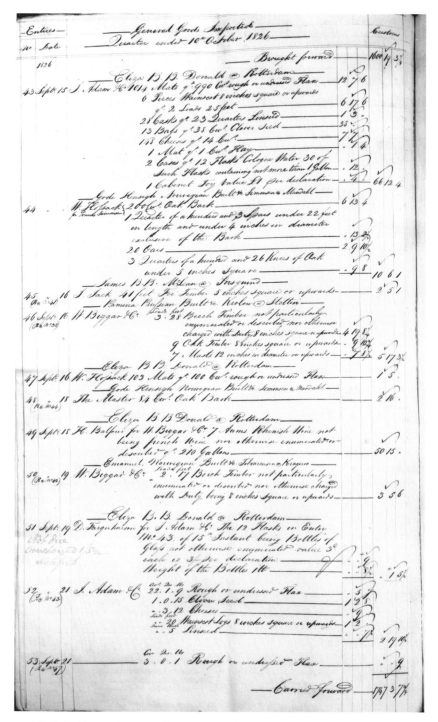

Fig 3.3b: Extract from Banff Customs Register quarter ending October 1829

Exports from Inverness and its surrounding ports were relatively low in volume compared with the Banffshire and Moray ports, albeit they followed a similar pattern. The reason for the difference in volume is that, for most of the period, Inverness had an effective rail link with the south which could transport goods, cattle, and passengers to Leith and London. The movement of goods to and from Inverness was probably greater than the Banff area if records of rail and steamer cargoes are taken into account. Inverness built a large number of small ships suitable for the movement of goods within the Firth and with the west coast but did not build large vessels until the 1850s and many of these according to newspaper records engaged in trading outwith Scotland.

Trade figures record the movement of ships between Banff, Macduff, Portsoy, Lossiemouth, Burghead, Nairn, Inverness, and Cromarty, but there was a considerable movement of goods by sea in addition to those recorded in the newspapers. Many cargoes of locally produced goods and coal were landed on the beaches and in other small harbours and this practice continued long after the 1880s.

IMPORTS 1850-80

The major import into the Firth was undoubtedly coal from the northeast of England and Fife, with England being the major supplier. There were several reasons for this – it produced coal more cheaply, had better facilities for loading, and the fuel was well suited to the domestic market. As northeast England purchased large amounts of pit props and railway sleepers, ship masters found trade with this part of England very profitable, in that with good agents they had cargoes both on the outward and inward voyage. Northeast England also purchased grain and timber from the Baltic, so that one of the regular routes was herring to the Baltic, grain to northeast England, and coal to the Moray Firth. The Scottish coal trade with the Firth was substantial, but coal price and quality (which was more suitable for industrial use) ensured that the market did not increase until the later part of the century.

The Firth's landward economy was largely based on agricultural fertiliser which consisted of bone dust from the Baltic, and guano which was transhipped from Liverpool and London. Some of the ships carrying guano came directly to Cromarty; the cargo was then carried by coaster to various local ports.

Exported timber was of a quality more suited to making pit props and railway sleepers, as the largest sizes and the best quality hardwoods were retained for use in the shipbuilding industry. Larger vessels were now being produced and the shipbuilders had to import better quality timber from the Baltic and North America to meet this demand. The fishing boats, being smaller, used home grown timber such as oak or larch.

Timber suitable for shipbuilding was available in North America and because of its strength and resistance to rot was largely used during the second half of the century. The Lloyds Surveys of ships give details of the timber used in their construction and it is possible to ascertain what particular type of North American timber was used. However, there appears to be no record of ships bringing in timber from that area. There are two possible reasons for this: the timber might have been landed at Liverpool or Aberdeen and shipped by rail to the Firth because of the size involved; or, like guano, the cargoes could have been taken directly to Cromarty and transhipped from there. The Baltic remained the major supplier of timber and the *Banffshire Journal* records that in 1869 there were ten cargoes from the Baltic and two from Russia and Sweden. The same newspaper comments on the considerable quantities of larch wood being taken into the area by rail.

THE BALTIC HERRING TRADE

Customs records of exports for the ports of Inverness and Banff up to 1830 devote a whole page every quarter to ships taking cargoes of herring to the Continent (Figure 3.2). As export records do not exist for the following 20 years it is not possible to state what volume was to the Continent during that time. Records of herring exports for 1850 show that trade had increased so it is reasonable to assume that the Moray Firth ports had continued to meet Continental demand.

Trade with the Continent had existed for a very long time but the Scottish fishermen's share of this market was small compared to that taken by the Dutch, who monopolised the market. The Dutch were proficient in catching and curing the fish and had built up a market for a high quality product. One reason for the success of the Dutch herring industry was that they produced a very high grade of salt for curing the fish with a consequently better flavour than fish cured by Scottish salt. They also had better methods of curing fish so that their product was still a marketable commodity by the time it reached its final destination.

The British Government was concerned about the methods the Scots employed in curing herring and so it set up the Herring Board in 1807, with the intention of improving standards and meeting the demands of Continental markets. This was done at the right time, as the Dutch hold on the market was weakening and the Scots were therefore well placed to exploit the situation. Their success in breaking into and improving their sales to the Baltic was due to two factors – their ability to catch and deliver fish to the market, and the improvement in their methods of curing these fish. There were other markets for herring, namely Ireland and the West Indies but the Continent was closer to hand and had the advantage that it was a larger market and cargoes could be obtained from the Baltic ports for the return journey.

Herring export records for 1860 show a decline in cargoes from ports served by the Inverness and Banff Custom areas. This was because, as the stocks of fish declined off the coast, fishermen had to go further out into the Firth in order to catch the fish. It was just as convenient, and made more sense, to land their catches in ports which had labour for curing and packing fish as well as a ready market for their product, such as Wick, Helmsdale, Fraserburgh, and Peterhead. The fish curers had well established trading links with Germany and the Baltic, because they had proved that their barrels of Scottish herring, with recognised trade marks, were of a high quality. There was also transport by ships with masters experienced in trading with European fish importers.

	Great Britain	Holland	Norway
1824	15,468	1,374	1,030
1825	18,160	4,255	6,758
1826	7,695	4,874	6,915
1827	15,082	5,010	9,948
1828	13,478	7,283	16,008
1829	14,449	4,422	28,485
1830	33,866	4,595	29,137
1831	13,077	3,802	21,924
1832	31,837	4,712	56,979
1833	31,177	2,756	77,758
1834	19,060	4,546	53,981
1835	26,875	1,943	39,730
1836	28,227	2,137	34,798
1837	36,309	6,722	77,851
1838	40,209	4,491	51,761
1839	49,456	1,059	46,282
1840	73,949	2,141	82,914
1841	50,732	850	43,433
1842	62,135	3,397	48,240
1843	143,659	1,119	44,092
1844	105,097	990	97,127
1845	81,189	2,457	44,264
1846	104,372	179	54,733
1847	112,260	348	42,828
1848	103,402	196	23,903
1849	147,103	1,313	26,962
1850	116,538	568	12,507

Table 3.1: Herring imports into Stettin (per barrel)

Table 3.1 gives the number of barrels of herring exported from Britain, Holland and Norway to Stettin – the centre for distribution of Scots herring in Northern Europe – for the period 1824-50. Despite the efforts of the Herring Board to improve standards, the increase in volume from Britain was slow in the early part of the century.

Quite apart from the quality of the product there was another factor which contributed significantly to the growth of the industry. The Zollverein – the trading market formed by the northern German states – charged much lower rates on herring than other Continental countries and consequently the Scots were able to sell at prices which still gave them a good rate of return. The extent of the area covered by this trading market was considerable as can be seen by the shaded area on Figure 3.1.

The four main centres for exporting fish were Wick, Helmsdale, Fraserburgh, and Peterhead and by the latter part of the century they had built up an effective system of curing, packing and transporting fish to the Continent. The Fishery Board's 'Crown Brand' mark was accepted throughout Europe as representing a good quality product. It was thus possible for merchants to obtain credit by holding bills of lading for 'Crown Brand' herring, ensuring that payment was made quickly to all involved in catching and processing. It is taken for granted that an international system for obtaining credit is a modern creation. However, an examination of the international finance system, which formed the basis for meeting the requirements of the Scots herring industry and the German merchants in the nineteenth century, shows that the system was as effective as modern methods of transferring credit, if a trifle slower.

MORAY SHIPS' TRADE

The Custom records for Banff record the names of vessels taking out cargoes of herring and returning with cargoes from various European ports. Many of the vessels were foreign built, but amongst the British vessels were ships which could be identified as being built in the Firth. There were not many locally owned ships at that time so identification was not a difficult task. The names of these ships, together with some of their cargoes and destinations undertaken during the period are listed in Table 3.2. The smallest vessel was the 41ft *Alpha* of Banff; average weight was 60-70 tons and 55-60 ft in length. The largest vessels – *Jessie* and *Mary* – would have been roughly 90 feet long. To reach their destination in the Baltic they had to cross the North Sea, go through the Kattegat and traverse the Baltic in order to get to Russia, a round voyage of 2,600 miles.

The 770 mile voyage to Stettin with a cargo of herring took between 10-14 days, and required a Master with considerable experience and navigation ability, a skill that could not have been common in those days. He had to deal with agents, Customs and port officials, and in addition arrange the purchase of food, water and supplies for the ship, and repairs if necessary. These transactions would have been carried out in a foreign language and currency.

The problems associated with speaking a foreign language in the Baltic ports and Germany may not have been so great for the Moray and Banffshire Masters, as the language spoken in these countries was 'Nieder Deutsch', which has many similarities to the dialect of northeast Scotland.

There would also be Scots in these ports who would have looked after the trading interests of their compatriots as well as their own. Masters and their crews would have been able to converse with agents and suppliers in any of these countries and that facility must have been of considerable benefit in the furtherance of trade there.

Vessel	Tons	Port of Registry	Destination	Cargo	Distance (Naut. Miles)
William	60	Portsoy	Hamburg	Herring	490
Helen	66	Garmouth	St Petersburg	Hemp	1300
Eliza	93	Portsoy	Rotterdam	Flax,Clover & Seed	570
Mary	153	Garmouth	Memel	Battens & Deals	910
Friendship	35	Portsoy	Hamburg	Herring, Iron & Fir	490
Marchioness	57	Portgordon	Gothenburg	Treenails	570
Lark	62	Banff	Stettin	Herring	770
Jessie	142	Garmouth	Stettin	Herring	770
Duchess of Gordon	65	Banff	Hamburg	Herring	490
Barbara and Ann	73	Spey	Azores	Herring, Birch & Spars	1900
James	47	Portsoy	Porsgrunn	Battens	360
Alpha	37	Macduff	Hamburg	Herring	490

Table 3.2: Some voyages by Moray Firth ships 1805-29

Overseas trade was only part of the maritime activities of these vessels which would also have been engaged in trading with Scottish and English ports. When one considers the size of the harbours and ships of Portsoy, Spey and Banff, it reflects the commercial drive of the merchants and their ship masters that they founded and built up such an extensive overseas trade.

STEAMER SERVICES 1840-1870

During the period 1840-65, local newspapers carried advertisements giving details of the regular weekly services provided by steamers between Inverness and Edinburgh. The steamers called at various intermediate ports, such as Fort George, Cromarty, Invergordon, Nairn, Findhorn, Burghead, Lossiemouth, and Banff.

The advertisements stated that the ships had spacious passenger accommodation and facilities for transporting cattle and other livestock, together with items of cargo all of which were 'carried at proprietor's risk.' They were also of great benefit to both passengers and farmers when one considers the state of the roads. Sutherland farmers were concerned about the effect of droving cattle overland to markets because of its effect on the value of their cattle. The services provided by the *Maid of Morven* and latterly by various steamships proved profitable to both farmers and ship owners (see Appendix 4). *Iris*, an early paddle steamer, was used for a short time in the north of Scotland but was later sold to Norway (Fig 3.4).

Apart from the steamer services, small ships advertised regular services to London, Newcastle, and Aberdeen in the 1840s and 1850s from Burghead and Findhorn. These services must have ceased by 1863 as Blacks' Directory for that year makes no mention of them. There were regular passages by small ships between Burghead and Littleferry – a much quicker journey than the overland route – from as early as 1866 (see Fig 2.2).

The early paddle steamers carried a considerable amount of cargo and passengers as, unlike sailing ships, they were not dependent on the wind for propulsion. They were driven by engines which, by 1870-80 standards, were low powered and inefficient, consuming large quantities of coal, and limiting the amount of cargo they could carry to short routes (e.g. Leith-Inverness). Steamships built after 1870 had many advantages over the early paddle steamers. Their hulls were built of iron, the engines were more powerful and reliable, and they were screw driven. Because of these factors their operating costs were much lower and, by the 1890s, maritime trade in the Firth was carried almost exclusively by steamships.

The railway companies, which could also reach inland areas inaccessible to steamers, were providing effective competition but they were not very popular because of their high charges, and small sailing ships continued to serve outlying communities up to the early part of the twentieth century.

Fig 3.4: Paddle Steamer *Iris* (Aberdeen Maritime Museum)

4 *ORIENT, HIGHLANDER,*
EXPRESS and *CALEDONIA*

Introduction

There is a wealth of books providing photographs of nineteenth century sailing ships, and records of their sailing capabilities are available for anyone wishing to do research on these vessels. Their design and method of construction are well documented and it is possible to examine many of the original plans of these ships. It is however difficult to obtain a detailed record of their operation which shows voyages undertaken during their working life, the cargoes obtained, the cost of maintaining the ships and the crew and, in the end, how profitable they were as an investment.

The scarcity of the records providing this information is not surprising when it is understood that these early sailing ships were owned by small groups of men including, in many cases, the Master of the vessel who, once it was sold or wrecked, would have no further interest in any records relating to it.

The records which are of interest are the ship's Log, which detailed the courses and the distances travelled to various ports, and the disbursement Ledger, which gave the income obtained from cargoes at different ports and all expenditure incurred by the Master. This last record provides the most useful information in that the income and expenditure were usually recorded in some detail, making it possible to analyse the costs and determine the functions that a Master had to carry out at each port in order to load and discharge cargoes and service his ship. The Ledger's primary purpose, however, was that of a record of stewardship by the Master and was used to ascertain the profit or loss at the end of each trading period.

The four Disbursement Ledgers which are examined in this chapter vary considerably in the amount of information that they provide. They do, however, enable a record to be compiled of the working lives of these ships which were representative of the many hundreds of sailing ships which carried out Britain's coastal and Continental trade in the nineteenth century.

ORIENT

The *Orient*, a 103 ton schooner, was built in 1855 and, until she was sold in 1867, was engaged in the coasting and Baltic trade. She was no different from the hundreds of schooners which were engaged in similar trade at this time and it is this type of ship whose cargoes and movements are described in Chapter 3 and Appendix A:5.

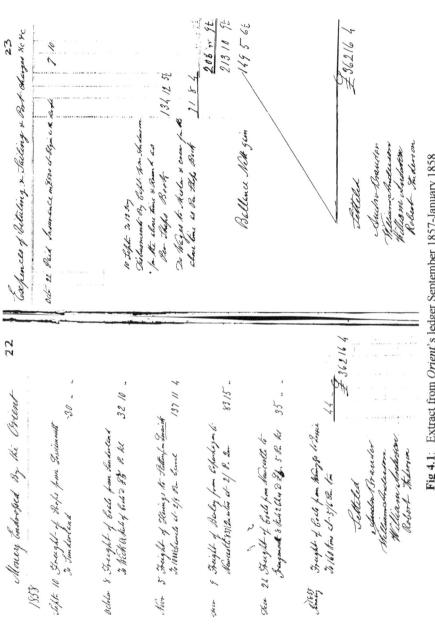

Fig 4.1: Extract from *Orient*'s ledger September 1857-January 1858
(Mr George Innes)

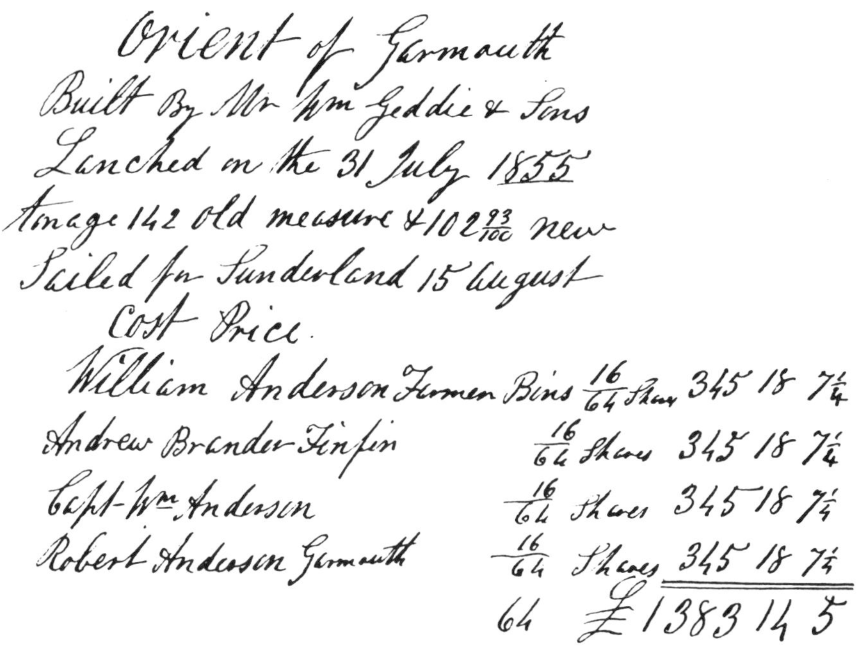
Orient of Garmouth
Built By Mr Wm Geddie & Sons
Lanched on the 31 July 1855
Tonage 142 old measure & 102 93/100 new
Sailed for Sunderland 15 August
Cost Price.

William Anderson Fermen Bins	16/64 Share	345	18	7¼
Andrew Brander Finfan	16/64 Shares	345	18	7¼
Capt Wm Anderson	16/64 Shares	345	18	7¼
Robert Anderson Garmouth	16/64 Shares	345	18	7¼
	64	£1383	14	5

Figure 4.2: *Orient* - cost of construction showing shares held by owners

An extract from *Orient*'s ledger (Fig 4.1), entitled 'The Money Engrossed by the Orient and Expenses of Victualling and Sailing and Port Charges etc', gives only a summary of monies spent on individual wages, food and materials. More detailed information was recorded in the ship's book, which sadly has been lost. Income from carrying cargo, insurance claims and major repairs is recorded, however, and this information is sufficient to provide an accurate picture of the vessel's economic life.

The value of the ledger is that, as far as is known, it is the only complete record in existence which gives the trading pattern of a Moray Firth ship engaged in the coasting and Baltic trade. It requires such a record of the trade carried out by one vessel to show that ships had to work hard from one year to another in order to make a living.

The *Orient* proved to be a profitable venture for her owners for she provided them on average a return of 12.6 percent per annum, an excellent rate at that time and perfectly acceptable even today – an investor would normally expect to get a five to six percent return on his capital in 1860-70. However, even that rate only applied to commercial ventures which carried a risk; British government securities only gave a return of two to three percent.

According to Lloyds Register, the *Orient* did not have a copper bottom, so she was only fit for voyages in northern waters. She did make one voyage to Figueira for salt but otherwise confined her activities to British coastal waters and the Baltic. Her pattern of trading was variable; some years she was confined to coastal trading but her later years found her more often in the Baltic. It is noticeable that she had a considerable number of voyages where there was a cargo both on the outward and inward journey. The ledger does not provide the names of the crew but it does give the names of the Masters and their period in command. With the exception of Captain Anderson, a part owner, their stay in every case was short. The Andersons were also ship brokers and therefore would have had good agents throughout the *Orient*'s trading area. This factor must have contributed to the high rate of return on their capital.

Master	From	To	Period of Stay
Anderson	August 1855	February 1859	3½ years
Ross	March 1859	September 1859	6 months
Barlow	October 1859	March 1861	1½ years
Crooks	April 1861	September 1862	1½ years
Farquhar	October 1862	February 1864	1½ years
Henry	April 1864	July 1865	1¼ years
Wilson	July 1865	February 1866	8 months
Weir	March 1866	November 1867	1½ years

Orient's Masters and their periods of employment

This pattern of employment was not uncommon, for records show that many Masters and Mates did not stay long on any one ship. It must be assumed that, as young men, they would have not wished to stay too long and would have sought employment on larger vessels once they had gained experience of being in command.

The *Orient*, like any other vessel, incurred expenditure on minor repairs, but this information was not recorded in detail. The cost of major repairs was recorded but little or no information provided. In March 1861 the *Orient* had repairs carried out in Leith which cost £865 4s 7d and the damage must have been considerable in view of the fact that her original cost in 1855 amounted to £1,383 14s 5d. As this work required her to be practically rebuilt the fact was recorded in Lloyds Register. The shareholders recovered £656 9s 3d from insurance companies as a contribution to the costs. The *Orient* ran aground in February 1862 and salvage and repairs cost £68 1s 7d and a similar incident in 1864 incurred a salvage bill of £269 2s 4d. The insurance companies paid £30 11s 7d towards the first claim and £178 1s 7d towards the second.

FROM	Cargo	No		TO	Cargo	No
GERMANY				**ENGLAND**		
Danzig & Stettin	Wheat, Barley	18		London	Wheat, Oats, Barley	9
	Timber	3			Salt	1
	Staves	2		Newcastle	Wheat, Oats, Barley	3
	Peas	1		Fareham	Wheat, Oats, Barley	1
				Exeter	Wheat, Oats, Barley	1
RUSSIA				Hartlepool	Wheat, Oats, Barley	1
Riga & Memel	Flax	1			Peas	1
Konigsberg	Oats	3			Timber	1
	Wheat	2		Weymouth	Wheat, Oats, Barley	1
	Peas	1		Hull	Wheat, Oats, Barley	1
				Grimsby	Timber	1
SCANDINAVIA						
Malmo & Nysted	Oats	1		**SCOTLAND**		
Copenhagen	Barley	2		Leith	Wheat, Oats, Barley	4
					Peas	1
PORTUGAL				Grangemouth	Wheat, Oats, Barley	3
Figueira	Salt	1			Timber	1
				Aberdeen	Wheat, Oats , Barley	1
				Dundee	Wheat, Oats , Barley	1
					Timber	1
				Kirkcaldy	Wheat, Oats , Barley	1
				Fraserburgh	Timber	1
		35				**35**

Table 4.1: Cargoes carried by the *Orient*: 1855-67

Foreign Trade

The *Orient* did not have a fixed trading pattern. In her early life, most of her voyages were between Scottish and English ports. In the last few years she traded mainly between Baltic and British ports. A record of her voyages is given in Appendix 5. Voyages to and from British ports and the Baltic, together with the one voyage to Portugal, are summarised in Table 4.1 and Table 4.2

Cargo	From	To
Coal	Newcastle	Stettin (2), Danzig (4), Konigsberg
		Malmo & Figueira
	Hartlepool	Danzig (2)
	Sunderland	Danzig
	Grangemouth	Lubeck & Stettin
	Clackmannan	Danzig
	Dundee	Stettin
	Dysart/Wemyss	Griefswald & Malmo

Cargo	From	To
Herring	Lerwick	Stettin
	Cromarty	Stettin
	Hopeman	Stettin (2)
	Wick	Stettin
	Portmahomack	Stettin
	Cullen	Stettin
	Helmsdale	Stettin (2)
	Peterhead	Memel
Pig Iron	Bo'ness	Copenhagen & Stettin
	Leith	Konigsberg
	Grangemouth	Stettin
Clay	Gillingham	Copenhagen

Table 4.2: Cargoes taken by *Orient* from British ports to the Continent 1855-67

HIGHLANDER

Costs and Voyages

The *Highlander* was a 74 ton schooner, built in Kingston in 1840. Its disbursement ledger only records expenditure and ports visited by the ship for the period 1847-48 and does not provide any details of cargoes or income received from transporting these cargoes. Whilst it is not possible to state the rate of return earned by the ship, it must have been profitable as Russels

1847	From	To	Assumed Cargo
14-28 Apr.	Spey & Banff	Peterhead	Ballast
3-16 May	Shields	Portsoy	Coal
21 May-4 Jun	Portsoy	Lowestoft	Marble
14-30 Jun	Sutherland	Lossiemouth	Coal
1-17 July	Portsoy	Maldon	Herring
30 Jul-6 Aug	Sunderland	Lossiemouth	Coal
12-23 Aug	Spey & Montrose	Queensferry	Timber
26 Aug-1 Sep	Cockenzie	Peterhead	Coal
13-26 Sept	Spey & St Davids	St Davids & Spey	Ballast & Slates
25-26 Oct	Spey	Guardbridge	Timber
4-8 Nov	Lossiemouth	Peterhead	Timber
	No record of any voyage during this period		
1848			
11 Jan	Peterhead	–	not known
15 Jan	Queensferry	–	not known
20 Jan-2 Feb	Guardbridge	–	not known
11-20 Feb	Sunderland	Peterhead	Coal
6 Mar	Portsoy	–	not known

Table 4.3: Voyages undertaken by *Highlander* 1847-48

Directory records her as still being registered in Garmouth during 1863. The Directory lists many small vessels belonging to various Moray Firth ports which were similar in size to the *Highlander* and engaged in transporting goods round the east coast of Scotland with occasional voyages into England.

The ledger did not record cargoes but gave the names of ports where cargoes were loaded and unloaded, so cargoes which are likely to have been exported from particular ports have been shown in Table 4.3. The ship was owned by A P Ross of Kingston but it is not possible to trace the crew from Census records, apart from a Thomas Brander who resided in Speymouth.

The monthly rates of pay for the Master and the crew were as follows:-

		£	s	d
Master	T Brander	5	0	0
Mate	J McGregor	3	0	0
AB	G Wishart	1	17	6
OS	J Brander	1	10	0
Boy	H Henry	1	10	0

It is noticeable that the rates of pay for the Master and Mate differed considerably from that paid to the crew, which increased significantly by the 1860s according to the ledgers of sailing ships for that period. The conditions were 'all found' – the owners provided all the food – the list of provisions purchased in June and July 1847 (below) seems gey plain fare; however, most people in Scotland at that time would have existed on a similar diet.

		£	s	d
17 June 1847	½ cwt Bread		15	0
	1 stone Flour		3	0
	42 lbs Beef	1	2	6
	2 lbs Coffee		3	6
	6 lbs Sugar		3	0
	15 lbs Molasses		5	0
	Barley, Peas & Matches		1	9
	Vegetables		1	9
	Water			9
22 June	½ cwt Bread		12	6
	8 lbs Sugar		4	0
	4 lbs Coffee		6	8
	2 Bushels Potatoes		5	0
	Vegetables		2	2
23 June	2 Bottles Whiskey		3	6
3 July	2 Bottles Whiskey for Stock		3	0
	1 lb Coffee		2	0
	Matches		4	0
	12 stone Flour		4	0
	1 lb Mustard	1	10	0
	Fish - Cod & Skate		3	6

Surprisingly, there is only one entry for the purchase of oatmeal which was a staple commodity in these days. The spelling of 'whiskey' is as used in the ledger.

The *Highlander* was not a large vessel and is an example of those trading between northern Scotland, the Firth of Forth and the north of England during the nineteenth century. She carried the produce of these areas for over 20 years and the fact that she traded for so long was a tribute to her builders and her Master in keeping her in a seaworthy state during that time.

EXPRESS - 1863-68

Voyages

The voyages undertaken by *Express*, a 135 ton schooner (Appendix 6), may be seen as mundane in that they were for the transportation of goods to and from British, Baltic and Mediterranean ports rather than more exotic destinations. The *Express*, however, was a ship which represented a development in the trading activities of Moray Firth shipowners that started in the late 1850s and was to continue for 30 years when shipbuilding on a large scale ceased in the Firth.

Shipowners in the 1850s had built vessels capable of limited voyages around the coasts of Britain with larger vessels capable of undertaking voyages to the Baltic. This period saw the introduction of changes which enabled shipowners to consider extending their area of trade in the 1860s with the possibility of obtaining a higher rate of return on their investment. These changes were:-

- ◆ Improvements in hull design; more extensive use of iron in the standing rigging; cotton rather than hempen sails; and more machinery – all reduced running and crew costs.
- ◆ Better trained ships' officers capable of taking ships anywhere in the world.
- ◆ The development of wireless telegraphy which enabled owners to communicate with agents and Masters.
- ◆ The international demand for coal together with the demand for wheat and other food products by Britain's increasing population which enabled shipowners to obtain cargoes both for the outward and inward voyages.
- ◆ An increase in the number of companies specialising in marine insurance enabling owners to obtain full cover for their ships and cargoes.

The tonnage of the *Express* could not be described as large but compared to the size of ships which were built for the coastal trade and transportation of cargoes within the Firth, she represented a considerable increase in size. Vessels such as the *Orient* (103 tons) were still being built for coastal and Baltic trading but more and more shipowners were building larger vessels and seeking cargoes in more distant ports.

The *Express* was not at sea every month of the year. For one or two months at the beginning or end of the year she was in port – presumably Kingston – in order to have necessary repairs and maintenance carried out as well as giving the crew essential home leave. This was more normal practice for deep sea ships in those days because of the amount of maintenance that wooden sailing ships required.

CALEDONIA - 1855-67

Voyages

Being larger than the *Express*, *Caledonia* – a 191 ton schooner – was capable of trading further afield, making several voyages to Romania by way of the Black Sea. She did undertake one voyage to Pernambuco for sugar but apparently this did not prove to be a profitable venture, for the she reverted to the Mediterranean and Black Sea trade. The cargoes carried by both ships were similar – coal, iron, wheat, barley, locust beans – but the *Caledonia* was more profitable, earning ten percent per annum, against the five percent earned by the *Express*.

The most likely explanation for the difference in profitability is not the owners, as the majority of the shareholders of the ships were the same men, nor the capabilities of the masters, or the Black Sea trade, but the fact that with the same number of crew the *Caledonia* could carry 40 percent more cargo.

The *Express* and the *Caledonia* were far from unique, for hundreds of ships of this size – and larger – were being built and operated at that time by British shipowners. They have obtained a place in history because of the existence of their disbursement ledgers which provide so much detailed information about their operations. The fact that these ships from a small port in the north of Scotland operated successfully in a trading area where there must have been considerable competition says a great deal about the ability of their owners and Masters and the quality of the ships themselves.

It is a matter of some concern that there are in existence so few written records of the trading activities of Scottish sailing ships. The four records which are analysed in this chapter are representative of many, but there were others who traded with European, American and African ports on a regular basis, and if these records had been available it would have been possible to compile a more complete record of Scottish maritime trade.

OPERATING COSTS

The disbursement ledger of the *Orient* does not show in detail many of the costs such as food and wages but does provide the essential figures to enable an assessment to be made of the rate of return which the ship provided for her owner. In order to make a comparison with the running costs and revenue earned by the *Orient*, the disbursement ledgers of the *Caledonia* and the *Express* – both built in Kingston – have been analysed and a summary is given in Table 4.4. They differ from the *Orient* in their trading patterns, which were mainly to North African and Mediterranean ports, and in being larger.

	Caledonia	*Express*	*Orient*
Vessel Type	Schooner	Schooner	Schooner
Tonnage	191	135	103
Year Built	1864	1868	1867
Trading Area	Baltic, Mediterranean, Black Sea & British coast	Baltic, Mediterranean, North Africa & British coast	Baltic & British coast
Net Income Earned	£3,657 10s 5d	£972 13s 5d	£2,942 3s 9d
Income from Sale	£1,250 0s 0d	---	£531 9s 0d
Insurance on Loss of Ship	---	£980 0s 0d	---
Total Revenue	£4,907 10s 5d	£1,952 13s 5d	£3,473 12s 9d
Less **Cost of Building**	£2,337 8s 3d	£1,556 8s 10d	£1,383 14s 5d
Net Income	£2,750 2s 2d	£396 4s 7d	£2,089 18s 4d
Net Return	110% or 10% pa	25% or 5% pa	151% or 12.6% pa

Table 4.4: Summary of operating costs and revenue

Analysis of the operating costs of both *Caledonia* and *Express* show that they were similar, if major repair costs are excluded. This was not an unreasonable position, given that the vessels were of similar design and managed by local men.

Ship Handling & Maintenance	30%
Wages & Food	35%
Insurance, Agent's Commission, Brokerage	35%
and miscellaneous	100%

The wage cost for the *Orient* amounted to 28 percent and reflects in part the difference in size of the vessels. If figures for food cost were available this element would increase the percentage to nearer the figure for the other two ships.

	Caledonia	*Express*	*Orient*
Master	£8 0s 0d	£7 0s 0d	£4 0s 0d
Mate	£4 10s 0d	£4 10s 0d	£4 0s 0d
Cook	£4 0s 0d	£2 12s 6d	–
ABs (3)	£3.15s 0d	£3 10s 0d	£3 0s 0d
OS	£2 0s 0d	£2 5s 0d	£2 0s 0d
OS	£2 0s 0d	–	–

Monthly Wage Rates

The rates of pay for the crew of these three vessels reflected in part the differences of the size of the vessels. The figures for wage rates paid to the crew of the *Orient* are estimates as the ledger does not provide these costs. The above rates – taken from maritime records – were those applicable to ships of that size during that period.

The rates of return for these three vessels show that even with the *Express*, shareholders were receiving a good return on their investment. The current rate of interest on investment during the 1860s was between five and six percent, so that five percent would have been acceptable. One shipowner – William Kinloch – stated that he expected a vessel to cover her costs within a three year period. This may well have been true in exceptional circumstances such as running the French blockade during the Franco-Prussian war in 1870, but a normal rate of return even for a well managed Moray Firth ship would have been much lower. Much would depend upon the economic conditions prevailing in Britain and the Continent, if there was a glut of ships, and whether or not the vessel was well managed both onshore and at sea. The rate of return on large ocean-going sailing ships of the period was much higher, but these rates reflected the greater risks and the fact that larger ships were operated at much lower cost per ton of cargo carried.

It is interesting to compare how many Masters these three vessels had in their lifetime. *Caledonia* had the first for 22 months and two others for five and four years respectively. The *Express* had only one Master. *Orient*, the vessel with the highest rate of return, had eight: one for 3½ years, five for eighteen months and two others for approximately six months. The *Orient* may have been profitable but it is unlikely that she would have been a happy ship.

Registered Owners

The registered owners of the three ships are given below and it is noteworthy that the majority of the shares in the *Caledonia* and the *Express* were in common ownership and that with the exception of Messrs Brander and Sutherland and Dr Geddie the remainder were either ship builders or ship masters.

Express		*Caledonia*		*Orient*	
Owners	**Share**	**Owners**	**Share**	**Owners**	**Share**
Dr Geddie	8	Dr Geddie	8	Wm Anderson	16
James Geddie	8	James Geddie	8	Andrew Brander	16
Alex Geddie	8	Alex Geddie	8	Robert Anderson	16
John Duncan	16	John Duncan	16	Captain	
James Geddie	8	James Geddie	8	WmAnderson	16
John Sutherland	8	Wm Marr	16		
Wm Geddie	8				

CONSTRUCTION COSTS

Alexander Hall & Sons of Aberdeen, and some of the large shipbuilders on the Clyde, kept records of ships and their costs but they do not exist for the Moray Coast yards. The only record of the cost of construction of ships is given in the disbursement records of the three Kingston-built ships – *Orient*, *Express* and *Caledonia*. The details are as follows:-

	Tonnage	Total Costs	Built	Cost per Ton
Orient	103	£1,383 14s 5d	1855	£13 8s 0d
Caledonia	191	£2,337 8s 03d	1864	£12 5s 0d
Express	135	£1,556 8s 10d	1868	£11 10s 0d

In order to make comparisons with ships built in Scotland at that time, the record of ships built by Alexander Hall & Sons were examined, but few examples of ships of a similar size were found, as most of the ships built at that yard during the 1860s were larger – 700-900 tons – with costs of between £17-£19 per ton. This cost per ton of the smaller ships was as follows:-

	Tonnage	Built	Cost per Ton
Enterprise	76	1852	£12 10s 0d
Agricola	158	1857	£15 0s 0d
Martinet	72	1856	£13 0s 0d
Colleen Bann	386	1861	£14 0s 0d

It appears from this small sample that the Speymouth builders were building ships of up to 200 tons at a lower rate than Alexander Hall, and the difference may be due to different timbers being used and, perhaps, higher labour costs in Aberdeen. There is no suggestion that the Kingston yards were turning out ships of an inferior quality as the records show that, given a competent master, they had a long life. They were built at a cost which local prospective shipowners could afford, whilst the Aberdeen yards were obviously dealing with men and firms who were prepared to pay for ships built to a higher specification and no doubt better equipped.

Halls were building large ships at this time at a much higher cost per ton. This was due to more extensive use of high quality timber (such as teak). Many shipowners were prepared to pay these costs however, because Lloyds allowed these ships a much longer period before they required them to be re-surveyed.

Vessels required to be surveyed after a specified period of years after they were built if they were to retain their 'Category A' rating. Lloyds set out detailed specifications on the method of constuction to be followed by shipbuilders, and the timbers to be used in various parts of the hull.

Depending on the method of construction and the quality of the timbers used, the Surveyor would determine how many years should remain in Category A before requiring to be re-surveyed. Appendix A.7 gives the timber required to be used in the construction of the frames , and an excerpt from the 'Rules to be Observed' in building ships taken from Lloyds Register for 1848.

There were also tables specifiying the timbers to be used for the outside and inside planking. The majority of the Moray Firth ships had a limit of seven years before requiring to be re-surveyed.

	£	s	d
Memel mast 59½ft X 14½in 86-10-5 @3/-	13	0	7
Bowsprit ex ship Superior cost	3	18	9
Crossjack (yard) ex ship Superior 42ft X 7in	1	5	0
Norway log topmast 36½ ft X 6¼in		18	0
Tops'l yard 31½ X 7¼in	1	10	9
Main Boom	4	16	8
Gaff		15	0
Trysail gaff and swing booms		13	0
Topgallant yard		6	6
Timber and plank	379	9	3
Tree nails	14	6	6
Iron bolts and nails	5	19	7
Copper nails &c	2	2	2
Pitch, tar and oakum	6	7	11
Carpenter's wages	149	11	10
Cash: carpenter's allowance 10/6; launch expenses £3 16s; carver 15/-	5	1	6
Boat building		4	6
Composition bolts &c	8	17	3
James Abernethy & Co - one set of 14ins windlass metal	3	10	
George Black - ironwork	12	15	2
Profit arising from this vessel	17	10	0
	£633	12	11

Table 4.5: Building costs of *Harmony* (source: James Henderson)

In the early part of the nineteenth century the Kingston yards and Alexander Hall were building ships of similar size (60-100 tons). One of these was a 74 ton sloop named *Harmony*, built by Halls in 1823; she had a square stern with dimensions of 53ft x 18ft x 10ft – very similar in appearance to the *Brothers* whose lines are given in Fig 6.4. The construction costs (above and Table 4.5) are taken from Hall's yard book, and show the amount of capital needed to purchase a ship. Considering the wages paid to masters and crew, it is surprising that so many vessels were owned by Masters and partners rather than by merchants with extensive commercial interests (such as Osbourne).

Express and *Caledonia*

A summary of the accounts rendered by the various Speymouth tradesmen involved in the construction of the *Express* and the *Caledonia*, including the builder (Geddie) are given in Appendix A.8.

Copies of two accounts exist, one from Alex Cairney giving details of the quality of canvas and cordage used for sail making, and the other from the ship chandler – William Geddie – probably a relative of the builder. The latter details the equipment which a ship of the size of the *Express* would have required. This is very limited when compared with the list of equipment supplied to the larger ships built by Alexander Hall & Sons in the 1860s. Their account includes the supply of 3 bottles of 'whiskey', then one further bottle, followed later by a gallon of the same. It can be assumed that some of the bottles were consumed during the fitting out, with the gallon measure being reserved for the launching ceremony. From contemporary newspaper reports this was an occasion for the consumption of substantial quantities of whisky and food by the builders, owners and their friends. Geddie's account is given in Appendix A.9. The spelling of 'whiskey' is taken from the accounts; they were not too particular about spelling in those days but there is little doubt that the bottles contained the local product and not an Irish import.

Crockery and cutlery were supplied in half dozens, and as there were two officers and six of a crew, it would appear that these articles were supplied for use by the master and the mate, leaving the crew to supply their own utensils – the standard practice on ships of that period. The list also records two kettles being supplied, one for the cabin and one for the forecastle, but only one tea pot.

The *Express* was supplied with food as well as equipment. The only item of note was the purchase of 5cwt of bread. Examination of the ledger of the *Express* shows that bread was not purchased in large quantities during her working life, for it is a commodity that does not keep for long periods. The only explanation is that bread was purchased in order to feed the guests and the shipyard workers at the launch.

The cost of the sails for the *Express* and the *Caledonia* were £290 4s 6d and £333 17s 8d, forming only 24 and 17 percent respectively of the hull construction costs of these ships. It would appear that the old joke that a ship was called a 'she' because her sails cost more than her hull had no foundation!

OVERSEAS TRADING

Many of the larger ships built in Inverness, Kingston, and Banff were built by shipowners intending to use them for trading outwith the Firth. British overseas possessions and her development as an industrial power required a large merchant fleet and shipowners were aware that it would be more profitable to have ships engaged on overseas trade than on the well-provided coastal and Baltic trade.

These large ships rarely returned to their home ports and operated from Scottish and English ports, with the crews returning to Kingston at the end of each voyage. From descriptions of the prospective trading areas given in Lloyds Registers, a large number traded with the Mediterranean and Continent, but larger vessels sought cargoes in the Far East and Australia. The owners would have been in telegraphic communication with British and Continental agents in order to arrange cargoes both for the outward and inward journey. However, in more distant ports, the Master would have had the responsibility for obtaining a cargo for the return journey. From researching copies of correspondence between a Master and the owner, a great deal depended upon the business acumen of the Master in dealing with import and exporting merchants.

Vessel	Type	Tons	Built	Trading Area
Abeona	Barque	295	1877	Australia and New Zealand
Afghan Chief	Barquentine	275	1885	Mexico and South America
Chieftain	Barque	339	1868	China. Claimed to have made very fast voyages
Clansman	Barquentine	382	1870	South America
Duke of Richmond	Schooner	294	1868	Australia
Freuchy	Barque	324	1875	South Africa and Japan
Letterfourie	Barquentine	348	1876	Australia
Morning Star	Barquentine	258	1877	White Sea and Australia
Moray Chief	Barquentine	314	1878	West Indies
Progress	Schooner	177	1866	Baltic, White Sea Mediterranean
Voyager	Barquentine	242	1873	South America

Table 4.6: Trading areas of several Speymouth ships

The voyages undertaken by the 209 ton schooner *Garmouth* (108ft 8 inches long and built in 1870) shows that size was not an obstacle in the search for trade. The following list of voyages undertaken by this ship between 1873 and 1879 show that she was a very well travelled ship during the last six years of her life.

♦ Commenced Goole October 1873, closed Dunkirk November 1874. Ports of call Cette, Messina, New York, Bari, Girgente and Stettin.
♦ Commenced Dysart January 1875, closed London May 1875. No complete itinerary for this voyage but there is evidence from a Consular Stamp that Cuba was a country visited.
♦ Commenced London June 1875, closed Hong Kong November 1877. Ports of call South Africa and Port Louis, Mauritius, Melbourne, Freemantle, Tiensin, New Chang and Whampoa.
♦ Commenced Hong Kong 1877, closed London December 1878. Ports of call Melbourne, Newcastle, Auckland and New Bedford USA.

♦ Commenced London January 1879, closed Southampton June 1879. Ports of call Gaudeloupe and Trinidad.
♦ Commenced Southampton June 1879, closed Banff June 1879. Direct voyage between these ports.
♦ Commenced Banff November 1879 - Vessel Missing

INSURANCE

The system whereby a ship and its cargo was owned by a group of people holding shares in the ship and cargo was an effective one, for it enabled losses and gains to be shared between a group of people. Such a system was formally approved by the British Government in 1824 but it meant that if the ship was lost or damaged the subscribers lost their investment or had to pay for the cost of repairs. Insurance could be obtained from the Royal Exchange Society and the London Assurance Society, both of whom charged very high premiums. When their monopoly came to an end in 1824, small groups of men formed themselves into Associations in order to provide cover for local ships and cargoes. This system, which was common throughout Britain during the nineteenth century, ensured that, in the event of loss or damage to the ship, the subscribers would be reimbursed either in whole or in part.

These Associations were small, with limited resources and they confined the cover provided to locally-owned ships and to a proportion of the value of the vessel. This was a safeguard against unscrupulous shipowners obtaining full cover and then wrecking the vessel – not an uncommon practice. Their members did not look for a high rate of return and kept administration costs low – another example of how maritime communities financed their trading activities in which, one way or another, they were all involved.

As ships became larger and undertook voyages to foreign ports with a substantial increase in risk, local companies could not provide the amount of cover needed and shipowners had to obtain cover from insurance companies who were prepared to take a larger share of the risk at, of course, higher premiums. These companies did not limit themselves to providing cover for local ships and with the growth of shipping, maritime insurance proved to be very profitable.

In order to reduce the risk involved in insuring ships, the early associations and the insurance companies would not accept a risk unless certain conditions were met; for example, the vessel had to be registered with Lloyds, the Master needed a Board of Trade Certificate, and the ship had to be maintained to specific standards. Where a cargo needed to be delivered to ports where there could be risks, such as the Baltic in winter, the insurers had to be notified and rates would be revised accordingly.

The ledger for the *Express* shows payments being made to the following insurance companies:-

Dundee Mutual Marine Insurance Association
Banffshire Mutual Marine Insurance Association ✦
Moray Firth Mutual Marine Insurance
Dundee Shipping Insurance Association ✦
Dundee Protection Assurance
Arbroath Assurance

In the case of the companies marked '✦' the value of the cover was limited to £300. Owners overcame these limits by taking out cover with several companies thus ensuring that the ship and its cargo were fully covered. The *Caledonia*, also from Garmouth, was insured with the same group of companies, with one exception – Dundee Protection Assurance.

Other insurance companies operated in Morayshire (such as the Spey Marine Assurance Association and the Elgin Marine Assurance Association), all adopting the standard rules regarding conditions under which insurance would be granted. The only information about these conditions is that percentage rates were applied to vessels classed A1 by Lloyds. Vessels not in that category were liable for a higher rate of premium.

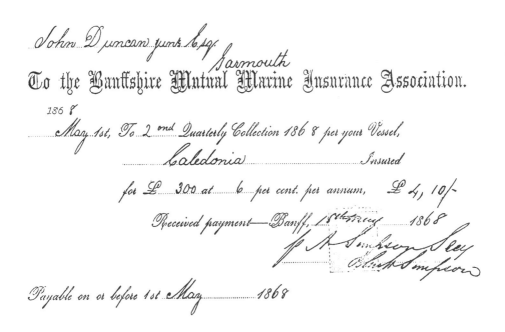

Fig 4.3: Insurance Receipt: Banffshire Mutual Marine Insurance Association

Fig 4.4: The brig *Henry* (Hull City Council)

5 SEAMEN, MASTERS AND OWNERS

Introduction

In the majority of books describing sailing ships currently available, apart from brief comments on the Master, there is often little or no reference to the other members of the crew or their owners; nor the sad fact that many ships with their crews were lost at sea.

The means whereby a young seaman could gain sufficient knowledge to be capable of carrying out the duties of mate, and eventually Master, of a vessel were vastly different to present day conditions. Much depended upon the willingness and the ability of individual Masters to train men in seamanship and navigation. In many small vessels, formal means of navigation by means of a sextant and charts did not exist, and Masters reached their destinations by 'dead reckoning' (i.e. estimating the ship's position by the course steered and the distance covered in a 24-hour period). It is unlikely that navigation would be taught unless he had a basic knowledge of mathematics and served on board a large vessel whose Master was experienced in navigation. It was not until 1854 that ships officers were required by law to show that they were competent in navigation and the handling of ships.

During the nineteenth century it was relatively easy for any person with a small amount of capital to obtain part ownership of a ship by means of the share system. With the majority of ships there were only three or four owners but many shareholders were willing to allow people to hold a small number of shares as a means of investment. Effectively the management of the ship lay with three or four men who managed it on behalf of the rest of the shareholders. As ships got progressively larger and therefore more expensive, the cost of individual shares increased, putting them beyond the reach of most people. The number of people holding shares in individual ships diminished and the number of people owning shares was largely confined to those with maritime interest.

The ships themselves provided living and working conditions for their crews which would not be acceptable by today's standards and they required a great deal of skill to operate and maintain in good condition. In bad weather and in winter, with poor food and inadequate protection against the elements, the lives of the crew would have been miserable. Regardless of losses and poor conditions the seafaring life proved to have a very strong attraction for young men, and ships were never short of crews and officers.

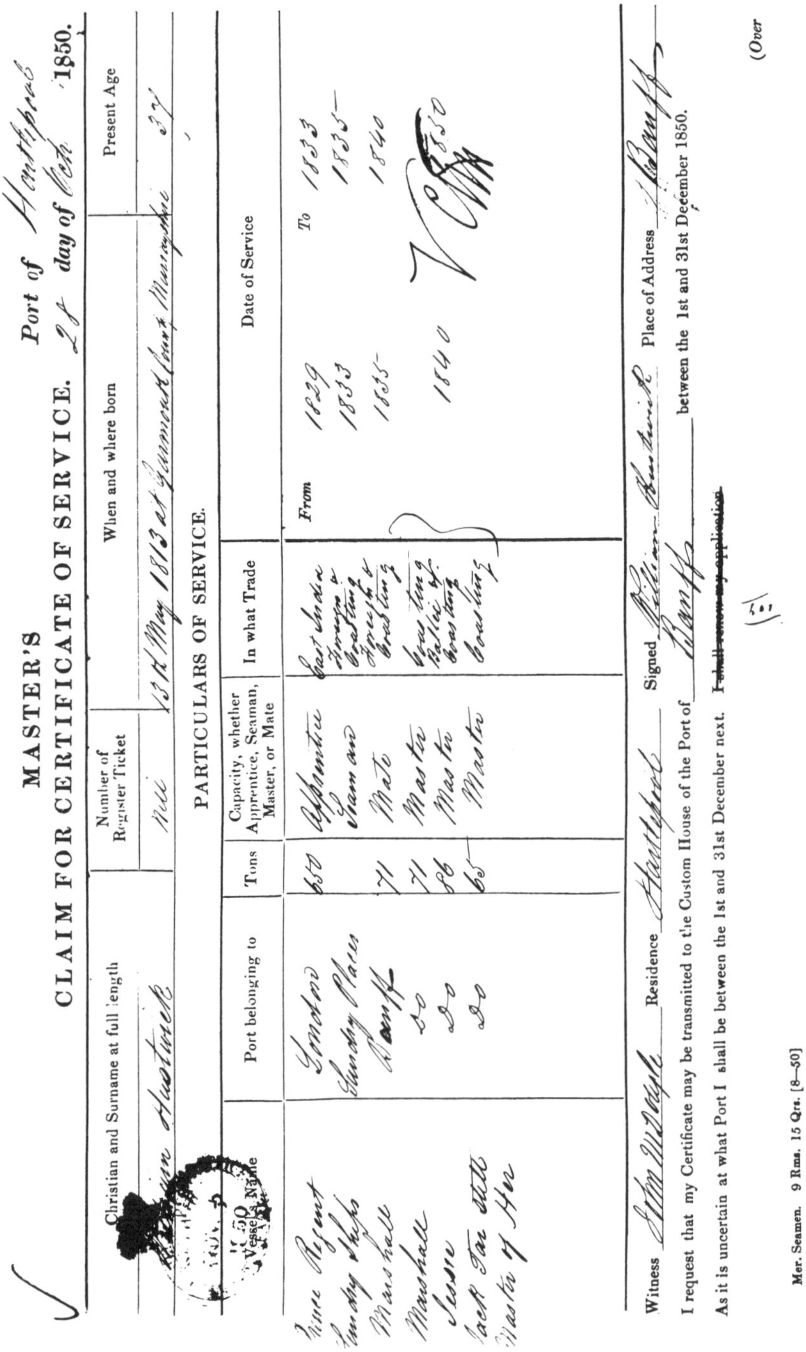
MASTER'S

CLAIM FOR CERTIFICATE OF SERVICE. Port of Hartlepool 28 day of Oct 1850.

Christian and Surname at full length	Number of Register Ticket	When and where born	Present Age
William Austwick	nil	13th May 1813 at Yarmouth County Murray	37

PARTICULARS OF SERVICE.

Vessel's Name	Port belonging to	Tons	Capacity, whether Apprentice, Seaman, Master, or Mate	In what Trade	Date of Service From	To
Prince Regent	London	650	Apprentice	East India	1829	1833
Sundry Ships	Sundry Places		Seaman	Foreign & Coasting	1833	1835
Marshall	Banff	71	Mate	Foreign & Coasting	1835	1840
Marshall	do	71	Master	Coasting	1840	1850
Jessie	do	86	Master	Baltic & Coasting		
Jack Tar still Master of Her	do	65	Master	Coasting		

Witness John McDougal Residence Hartlepool Signed William Austwick Place of Address Banff

I request that my Certificate may be transmitted to the Custom House of the Port of Banff between the 1st and 31st December 1850.

As it is uncertain at what Port I shall be between the 1st and 31st December next. ~~I shall renew my application~~

(Over

Mer. Seamen. 9 Rms. 15 Qrs. [8—50]

Fig 5.1: Claim for Master's Certificate of Service

SEAMEN

In the early nineteenth century a young man in a coastal village would have had little or no choice but to go to sea with a relative who was a master and learn the trade, first as a cabin boy advancing to Ordinary Seaman, and then to Able Seaman. There were no formal training courses but if he had a good basic education it would have been possible for a young man to obtain a sound training in seamanship and navigation under the tutelage of the Master. He would then be able to apply for the post of Mate and progress to Master. In the early part of the century there were no formal examinations set by the government to test the proficiency of aspiring Mates and Masters, so the responsibility for teaching men resided solely with the Master.

Young men went to sea at an early age – 12 or 13 – and, with reasonable ability, could expect to be a Master of a vessel by the age of 22 or 23, by which time they would have acquired considerable experience in the coastal and European maritime trade. If they were ambitious, seamen did not stay very long with one ship. With the growth in the number of sailing vessels in the nineteenth century a man who was prepared to take responsibility would have plenty of opportunity to achieve command.

The Merchant Shipping Act of 1854 introduced much needed improvements in the welfare and training of seamen and officers, by consolidating features of previous Acts relating to Maritime matters and repealing outdated statutes. One such change was the requirement for Masters and seamen to sign a 'Certificate of Discharge and Character' on the termination of each voyage.

These certificates provided a record of experience and conduct as well as stating the capacity in which the seaman had served on individual ships (for example, as an ordinary or able-bodied seaman). Both Masters and men benefited from this system; the seaman could prove that he had the necessary experience, whilst the Master could satisfy himself that he was signing on a seaman with a proven level of ability.

A copy of a Certificate of Discharge for James Munro, a Moray Firth seaman, recording his service on the *Flora Emily* – a Kingston built ship – is given in Figure 5.2. The words 'very good' are barely discernible in the spaces for character of conduct and ability.

Because of the heavy losses amongst sailing ships – due in part to lack of navigation skills – a system of examinations was introduced in 1845 for Mates and Masters. This was initially a voluntary scheme and applied only to officers of foreign-going vessels. With the passing of the 1854 Act, the system became compulsory for officers of all ships, regardless of whether they sailed in coastal or foreign waters. From as early as the eighteenth century, however, many of the Moray Firth schools included navigation as part of their curriculum since so many of their pupils intended going to sea.

The 1854 Act stated that no ship could leave harbour unless the Master and, in the case of a foreign-going ship, the First and Second Mate had obtained and possessed a valid certificate of either competency or service.

No ship of 100 tons burden or upwards could legally proceed to sea unless at least one officer besides the Master possessed a certificate appropriate to the grade of Mate. This limit of 100 tons meant that many owners specified that vessels be constructed with a tonnage of 99 tons or less in order to save the expense of having a certificated Mate.

The certificate could be endorsed with the words 'fore and aft rigged' – limiting a Master's command – if he had no experience in sailing square-rigged vessels. This condition did not apply to Mates who, being younger, were expected to gain all-round experience. The examinations which Mates and Masters were required to take under the requirements of the Act is shown in Appendix A.10.

Topsail schooners fell into the category of fore-and-aft rig. However, although efficient, it is doubtful if their use would have been so widespread if the Merchant Shipping Act had not enabled Masters to obtain an endorsed certificate. Figure 5.1 shows a claim by William Hustwick for a Certificate of Service, as he had already served as Mate and Master in British and foreign going ships before 1 January 1851. The Certificate of Service granted is shown in Figure 5.3.

Living conditions for Mates and seamen must have been very basic, with seamen eating, living and sleeping in the fo'c'sle, usually in badly ventilated, poorly lit damp spaces. The men made their own clothing out of canvas which they coated with oil – effective but not very comfortable. Good protective clothing was not available until later and conditions must have been barely endurable in long periods of rough weather. Small ships did not carry a cook, an essential crew member in large ships, and the task of preparing food would not have been easy without a galley and when the ship was under way in heavy seas.

The food supplied for the Master and crew would not have provided a varied diet. This is shown (Figure 5.5) by an extract from the Customs record of food supplied to the *William* of Portsoy and the *Barbara & Ann* of Spey in January 1817. The *William* was taking herring to Hamburg and the *Barbara & Ann* had a cargo of herring for the Azores – a journey of 1900 nautical miles.

Scottish salt was used when supplying meat and pork for use on board ship; it was not highly regarded as a commodity for preserving meat (for export) because it contained so many impurities – 'bay' salt from France, Portugal and Spain was much preferred. The list does not include vegetables, and was deficient in certain vitamins, but was no doubt the basic provision for seamen at that time – by the time the *Barbara* reached the Azores the crew would no doubt have welcomed a change in their diet. Both ships were carrying cargoes of surprisingly high value; in the case of the *Barbara*, the cargo was worth as much as the ship. 'Red herring' was the term used for smoked fish.

Dis. I.

CERTIFICATE OF DISCHARGE

FOR SEAMEN DISCHARGED BEFORE THE SUPERINTENDENT OF A MERCANTILE
MARINE OFFICE IN THE UNITED KINGDOM, A BRITISH CONSUL, OR A SHIPPING
OFFICER IN BRITISH POSSESSION ABROAD.

**ISSUED BY
THE BOARD OF TRADE.
1890.**

No. 170

Name of Ship.	Offic¹. Number.	Port of Registry.	Reg. Tonnage.
"Flora Emily"	YY. 539	Inverness	99

Horse Power of Engines (if any).	Description of Voyage or Employment.
—	Baltic

Name of Seaman.	Age.	Place of Birth.	No. of R.N.R. Commission or Certif.	Capacity. If Mate or Engineer, No. of Cert. (if any).
James Munro	33	Fuidhorn	—	Bosun

Date of Engagement.	Place of Engagement.	Date of Discharge.	Place of Discharge.
13. 9. 96	Burghead	19. 11. 96	Montrose

I certify that the above particulars are correct and that the above named
Seaman was discharged accordingly,* and that the character described hereon
is a true copy of the Report concerning the said Seaman.

Dated this 19th day of Nov. 1896.

George Mason   MASTER.

AUTHENTICATED BY
W. R. Lovell
Signature of Superintendent, Consul, or Shipping Officer.

* If the Seaman does not require a Certificate of his character, obliterate the following Words in lines two and three, and score through the Discs.

**CHARACTER
FOR CONDUCT.**

**CHARACTER
FOR ABILITY.**

NOTE.—Any Person who forges or fraudulently alters any Certificate or Report, or who makes v
of any Certificate, or Report, which is forged or altered or does not belong to him, shall for each such
offence be deemed guilty of a misdemeanor and may be fined or imprisoned.
N.B.—Should this Certificate come into the possession of any person to whom it does not belong v
will be handed to the Superintendent of the nearest Mercantile Marine Officer, or be transmitted to t
General of Seamen, Custom House, London, E.C.

Fig 5.2: Seaman's Certificate of Discharge (Mr R Clunas, Nairn)

MASTER'S CERTIFICATE OF SERVICE.

(Issued pursuant to the Act 13th and 14th Vict., cap. 93.)

Nº. 40.750

Number Forty Thousand Seven Hundred and *Fifty*

William Huntwick

Born at *Garmouth* County of *Murray* on the *13 May 1813*

Has been employed in the Capacities of *2nd Mate & Master* *21* years in the
British Merchant Service principally in *Coasting Foreign* Trade.

Bearer's Signature *William Huntwick*

Granted by the REGISTRAR GENERAL OF SEAMEN, LONDON. By order of the BOARD OF TRADE.

M Brown Registrar.

Issued at *Garmouth*
this *Sixth* day of *January* 1857   *Capt. Grieve J. Ph.*

No. OF REGISTER TICKET.

. Any Person Forging, Altering, or Fraudulently using this Certificate, will be subject to a penalty of FIFTY POUNDS, or THREE
MONTHS' Imprisonment with or without HARD LABOUR; and any other than the Person it belongs to becoming possessed of this Certificate,
is required to transmit it forthwith to the REGISTRAR GENERAL OF SEAMEN, LONDON.

Fig 5.3: Master's Certificate of Service

MASTERS

By the time a first mate had passed his examinations for Master he would have been at sea for at least 10-12 years, serving in different capacities on several ships. Masters ensured that he gained experience in all aspects of ship management, such as handling men, maintaining ships, loading and unloading of cargoes, as well as the art of navigation.

On becoming Master his responsibilities were far wider, for he had to ensure that the vessel operated efficiently and produced a profit for the shareholders. As Master he had to deal with pilots, customs officers, consuls, ship chandlers, repairers, labour for unloading and loading cargo, agents in order to obtain cargoes for the return voyage, pay the crew and maintain a proper record of income and expenditure for submission to the shareholders. It was this side of ship management, quite apart from his ability as a seaman, that identified a good Master. He would also have to prove that he could deliver cargoes in good condition without undue delay. It was this ability which would prove essential in maintaining good relations with agents and the brokers whose function was to arrange for the efficient transport of cargoes from one port to another, without damage.

Fig 5.4: The schooner *Nairnshire* (John Gordon & Son, shipowners and timber merchants, Nairn)

Nᵒ and Date of Entry — Goods Exported — Quarter ended 5ᵗʰ January 1817. —

1 (1810) 11 In the William of Footsey, (B.B.) William Blackhall Master for Hamburgh. —
Victuals for the Vessel — 1 Barrel qt 1½ cwt Beef cured with one fourth Bushel Scots Salt, Excise and Equalizing Duty paid as per Certificate produced, 3 cwt Bread 12 pounds Butter, 2 cwt Potatoes, 2 Bushels Oatmeal, 1 cwt Barley, 14 pounds Groceries 2 dozen pound Candles, 2 Gallons Oils, 3 cwt Coals. — Free "

2 " 11 In said Ship —
                                    Joseph Green —
300 Barrels White Herrings —
— Barrels Value £90. 0. 0 —
— British — Total Value £345. 0. 0 — 1

3 " 11 In said Ship —
                                    Joseph Green —
60 27/94 Tons Burthen pr Register — 3

4 " 16 In the Barbara & Ann of Spey (B.B.) William Kustwick Master for St Michaels —
Victuals for the Vessel — 2 Barrels qt 9 cwt Beef and Pork cured with half a bushel Scots Salt, Excise and equalizing Duty paid as per Certificate produced, 4 cwt Bread, 4 cwt Flour, 5 cwt Potatoes, 2 Bushels Oatmeal 1 cwt Barley 1 fourth cwt Groceries, 1 dozen pound Candles 2 Gallons Oil 10 cwt Coals — Free —

5 " 16 In said Ship —
                                    George Stronach —
300 Barrels White Herrings —
— Barrels Value £90. 0. 0 —
200 Barrels Red Herrings —
— Barrels Value £30. 0. 0 —
— British Total Value £550. 0. 0 — 2

Fig 5.5: Extract from the Customs Record, quarter ended Jan 1817

A page from the disbursement ledger of *Caledonia* is given in Fig 5.6A, showing entries over a four month period (note the variety of people to whom the Master had to make payment for various services rendered). The ledger for four years prior to this period observed the rules of double-entry book-keeping, but for the period in question the record, whilst it is very neatly kept, shows expenditure on both sides of the page. The income obtained from transport of cargoes was recorded on following pages. The shareholders approved the balance at the end of the voyage; therefore it was a correct record, even if book-keeping principles were not strictly observed. Some of the expenditure incurred was in foreign currency but the ledger only records payments in sterling. A further example of the same ledger, following standard methods of recording income and expenditure, is shown in Figure 5.6b.

If the ledgers of *Orient, Express* and *Caledonia* are examined, it will be seen that they all have one thing in common – the handwriting. Prior to undertaking research for this book it had been assumed that the ships' Masters maintained the entries in their disbursement ledgers before returning to their home port; but on investigation it appears that they only kept a rough record of receipts and payments, and entries in the Ledger were recorded on their return by someone with more experience in book-keeping. The handwriting in each ledger does not alter as one would expect if they were written by different masters – *Orient* had eight masters, *Express* one, and *Caledonia* three. In addition it is obvious that the handwriting in the ledgers for the last two named ships is the same. This is not surprising as these ships had several shareholders in common and one person would have maintained both records.

Examination of these ledgers shows that there was a considerable amount of expenditure and income which was not initiated by the Master – such as major repairs, insurance claims, agents' fees – and these transactions would have been carried out by one of the shareholders who acted as Manager. It can be imagined that the Masters would not have looked forward to being questioned by the 'recorder' on some of the entries in their rough ledgers, and the preparation of the final record would not have been an easy task.

Correspondence shows that the Master had to act as agent for the owners in all matters when in foreign ports and that to be effective he would have had to make arrangements on occasion to obtain a cargo for the return voyage. Vessels engaged solely on coasting traffic would not need to act independently as they could easily communicate with their owner or agent dealing with the problem of obtaining a return cargo. This position changed after the 1860s with the continuing development of the international telegraph system but a great deal still depended on the judgement of the Master.

OWNERS

The General Registry Act of 1786 introduced a system of statutory registration of ships, recording where it was built, its builder and owner, together with details of size, rig and tonnage. It did not require owners to give details of other interests in the ownership of the vessel. However, the Merchant Shipping Act of 1854, in limiting the number of shares in any one vessel to 64, required this information to be recorded.

Until that date there was no recognised system for shared ownership, although records do exist which show that a system based on eighths and sixteenths was in use by the end of the eighteenth century. The practice of sharing ownership of a ship and its cargo was in general use as early as the twelfth century and was recorded in early maritime law.

The Act was important because it gave people with limited capital, such as seamen, an opportunity to share in the ownership of the ship which they worked and maintained. Much of the population in the seaport participated directly or indirectly in the construction, provision and manning of ships, and the share system allowed the community to continue that participation.

An analysis of the Banff Register of Shipping for the period 1867-87 is shown in Table 5.1 indicating a wide range of occupations. People with maritime interests, such as shipbuilders, Masters, and seamen, took 62 percent of the share total, with shipmasters having the highest proportion. Amongst people with no maritime interests, merchants, farmers, spinsters and widows predominated. The occupation of individual merchants is not given, so it is impossible to state whether they were connected with the construction of ships. However, they had capital to invest and, as a result of their business activities, were well placed to obtain information about the possible rates of return of these maritime ventures. There were not many opportunities for investment, and owning ships provided a higher rate of return than Government securities.

Many people, who did not have large amounts of capital, only took one or two shares in a ship and were no doubt quite satisfied with their rate of return. However, with the relatively high rate of loss of vessels, coupled with the fact that some were not fully insured, many people lost their investment. It is noticeable on examining the Register how often the Bank Agent was involved in the purchase of shares and in lending money to prospective shareholders. The Banks did not remain shareholders for long, and limited their role to that of providing the builder with working capital until other shareholders could be persuaded to make an investment.

Income & Disbursements of Caledonia of Spey

1872		Newport								
Aug.	9	To Pilotage out & one days attendce of pilts	£ 3	4	0					
,,	,,	,, Passage from Newport to ship		10	0	£ 3	14	0		
		Gibralltar								
Sept.	4	,, Half Gratuity	$	7	7	-				
,,	5	,, Shipchandler, port charges a/c	38	1	12					
,,	,,	,, Discharging Cargo	17	9	12					
,,	,,	,, Butcher &.c.& Vegetables & potatoes 3.2	17	8	11					
,,	,,	,, Water 3 Personal charges 2.6	5	6	,,					
,,	,,	,, Postages & Registering Letter	1	,,	,,					
		Ex. at /50° pr Dollar	87	9	3	18	5	7		
		,, 2% Commission	£ 3	8	5					
		- Advance at Newport	₮	,,	,,					
		- Bill on London	₮	-	-					
		,, Ballast	12	3	9					
		,, Advance Ins. at Casablanca		3	2	15	15	4		
Octr.	7	Casablanca								
,,	,,	,, Consuls charges 8.12. 4.2 & 15° pr 8	£	2	10	11				
,,	,,	,, Brushwood dunnage 12/12 lbs butter 14/	1	6	,,					
,,	,,	,, Provision Bill	4	,,	5					
,,	,,	,, Customary present to H last lighters		8	,,					
,,	,,	,, Capt of Port & Labourage at Ball & barge 3	2	13	,,	16	16	4		
		Queenstown								
Nov.	4	,, Stationary 2/. & Noting Protest 3/4		6	2					
,,	5	,, Frying pan 9/ Binnacle Lampglass 1/-		2	6					
,,	,,	,, Pint Measure 3. Druggist charge 1/9		2	5					
,,	,,	,, Personal expenses	1	15	,,					
,,	,,	,, Pilotage & Boat assistance mooring	1	10	,,					
,,	14	,, Butchers &c including sundry &c	11	7	6					
,,	,,	,, Harbour dues & Pilotage inwards 13.2	3	10	6					
,,	,,	,, Light Bill £2-4. Telegrams 2/-	2	6	4					
,,	,,	,, Bill stamp & postage & Agency 18/-	18	8	22	1	1		
						£ 76	14	4		

Fig. **5.6a**: Disbursement ledger of *Caledonia*

George Proctor Master

1872		Brought Over				£ 70 14 4		
		Liverpool						
Nov	22	To Labourer cleaning ship outside	£	..	12 ..			
"	"	" Tidesmen shifting in Dock 3 m. 3/6		"	10 6			
"	"	" Tidesmen shifting in Graving 3 men 6/		"	18 ..			
"	"	" Labourer taking old metal out of ye Dock		"	10 ..			
"	"	" Tidesmen ship from G Dk. to Georges Dock		"	18 ..			
"	"	" Red Herrings 10/5 Fish 1/2		"	11 5			
"	"	" Coopers Account		"	15 3			
"	"	" Two Table Cloths		"	6 ..			
"	"	" Carriage of Sails from Glasgow		"	2 6			
"	"	" Meters Labourers Allowance at discha		"	9 6			
"	"	" Soft Bread Whilst in Port		"	12 ..			
"	"	" Dock gatemen Both Masters		"	10 ..			
"	"	" Water account		"	6 6			
"	"	" Tide Table		"	1 ..			
Decr	13	" Butchers account		6	12 1			
"	"	" Half of Inward Gratuity		2	10 ..			
"	"	" Cash paid to Carpenter as advance		20	.. ..			
"	"	" Tide Watchman as pr Receipts		1	7 ..			
"	"	" Bending Sails & fitting New jib boom		"	15 ..			
"	"	" W. H. Stott & Co's Account		225	6 4	£266 13 1
		Wages						
		Master from Aug 5 to Decr 5; 4 m. 1d. at £8.—	£	32	5 4			
J. Jones	Mate	— . £ 5 — .. 5.4 — 1 .. at 5.—		20	3 4			
Henwright	bosn	— . — 7 — Nov. 3 . 14 — at 3.5/-		11	5 4			
George	A. B.	— . — 7 . — — 20. 3 . 14 — at 3.—		10	8 0			
Smith	A. B.	— . — 7 .. — 20. 3 . 14 — at 3.—		10	8 0			
Willis	O. B.	— . — 7 — . — 20. 3 . 14 — at 3.—		10	8 0			
Barlow	O. S.	— . — 7 — . — 20. 3 . 14 — at 2.5/		7	16 0			
H Osborne	App	— . — 7 — Dec 12. 4 . 8 —		3	2 10			
				105	16 10			
		Shipping Fees			13 ..	£105 3 10

Fig. 5.6a: Disbursement ledger of *Caledonia*

87

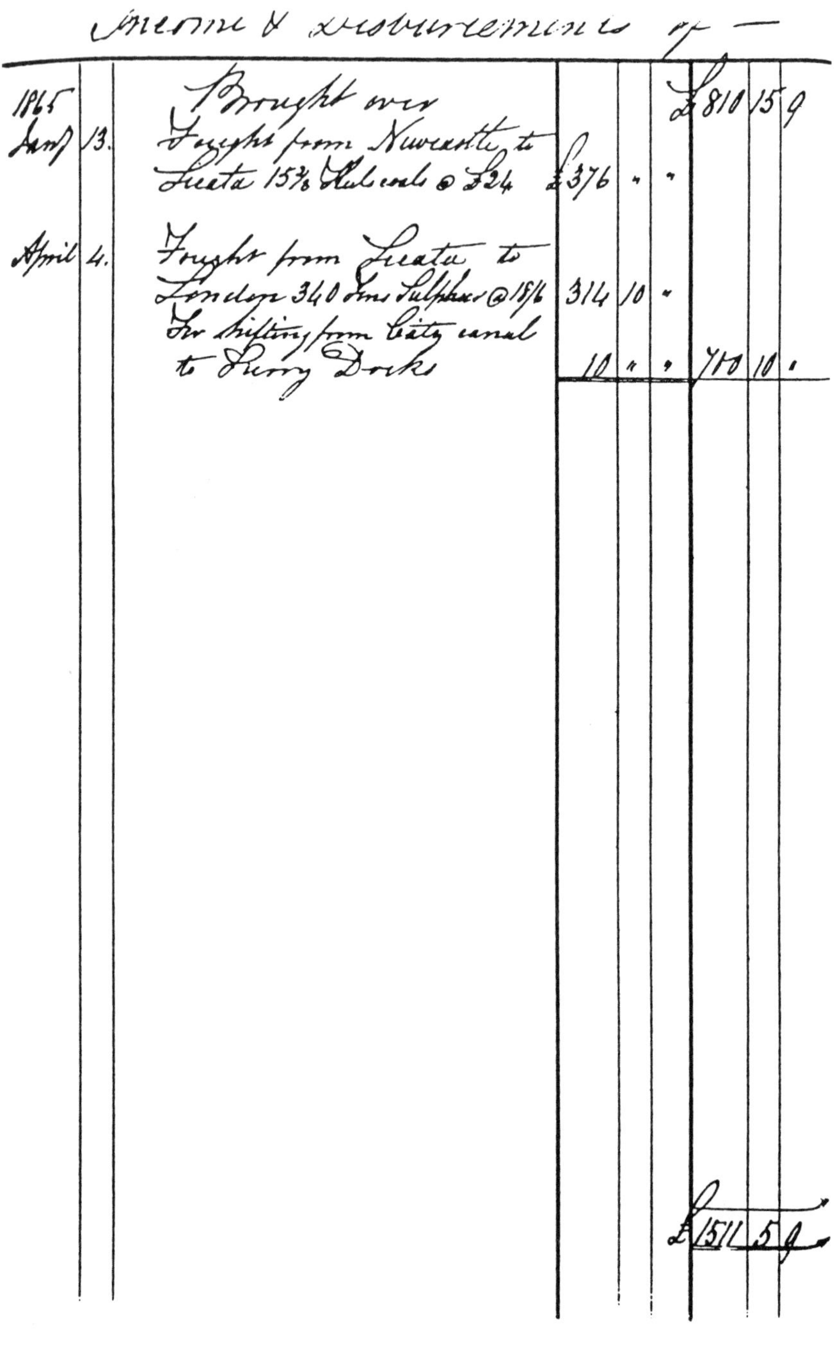

Income & Disbursements of —

1865		Brought over				£810	15	9
Jany	13.	Freight from Newcastle to Licata 15⅔ Keels coals @ £24	£376	"	"			
April	4.	Freight from Licata to London 340 Tons Sulphur @ 18/6	314	10	"			
		For shifting from City canal to Surrey Docks	10	"	"	710	10	"
						£1511	5	9

Fig. 5.6b: Disbursement ledger of *Caledonia*

Fig. 5.6b: Disbursement ledger of *Caledonia*

Occupation	Number	Shares
Non-maritime owners		
Accountant	5	64
Agent	2	12
Baker	6	228
Banker	32	652
Blacksmith	5	89
Cabinet Maker	1	68
Chemist	5	68
Clerk	8	92
Draper	4	30
Farmer	36	737
Flesher	1	16
Grain Merchant	3	64
Hotel Keeper	1	30
House Carpenter	2	12
Landowner	1	48
Manufacturer	4	58
Merchant	63	1453
Residenter	3	16
Shoemaker	1	38
Slater	3	66
Solicitor	9	86
Spinster	15	157
Stonemason	2	22
Surgeon	4	44
Watchmaker	2	40
Widow	4	118
Sundry	17	116
		4324
Maritime owners		
Fish Curer	8	220
Fisherman	4	78
Fishery Officer	2	20
Iron Founder	3	12
Master Mariner	104	2933
Rope Maker	3	12
Sail maker	3	80
Seaman	13	192
Ship Broker	3	80
Ship Builder	60	885
Ship Carpenter	7	103
Shipowner	68	2602
		2920
		7244

Maritime Owners 63%; **Non-maritime Owners** 37%

Table 5.1: Ownership of Vessels Registered at Banff 1867-87

MAINTENANCE OF SHIPS

A wooden sailing ship required constant attention throughout her working life, as all parts of the vessel were constantly under stress to a greater or lesser degree depending on the circumstances. The hull was subjected to strain when grounded or lying alongside the quay in a harbour – Masters needed to ensure that the cargo was evenly distributed and that the harbour floor or beach was level so that it would not be over-stressed. Deck timbers were soaked for days on end and then dry for long periods, giving rise to swelling and shrinkage, leading to gaps appearing through which water could enter and damage the cargo. The crew caulked these gaps with oakum, which was then covered in tar, producing a waterproof joint. Water penetration into end grain was the greatest cause of damage, and when water got into the covering board – the timber which covered the top of the frames – or between the frames, rot was inevitable.

The rigging was made of hemp and the sails of flax, materials which stretched and, because they were subject to constant movement, required a considerable amount of time to be spent on repair and replacement. It was not until iron wire was used for the standing and some running rigging, and cotton canvas replaced flax for sails, that the work of maintaining rigging and sails was reduced. If the ship was not well maintained and met with bad weather, rotten timbers could give way causing greater quantities of water to be taken on board than could be dealt with by the pumps. Pumps in those days were worked manually and could not cope with large quantities of water.

Maintaining a ship in good working order was a never ending task requiring the Master and Mate to keep constant watch on every part of the hull, rigging and sails. It also required a competent crew capable of carrying out normal maintenance and repairs, for the cost of repairs in the shipyard was high and vessels in a yard earned no money. Ships in general did not earn very much so there was no extra money to spend on having work done which could be done by the crew. Many vessels were laid up during the winter months,and this gave an opportunity to carry out repairs which could not be done at sea.

As mentioned earlier, every vessel was required to undergo a survey at stated intervals, and ships frequently returned to the yard where they was built in order to get the necessary work done. A surveyor would state what work was necessary; the amount of repair would depend very much on what had been done by the crew in maintaining the ship prior to the survey. When the work was completed and passed as satisfactory, a certificate was issued which stated that the vessel was in good condition and did not require to be surveyed again for a stated period of years. Examples of a Lloyds certificate are given in Figure 5.7. It appears that shipowners often took the opportunity, whilst the ship was in the shipbuilder's yard, to have extensive alterations carried out, such as re-rigging, applying copper sheathing, or even lengthening.

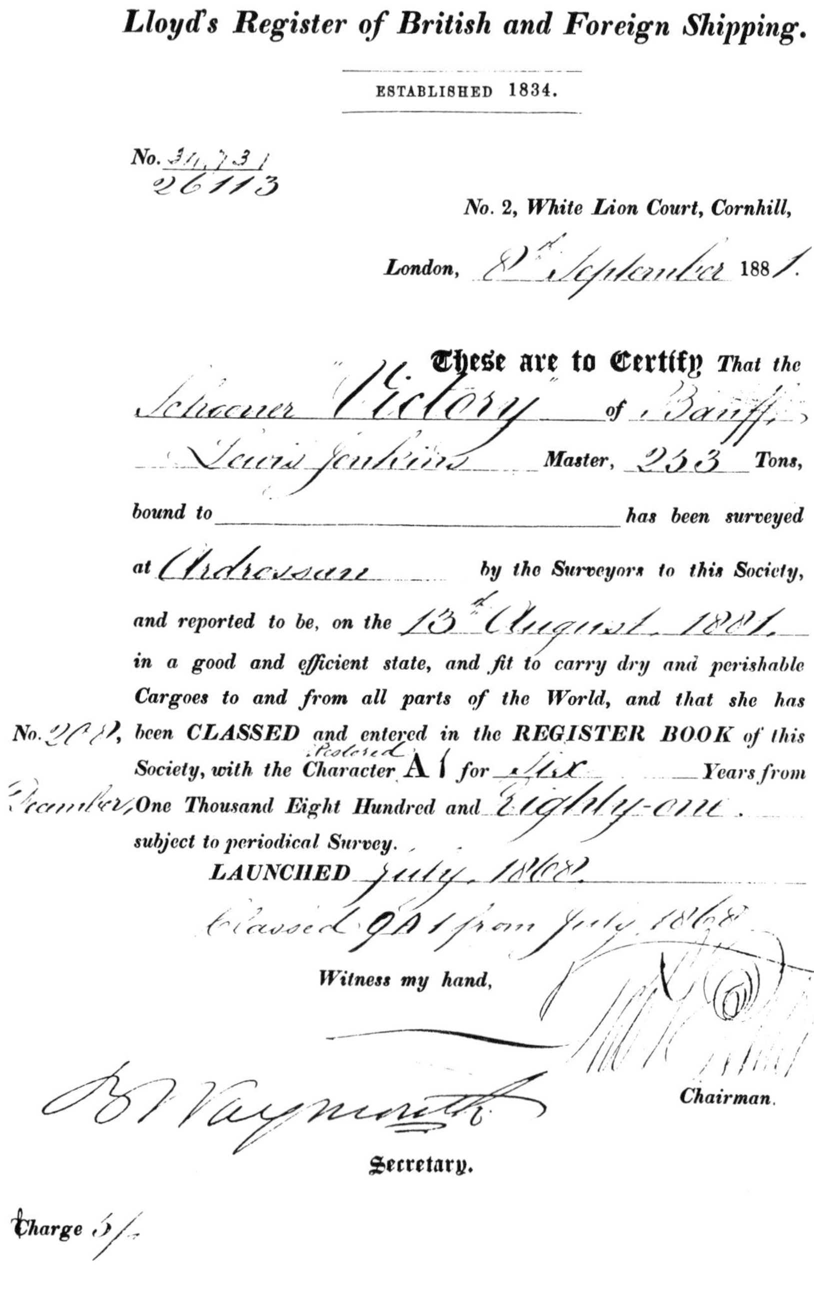

Lloyd's Register of British and Foreign Shipping.

ESTABLISHED 1834.

No. *34,731*
26113

No. 2, White Lion Court, Cornhill,

London, *8th September* 188*1*.

These are to Certify That the

Schooner "*Victory*" of *Banff*,

Lewis Jenkins Master, *253* Tons,

bound to _____ has been surveyed

at *Ardrossan* by the Surveyors to this Society,

and reported to be, on the *13th August 1881*,

in a good and efficient state, and fit to carry dry and perishable
Cargoes to and from all parts of the World, and that she has

No. *2631*, been CLASSED and entered in the REGISTER BOOK of this
Society, with the Character A 1 *Restored* for *Six* Years from

December, One Thousand Eight Hundred and *Eighty-one*,

subject to periodical Survey.

LAUNCHED *July 1862*

Classed 9A 1 from July 1862

Witness my hand,

Waymouth Chairman.

Secretary.

Charge *5/-*

Fig. 5.7a: Lloyds Surveyor's Certificate - *Victory*

I Michael Iron Harbour Master and Ship Survey-
er, having been called upon to Survey & report upon the
seaworthyness of the Schooner Victory of Yarmouth, James
Falconer Master bound on a voyage from Dover to New
York in Ballast.

And upon such survey I found the vessels
hull and standing rigging in perfect order the spare sails
require to be overhauled and there is on board sufficient
new canvass and twine for that purpose

The running gear is well worne and I therefore
recommend that 1 Coil of $2\frac{1}{3}$ Inch rope, one of 2 Inch and
45 fathom Lanyard rope to be put on board to replace
any Defects in the running rigging or Lanyards

And when this is supplied I am of opinion
that the vessel is in a fit and sea worthy condition
to proceed upon her voyage to New York.

Given under my hand
at Dover this 11th Sept 1873

(signed) R Iron

Fig. 5.7b: Lloyds Surveyor's Certificate - *Victory*

PERILS OF THE SEA

Sailing vessels without auxiliary power were at the mercy of the wind, weather and tides, and were at considerable risk during storms, often finding it difficult to make for safe anchorage unless the wind was favourable. Navigational aids were limited and their use depended upon being able to obtain daily sight of the sun. Charts were expensive and in many cases not used, as Masters relied on their own knowledge of landmarks and dead reckoning to guide the ship to safety.

Name of Vessel	Tons	Home Port	Built	Years
Rosie	34	Findhorn	1837	19
Violet	74	Kingston	1839	28
Sir James Gordon	79	Kingston	1841	3
Barbara		Banff	1844	19
Industry	83	Beauly	1847	10
Countess of Cawdor	125	Nairn	1850	9
Soho	48	Kingston	1853	23
Caledonia	70	Portsoy	1856	24
Ocean Gem	79	MacDuff	1857	4
Countess of Caithness	71	Kingston	1857	1
Alert	96	Kingston	1858	16
Agnes Smith	64	Portsoy	1859	10
Olive	87	Kingston	1860	18
Isa	87	Kingston	1861	28
Diadem	307	Banff	1862	3
Osprey	16	Fortrose	1862	3
Wanderer	235	Kingston	1863	10
Surprise	87	Kingston	1866	26
Robert Anderson	80	Lossiemouth	1867	18
May Queen	277	Kingston	1870	2
Pet	161	Wick - later Chester	1871	55
Earl of Moray	100	Kingston	1872	3 mths
Viscount MacDuff	290	Kingston	1874	8
Flower of Portsoy	75	Portsoy - later Plymouth	1875	53
Nile	333	Kingston	1876	5
Abeona	295	Banff	1877	1
Afghan Chief	275	Kingston	1885	6
Dispatch	109	Kingston - later England	1888	47
Volant	99	Wick	1875	71
Janet Storm	113	Findhorn	1890	2

Table 5.2: Life span of vessels

Mary Nish

This vessel, owned by John Gordon, timber merchant of Nairn, was one of the last schooners operating from that port. She was engaged for most of the year in taking pit props to the north of England, returning with coal. In 1915 the *Mary Nish*, together with several others, was stormbound in Sunderland with a cargo of coal. Nairn was 'out of coal' and the owner, John Gordon, wired the Master to sail if it was possible to do so. There was a break in the weather and seven ships sailed. A gale blew up and most of the ships were dismasted or lost their sails. The *Mary Nish* had been re-rigged and had new sails; she capsized with a cargo of 180 tons of coal – her Master and crew were lost. One of the crew was known as 'Peter the Russian'. His next of kin were never traced and his wages – about £8.00 – are still held by Gordon's.

Table 5.2 gives the life span of 30 ships showing considerable variation in their working lives. It is noticeable that the larger ships had a relatively short life; they traded much further afield than the smaller vessels and incurred far greater risks than the coastal traders, who sailed in relatively sheltered waters. The four ships with life spans in excess of 40 years must have had very competent Masters and been well maintained. The *Volant* is particularly noteworthy, with a life span of 71 years, all of which, with the exception of a few months, were spent in northern waters. According to records, up to 1946 she had only two owners, after which she was sold.

Seafaring has always been a hazardous occupation and official records show losses of sailing ships and their crew were very high. They were lost because of bad weather, springing a leak, catching fire or, more often than not, simply running aground in bad visibility. The following reports are extracts from local newspaper accounts of shipwrecks, which illustrate more clearly than statistics the dangers facing ships and the men who sailed in them.

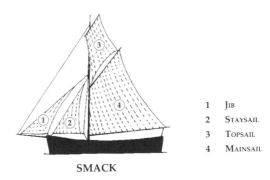

1	JIB
2	STAYSAIL
3	TOPSAIL
4	MAINSAIL

SMACK

My first voyage, said Major Anderson, was on the Spinaway, a barque built and owned by the Geddie family. We loaded with coals at Grangemouth and left for Demerara at the same time as a Sunderland barque, the Invincible. We went north through the Pentland Firth and she took south through the English Channel.

We met with adverse winds and Captain George Geddie, who was not in the best of health, put into Queenstown, in the south of Ireland. We were windbound there for three weeks and at the end of that time the captain was so ill that another skipper was sent for. He was Captain Stewart who took command. We eventually left Queenstown and had a good passage thereafter. The Invincible, which had left with us, should have been far in front, but the two vessels actually entered Demerara on the same day. Both ships discharged cargoes, and left on the same day for Barbados for orders. We then proceeded to Forth Liberty in San Domingo, where the Spanish fleet took refuge during the Spanish-American War. We both sailed from there with cargoes of log wood for Rotterdam. One night, however, we struck a reef and were stranded for a couple of days before we were taken off. Our ship, however, became a total wreck and we were landed at Turk's Island, which contained only one white inhabitant and had to wait there for six weeks before a boat called to take us to New York.

ജ

Shipwreck at Wick. – About 2 o'clock on the morning of Saturday last the 3d inst, the inhabitants of Pultneytown, in the immediate vicinity of the harbour, were alarmed by loud and prolonged cries of distress proceeding from near the mouth of the harbour. All who heard were immediately astir, and in a brief period a large crowd had collected, on finding that the cries proceeded from off a schooner which, in attempting to enter the harbour, had been driven ashore among the boulders at the back of the North Quay. There was a heavy sea running at the time, and occasionally making a clean breach over the deck of the vessel. As the crowd gathered the excitement increased, and the cries of the crew and of a crowd of women that had gathered on the braes were heard in the burgh, from which many of the inhabitants were also drawn to the scene. Efforts were immediately made to have the crew rescued, and in a comparatively short time both they and the pilot in charge of the vessel were safely rescued by means of ropes fastened round their waists. The vessel turned out to be the new schooner Countess of Caithness of Wick, belonging to Mr Donald Robertson, Staxigoe, and commanded by his son-in-law, Captain Charleson, jr. She was built at Spey last year, and has consequently only as yet make a few voyages. She had on board a cargo of coals for Wick. Soon after striking, the vessel was pitched heavily on the boulders by the force of the waves, and in a short time one of her masts had fallen overboard, and all along the north shore and up the back of the North Quay, portions of the vessel's bottom and other portions of the wreck, were washed ashore. The crew saved their clothes, and at low water a part of the rigging was got ashore; but the vessel is a total wreck. We learn that the Countess of Caithness was insured, though not to full value. - *Northern Ensign*

ജ

Wreck of a Beauly Vessel. – The schooner, Industry of Beauly, Paterson, master was stranded on the sands at Aberdeen on Saturday night. The schooner was on her passage from Sunderland to Beauly, and having sustained considerable damage in the previous part of her voyage, made for Aberdeen on Saturday afternoon. There was a heavy wind from the south-east, and the Industry attempted to cross the bar, and failing, was beached upon the sands on the north side of it. The crew were all saved. Two other vessels belonging to Inverness attempted the passage of the bar almost at the same time with the Industry and with success. The Industry was the property of Mr Maclennan, shipowner, Beauly. We understand that she was fully insured. There is no hope that she will be got off the beach.

6 HULL DESIGN AND RIGGING

HULL DESIGN

Prospective shipowners in the early nineteenth century demanded the following specifications for their vessels – good cargo capacity, a rig which did not require a highly certificated Master or a large crew, and a square cross-section so that she could sit upright (allowing cargoes to be moved in harbours which dried out at low tide, or when the ship was beached). Speed was not a prime requirement; it was more important to get cargoes delivered in good condition.

The hull plan (Figure 6.3) of the schooner *Brothers* – built in Kingston in 1838 – shows a vessel very similar in overall form to those built from the 1760s to the 1840s. It had a cargo-carrying capacity of approximately 120-140 tons, with a cross section which had reasonable deadrise, giving her good sailing qualities but still allowing her to load and discharge in the small harbours of northern Scotland. Her rig was economical to work and she lasted for a considerable period carrying cargoes around the coast of Britain with occasional voyages to the Baltic. She was typical of the type of vessel built in the Firth and elsewhere during this period when speed in delivery of cargo was not a prime requirement. The lines of the *Brothers* would have been similar to those of *Marshall of Spey*, which is shown on the front cover of this book.

Examination of Lloyds records show that ship owning was a risky business, and as capital was limited prospective owners and builders were unwilling to try new designs. The merchant class of the Moray Firth had the same approach to change as their compatriots in the rest of Britain and the Continent. Rigs could and did change and the size of vessels gradually increased, but hull forms remained unchanged.

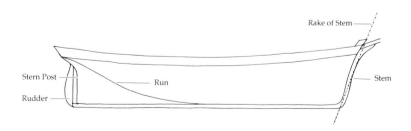

Fig 6.1: Hull of a wooden schooner

By the 1840s there was a move amongst a few progressive owners to build schooners with finer lines but this change was limited and it was not until the Government altered the method of calculating the tonnage of vessels that there was any financial incentive to introduce developments in hull design. In 1773, the formula used for the calculation of tonnage needed only two measurements, depth being assumed as half the breadth.

$$\frac{(\text{LENGTH} - 3/5 \text{ BREADTH}) \times \text{BREADTH} \times \frac{1}{2} \text{ BREADTH}}{94}$$

The figure produced by the calculation bore no resemblance to the actual tonnage which could be carried by a ship. It was, however, a standard measure applicable to all ships and one which could be applied by people with no formal training. It was the basis on which a vessel paid dues when being registered by Customs, and it was also used to determine pilotage, light and harbour dues, which were a significant element in the operating costs of a ship. As the depth of vessels was not a factor in assessing tonnage, many vessels were built with hulls which were very deep and narrow with a square cross section. These ships proved to be less stable and much slower than later vessels, and required a gale of wind to drive them.

After many years of deliberation the government introduced a new method of calculating tonnage which came into effect in 1836. This required surveyors to take measurements of two breadths and one depth for three cross-sectional areas of the hull, and introduced the measurement of hull depth for the first time. The divisor for the new formula was 3500 and this caused some awkward fractions to appear on the records.

Vessel from Banff to Australia.

THE Fine First-class Fast-sailing Schooner "WITNESS," of Banff, 10 years A 1, 200 Tons Burthon, Coppered, and Copper-fastened, will sail from BANFF direct for MELBOURNE, AUSTRALIA, on or about 2d AUGUST next.

For rates of freight and passages, apply to

JAMES WOOD.

Banff, 19th July, 1852.

RETURN TICKETS AT REDUCED RATES

Fig. 6.2: 1852 advertisement for the sailing to Australia of the schooner *Witness*

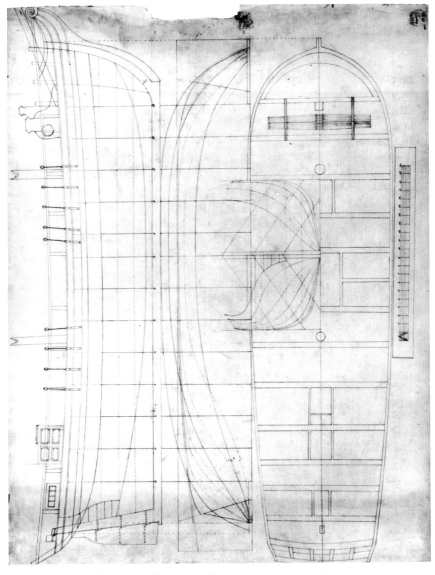

Figure 6.3: *Brothers* hull plan (Science Museum, London)

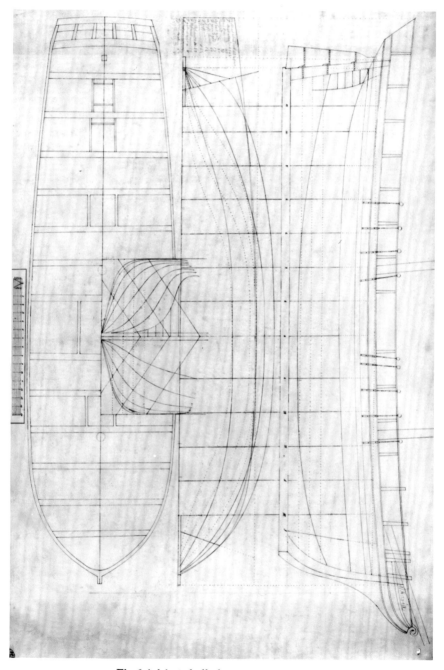

Fig 6.4: *Maria* hull plan (Science Museum, London)

The committee which recommended the new method of calculating tonnage could never have envisaged that their proposal would, over a period of years, bring about such a radical change in hull design. By lengthening the hull and making it shallower the builders were able to provide the same amount of cargo space with a reduction of measured tonnage. One of the first builders to construct a ship with a longer bow and narrow hull was Alexander Hall & Son of Aberdeen, who in 1839, built the *Scottish Maid*, a schooner of 145 tons, to serve the Aberdeen–London route. The effectiveness of the new design in reducing tonnage can be shown by the fact that under the old formula *Scottish Maid* would have 'measured' 195 tons – a difference of 25 percent. Not all ships benefited to such an extent, with the average being between ten and twenty percent.

Acceptance of the new design did not come about immediately, and even Halls continued for a time to build ships with the original hull form. As the design proved to be effective in producing ships which were much faster and therefore more economical to operate, shipowners were eager to accept the change. Many builders went to the other extreme in building ships with raking stems and masts, all in keeping with the new demand for speed and hopefully greater profit. The Merchant Shipping Act of 1854 introduced another formula which this time took account of the internal dimensions of a vessel and of the enclosed spaces above deck. This formula gave the capacity of the vessel in cubic feet which, divided by 100, converted to tonnage. This gave the gross figure, and deduction of certain spaces, such as accommodation, gave net tonnage. This method of calculation meant that there was no benefit to be gained by having extreme bows, as the length was taken from inside the stem and stern timbers.

During the 1840s and early 1850s, Geddie was building hulls with less beam, and bows which, while still blunt, were much sharper than vessels built in the previous decade. An example of this new type of hull is given in Figure 6.4 which shows the lines of the *Maria* – a 68 ton schooner. The lines of this vessel are similar to that of the *Orient*, whose trading activities are described in Chapter 4. The trend towards producing ships with slimmer, longer hulls continued into the 1850s, and by the next decade Geddie was building a standard hull form regardless of vessel size. They had much sharper bow stems with a moderate rake, straight floors and little deadrise. These factors, combined with a reasonable beam and draught, produced cargo carriers with good speed and low operating costs. One of Geddie's ships was the *Clarissa*, a 124 ton barquentine built in 1858, which typifies the Moray ships of that era, and her lines are given in Figure 6.5. They show a ship with a very different hull compared to vessels that were typical of the period up to 1840.

Whilst Garmouth and Kingston were still producing '99-tonners', the increased demand in seaborne trade, both within Britain and overseas, together with increased trade with the Empire, resulted in an increasing number of vessels being built of 150-450 tons.

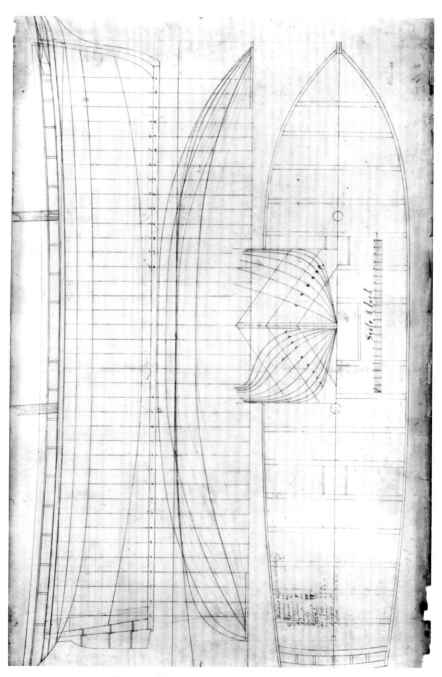

Fig 6.5: *Clarissa* hull plan (Science Museum, London)

Increases in the manufacturing capacity of industry ensured that goods were being produced in much greater quantities than in the early part of the century. This required bigger vessels and, in time, larger harbours with cargo handling facilities. Certain harbours, such as Findhorn, Banff, and Portgordon, lost considerable trade because they were too shallow to take these larger ships.

RIGS USED BY MORAY FIRTH SHIPS

The majority of the ships of under 280 tons listed in Appendix B were rigged as topsail schooners as they had a topsail or square sail on the foremast. This rig was in general use because it had good handling qualities, the square sail on the foremast giving the schooner extra sail area where it really counted. These sails were the equivalent of the modern yacht spinnaker, and Masters preferred the schooner to the ketch rig because a two-masted schooner could be handled in confined waters with just the gaff foresail set. In heavy weather, this could be stowed and only the reefer mainsail and fore stay sail used. The advantage of having the largest sail at the after end of the vessel was that it helped to push the vessels bow up to the wind.

Not all the smaller vessels of between 40-70 tons were rigged as topsail schooners. Some, whilst they had two masts, were fore and aft rigged; that is, the sails were parallel to the vessel's length and did not possess a topsail. They were classed as 'schooners' in the Registers, although the correct term would have been 'ketch'. They were small, manoeuvrable ships, employed on short voyages and because the rig was easily handled required only a very small crew. An example of this rig is given in Figure 6.6 where a ketch is shown taking on herring barrels at Holmsgarth in Shetland.

Many of the ships built at Kingston during the period 1785-1810 were square rigged and larger than the vessels which had been previously constructed on the Firth. Osbourne – a Hull merchant – required large vessels for his trading operations between Hull and the West Indies. Other local shipbuilders, who did not possess the skill or experience to construct vessels of that size, built vessels suitable for local needs, such as smacks (15-40 tons) and sloops (50-60 tons). The majority of their trade was limited to small cargoes, travelling relatively short distances on the coastal routes.

However, as trade developed between Scotland, England, and the Baltic, larger vessels were rigged as brigs requiring large crews and a Master experienced with square rigged vessels. This rig gave the power necessary to move these clumsy, deep hulled, bluff bowed vessels. As hull design improved, this rig became obsolete, being replaced by the schooner rig which, due to its economy in operation, continued in service throughout the century on vessels ranging in size from 70-250 tons.

As the century progressed and the need for vessels of 200 tons and more increased, ships were generally rigged as barque or barquentine. It is not possible to be precise and state that vessels under a certain tonnage were rigged as schooners, or over a higher tonnage were rigged as barquentines, as so much depended upon the personal preferences of the builder and owner. However, in the latter part of the century, Moray Firth ships of 250 tons and over generally used the barquentine rig.

One other early rig worthy of mention was the hermaphrodite, which used features common to rigs used by both schooners and brigs. It was fairly common up to 1840, but was superseded by the topsail schooner.

Masters, unlike ship owners and builders, had the opportunity to observe many different rigs during their voyage and would have been able to assess their effectiveness in speed and ship handling. Rigs were frequently changed when a vessel came into yards for repair, or to pass the Lloyds survey, and in many cases the ship itself was increased in length and an additional mast added. Ship owners were loath to accept changes in hulls, but rigs were changed regularly during the early part of the century, becoming more standardised as vessels became larger and the effectiveness of rigs for certain sizes of vessel was tested over long periods.

SHIP BUILDING RECORDS

Appendix B lists ships built in various ports of the Moray Firth. The individual details of each ship was taken from the Register of Shipping maintained by H M Customs for Inverness, Banff and Peterhead, and from Lloyds Registers (1785-1890). W Barclay, in his book *A Lost Industry* (1906), lists a considerable number of Banffshire ships. Some of these, such as the *General Gordon, Osman Pasha*, and the *Lavinia* do not appear in either Lloyds or the local shipping registers and, accordingly, are not included in the list.

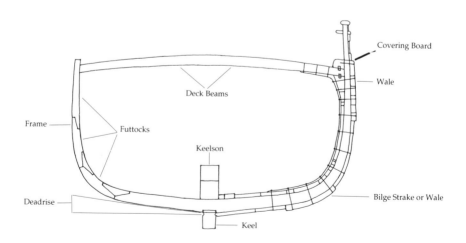

Fig 6.6: Midship section of a wooden schooner

Fig 6.7: Ketch loading herring, Holmsgarth, Shetland
(University of Aberdeen, George Washington Wilson Collection)

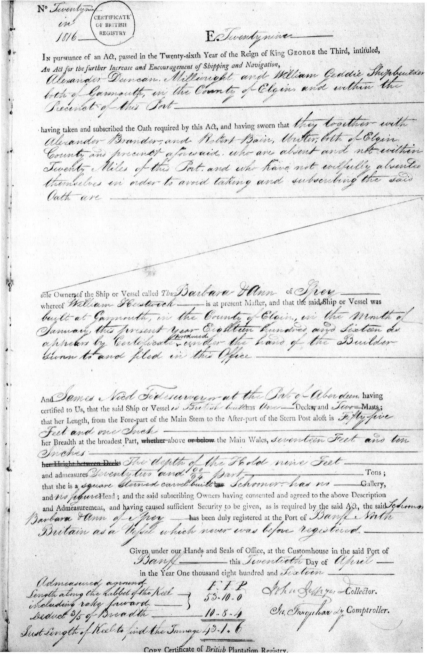

Fig 6.8: Extract from Banff Register of Shipping for *Barbara & Ann*

Lloyds Register contains a listing of all ships built and surveyed by them in any particular year, regardless of where they were built and registered. However, as shipowners were not obliged to have their ships classed at Lloyds, many vessels did not appear on these lists. This may be the reason why some ships known to have been built in Speymouth were not recorded. It was to an owners advantage to have a vessel registered with a good classification, so that shippers would use if for certain cargoes — for example fruit. Some vessels appear in Lloyds Register only once; thus, as not all records were available for the early part of the nineteenth century, this method of compiling a comprehensive list of ships was not particularly effective .

Lloyds registers for the years prior to 1812 did not recognise Garmouth as a ship building area. Using information from the OSA and other sources, several vessels – such as those owned by Osbourne or Leslie – known to have been built in Speymouth were recorded in Lloyds Register under the designation 'Scotland Fir', so this term was the only means of identifying Speymouth-built ships. It was only possible to state that vessels were Spey-built when records of the ships appeared in the Shipping Register stating that they were built in Garmouth or Kingston, or when Lloyds Register gave the location as Spey. After 1812 Lloyds Register used the location Spey – later Garmouth – but it was not until well into the 1850s that Kingston was given credit for the construction of ships.

Lloyds Register did give one piece of information which was not provided in the shipping register and that was the intended trading area of the new ship. In the early part of the century voyages were limited to Banff-Baltic, but from the 1860s onwards countries such as Brazil, China, South Africa, and Romania began to appear.

Shipping registers for individual ports are easier to check than Lloyds, but they do not provide a complete source of information – they do not include ships built in the area but registered in a different port. However, it is possible to obtain the names of a considerable number of ships, not listed in Lloyds, from these registers; they also list alterations to hull, tonnage, and rig, and the names of individual owners and the number of shares held by them. In many cases these shareholders took out loans, and the interest of the lender was recorded in the register together with the rate of interest charged. If she stayed in one port's registry it is possible to see on one page the life history of a ship, including the names of Masters, and details of when and where the ship was lost. The shipping register details the ownership of two Kingston ships – *Barbara & Ann* and *Marshall of Spey* – showing that William Hustwick was Master and part owner of the *Barbara & Ann*, and Master and sole owner of the *Marshall of Spey*. The *Marshall* would have cost about £600 – equivalent to £130,000 today. It seems that being a Master was a profitable business. Three of William Hustwick's sons went to sea on the *Marshall*, all eventually became Master before moving on to other ships. A copy of the entry in the Banff Register of Shipping for the *Barbara & Ann* is given in Fig 6.8. This shows details of the ship, its owners and Masters, and a transfer of shares eight years after she was built to her then Master, William Hustwick.

In compiling the list of ships, the spelling used is that taken from the original source (Customs register or Lloyds). If any differences occurred in the spelling of names between the two Registers, the entry in the Customs Register has been used, as this information was supplied by the builder directly to the clerk compiling that Register. The large majority of names only had one spelling, but there was the occasional exception. In Fig 1.5, Lloyds Survey gave the ship's name as *Lass o' Down*, Lloyds Register gave *Lass of Doon* and the Register of Shipping *Lass o' Doune*. *Rob the Ranter* is shown by that name in the Lloyds Register but in the Customs Register as *Rob o' the Ranter*.

The tonnage given for each ship is the registered tonnage, and the formula for calculating this measurement changed in 1836; where the new measurement is used in Lloyds or the Shipping Register this has been taken, but there is a period of overlap and vessels registered before that date have the tonnage recorded using the old measurement.

Many of the old records and newspaper reports used the term 'tons burden' which is equivalent to the deadweight tonnage (the weight of the ship plus the weight of the cargo she could carry). For example, the *Abraham Newlands*, launched at Kingston in 1806, had a 'tonnage' of 613 tons, but her dimensions are equivalent to a vessel of only 300 tons. Some of the tonnages ascribed to large ships built between 1786 and 1810 should be treated with some reserve because their dimensions are not available. However, there are proven cases of large ships being built at Kingston, for example *Sarah*, a 572 ton Hull-registered ship.

THE GEDDIE COLLECTION

The Science Museum in London has a collection of 24 plans of named ships, built by the Geddie family in Kingston between 1832 and 1867. The majority of them, ranging in size from 66-343 tons, are schoooners, with one barquentine, one brig and two barques. These vessels are not in the same category as the larger clipper ships built by Alexander Hall, Hood, and other Aberdeen shipbuilders, which were constructed to a much higher specification, as they were required to carry larger cargoes for much longer periods. The Geddie ships, however, were capable of dealing with the trading conditions for which they were built and, as records show, carried out their work successfully for many years. In general they were similar to ships built by British and Scandinavian countries for trading in European waters. (Appendix A:11 contains a list of these plans, together with a list of rigging plans.)

It was not the practice of shipbuilders in the nineteenth century to draw plans of ships, and the accepted method of determining the lines of a proposed vessel was to construct a half hull or scale model showing one side of the ship. Few shipbuilders had any skill in draughtsmanship and were able to construct ships without the necessity of drawings. For this reason very few plans exist of small ships of this period and, accordingly, the plans in the Geddie Collection occupy a unique position in British maritime history. Whilst the majority of the plans are ascribed to James Geddie (1820-95), it is assumed that the plans for the 1830s must have been drawn by older members of the same family.

Quite apart from their importance as a record of ship type, they are of considerable interest to marine historians, showing the development of hull design from the bluff bowed ships of the early nineteenth century to the fine bowed ships of later years. It is interesting to note that, while Aberdeen was an important and successful centre for development in ship design from 1840 onwards, the Speymouth shipbuilders did not rush to copy the Aberdeen bow. It was not until twelve years after the *Scottish Maid* (1849) was built that the Geddie yards built vessels which were similar to their counterparts in the south.

The 24 plans of named vessels can be classified by hull form into three distinct groups (Appendix A:11). The first comprises ships built from 1832 to 1841 which were of the traditional bluff-bowed design. The second group is made up of ships built over a seventeen year period, commencing 1844, and are examples of the transition from the hull design which was typical of the first group, to the longer shallow-draughted ships which became the standard design for ships which were built from 1861 (third group).

The common feature of all vessels in the first group is that they have deep hulls, and little or no deadrise. This, together with their square cross-section, made them slow and not very manoeuvrable. Records show that they were engaged in coastal Baltic and European trade and, whilst not as efficient as later ships, were effective cargo carriers.

With the introduction of the revised method of calculating tonnage in 1836, hulls became longer and shallower. As the design proved to be more efficient, the major yards in Britain started to build ships with these characteristics for owners whose ships were employed in deep-water routes. Owners whose vessels were used in coastal and Continental trade, where returns were not so high, were slow to change. However, they were aware of the advantages of the new type of hull, and ships constructed by Geddie from 1844 show distinct changes from the standard design of the previous decade.

Vessels in the second group indicate the change towards the slimmer, shallower hull shape which was becoming common elsewhere in Britain. Hulls still had a good beam and bows, and the early ships had a tendency to roundness. One important change was that the lower lines became more concave at the bow and stern. This trend became more pronounced with later vessels, and bows accordingly became sharper.

It was not until *Eident* was built in 1861 that there was a definite change in hull shape. The ratio of hull length to breadth which had not varied significantly within the previous group now increased as ships became narrower. In addition, the ratio of hull length to depth also increased as hulls became less shallow. Geddie continued to use this design for a series of ships ranging from small schooners to barques. These ships all had the same characteristics: *a*) well-balanced ends – the angle from the waterline to the ends of the stern and the stern was more or less the same; *b*) the bows were slightly concave and their run (the underwater part of the hull at the rear of the vessel) was also concave; and *c*) their hulls had limited deadrise with a square cross section which gave them a good cargo capacity.

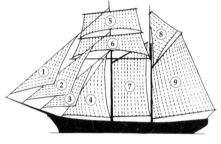

1	Flying Jib
2	Outer Jib
3	Inner Jib
4	Fore Staysail
5	Fore Upper Topsail
6	Fore Lower Topsail
7	Fore Sail
8	Gaff Topsail
9	Mainsail

TOP SAIL SCHOONER

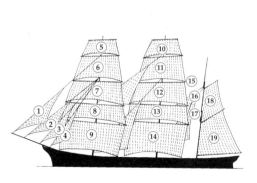

1	Flying Jib
2	Outer Jib
3	Inner Jib
4	Fore Topmast Staysail
5	Fore Royal
6	Fore Topgallant
7	Fore Upper Topsail
8	Fore Lower Topsail
9	Fore Course
10	Main Royal
11	Main Topgallant
12	Main Upper Topsail
13	Main Lower Topsail
14	Main Course
15	Mizzen Topgallant Staysail
16	Mizzen Topmast Staysail
17	Mizzen Staysail
18	Spanker Topsail
19	Spanker

BARQUE

GLOSSARY

CARGOES

Battens	Timber 9" wide, 2"-5" thick and 6ft or over in length.
Birch	According to the *NSA*, the timber used to make barrel staves.
Chaldron/ Chalder	Equivalent to 2 tons 13 cwts; a measurement used by the coal industry in the North of England
Clapboard	Small pieces of good quality oak suitable for panelling, barrels and staves.
Deals	Timber 9" wide, 2-4" thick and 6ft and over in length.
Harrowbills	Crossbars or spars of a harrow made from birch
Hemp/Flax	Natural fibres used in the production of linen rope.
Keel	8 chaldrons (21 tons 4 cwts) - the capacity of Tyne coal barges or lighters.
Oak/ Fir /Beech	Timber used in ship building. Beech was used to make blocks.
Oak bark	Added to water to produce a fluid used for preserving sails.
Treenails	Wooden pins for fastening timber - extensively used in building wooden ships.
Wainscotting	Oak of good quality suitable for panelling.

SHIP BUILDING

Adze	A tool used to shape timber. Shipwrights used an adze with a different handle from other trades. 'Eitch' is the term normally used in the north of Scotland for an adze.
Bilge	That part of a ship on which the hull would rest if the vessel were aground.
Deadrise	Deadrise is the angle by which the floor of a ship rises from the keel. Fast clipper ships – the *Cutty Sark* and the *Caliph* – had considerable deadrise; the Geddie ships had far flatter floors.
Floor	That part of the frame of a ship that extends from the keel to the bilge.
Frames	The ribs of a ship similar to the ribs in a human body. They are appendages to the ship's keel.
Futtock	The parts which make up the ribs of a wooden ship. The lowest of these is called the floor futtock.
Keelson	An addition to the keel inside the ship which rests upon the keel and which takes the stepping of the mast. It also secures the feet of the ribs laid out on each side of it.
Oakum	Strands of hemp or old rope which were used to seal or caulk gaps in hull and deck planks.
Planking	The covering of the ribs of a ship.

Rake	The term used to describe any vertical part of a ship which inclines from the vertical, i.e. masts or stem. Early clipper ships had masts and stems which had extreme rake
Run	The backward sweep of the after part of the hull. A fine run meant that a ship could move well in all weathers. Too fine a run meant that the cargo carrying capacity of the ship was reduced.
Shipwright	The man responsible for all work in the building of a ship.
Squarewright	In the north of Scotland this term was applied to craftsmen who used a square in the course of their carpentry work; nowadays they would be described as cabinet makers.
Stem	The foremast timber of a ship rising from the forward tip of the keel.
Stockholm/ Archangel tar	Tar derived from distillation of turpentine obtained from pine timber. It was used for caulking ships and as a basis for certain ointments used in the treatment of skin diseases.
Wales	Thick planks extending the length of the ship which protect the topside and the hull, where they are likely to come into contact with the quay or other ships, and around the bilges where the hull would rest on the ground.

BIBLIOGRAPHY

Moray Firth
Ash, Marinell. *This Noble Harbour*. John Donald 1991
Baldwin J.R. *Firthlands of Ross & Sutherland*. The Scottish Society for Northern Studies 1986
Barron J. *The Northern Highlands in the 19th Century*. Inverness 1907
Clew R. *The Dingwall Canal*. Dingwall Museum Trust 1988
Cook G. A. *A Topographical Description of the Northern Division of Scotland*. London 1810
Fraser F. Munro F. *Tarbat Easter Ross*. Ross & Cromarty Heritage Society 1988
Graham A. Old harbours in the East Coast of Scotland. *Proc.Soc.Antiq.Scot.*, Vol 108 & 117
Grant & Leslie. *Survey of the province of Moray*. Elgin 1798
Haldane A.R.B. *The Drove roads of Scotland*. Nelson 1952
    New ways through the Glens. Nelson 1962
MacDonald J. & Gordon A. *Down to the sea*. Shandwick Heritage Society
McKenzie G S. *A general view of the Agriculture of the Counties of Ross & Cromarty*. London 1810
Maclean C. *The Fringe of Gold*. Cannongate 1985
Moir C. *Mercat Cross & Tollbooth*. John Murray 1988
Morris R & F. *Scottish Harbours*. Everton 1983
Mowat I.R.M. *Easter Ross 1750 - 1850*. Edinburgh 1981
Munro R.W. & J. *Tain through the Centuries*. Tain Town Council 1966
New Commercial Directory of Scotland 1825-1837. Pigot & Co
North Sea Pilot Part 2, *1915 &1935*. HMSO
Ogilvie A.G. Physiography of the Moray Firth. *Trans.Royal Soc.Edinburgh* 1986
Omand D. *The Moray Book*. Edinburgh 1976
Ross S. *The Culbin Sands*. Centre for Scottish Studies, University of Aberdeen 1992
Seton M. *Laich O'Moray Past & Present*. Moray District Libraries
    Buckie Area Past & Present. Moray District Libraries
    Speyside Past & Present. Moray District Libraries
Sellar M. *Moray Province & People*. Scottish Society for Northern Studies 1993
Simpson E. *Discovering Banff Moray & Nairn*. J. Donald 1992
Smith J. S. Coastal Topography of the Moray Firth. *Royal Society of Edinburgh* 1986
Wilson M.G.T. *Golspie's Story*. The Northern Times 1983

Speymouth
Aberdeen Centre for Land Use. *Land use in the River Spey Catchment*. Aberdeen University 1987
Anderson, G. *Kingston on Spey*. Oliver & Boyd 1957
Forsyth, Rev A. *In the Shadow of the Cairngorms*
Lauder, Sir D. *The Moray Flood*. McGillivray & Son 1830
Mitchell A. *Gravestone Inscriptions of Speyside*. Scottish Genealogy Society
Murdoch J. *Speyside*
Rampini C. *A History of Moray and Nairn*. Blackwood 1897
Shaw L. *History of the Province of Moray*. Adams & Co Ltd, Edinburgh 1886
Skelton, J. *Speybuilt*. 1994
Strachan Lady. *Memoirs of a Highland Lady*. John Murray 1898

Trade
Alston D. *The Burgh of Cromarty - The Town and its Trade*. (unpublished)
Clark A. *A Short History of the Shipmaster Society*. WH Smith 1911
Davis R. Merchant Shipping in the Economy of the late 17th Century. *Econ.Hist.Rev.* 1956-57
Donaldson G. *Northwards by Sea*. Edinburgh 1961
Jackson G. *The Trade and Shipping of Dundee*. Abertay Historical Society 1991
Keith A. *1000 Years of Aberdeen*. Aberdeen University Press 1972
Lillehammer. 'The Scottish Norwegian Timber Trade in the Stavanger Area in the 16th and 17th Centuries'. In: Smout T C (ed). *Scotland and Europe*.
McNeil P & Nicholson R. *An Historical Atlas of Scotland 400-1600*. Conf. of Scot. Medievalists 1975
O'Dell. *The Highlands and Islands of Scotland*. Nelson 1967
Riis T. 'Long Distance Trade or Tramping: Scottish Ships in the Baltic in the 16th and 17th Centuries'. In: Smout T C (ed). *Scotland and Europe*.
Simpson G G. *Scotland and Scandinavia 800-1800*. John Donald
Smith G. *Something to Declare*. Harrap 1980

Smout T C (ed). *Scotland and Europe 1200-1800*. John Donald
Scotland and the Sea. John Donald
Turner J R. 1986. *Scotland's North Sea Gateway*. Aberdeen University Press
Wheeler P T. 1963. The development of shipping services to the east coast of Scotland. *J.Transport His.*

Fishing

Dunlop J. *The British Fisheries Society 1786-1893*. John Donald 1978
Gray M. *The Fishing Industries of Scotland 1790-1914*. University of Aberdeen 1978
Mitchell J. *The Herring - Its Natural History and National Importance*. Edinburgh 1864
Smith J S. *George Washington Wilson in Caithness and Sutherland*. University of Aberdeen 1988
Sutherland I. *From Herring to Seine Net Fishing*. Camps Bookshop, Wick
Whatley C A. *The Scottish Salt Industry 1570-1850*. Aberdeen University Press 1987
The Salt Industry and its Trade 1570-1850. Abertay Historical Society 1984

Ships & Shipbuilding

Albion R I. 'The Timber Problem of the Royal Navy 1652-1862'. *Mariners Mirror* 1952
Anston A. *A Dictionary of Sea Terms*. Brown, Son & Ferguson 1991
Barclay W. *A Lost Industry*. Banffshire Journal 1906
Buchan A R. *The Peterhead Whaling Trade*. The Buchan Field Club 1993
Cable B. *The world's first clipper*. *Mariner's Mirror*. 1943
Carnegie H. *Harnessing the Wind*. Centre for Scottish Studies 1991
Carvel J. *Stephen of Linthouse*. Alex Stephen & Sons Ltd, Glasgow 1950
Chapelle H.I.*The Search for Speed Under Sail*. Allen & Unwin 1968
Dobson D. *The Mariners of Aberdeen & North Scotland*. Wyre Forest Press
Ferguson D.H. *Shipwrecks of North East Scotland 1444-1990*. Mercat Press 1993
Frost T. *From Tree to Sea*. T Dalton 1985
Graham G S. 'The Ascendancy of the Sailing Ship 1850-1885'. *Economic History Review* 1956-57
Greenhill B. *The Life and Death of the Merchant Sailing Ship*. National Maritime Museum 1965
The Merchant Schooners. Conway Maritime Press. 1988
Greenhill B & Stonham. *Seafaring under Sail*. Conway Maritime Press
Greenhill B. *The evolution of the wooden ship*. Batsford 1988.
Jarvis R C. 'Fractional Share Holding in British Merchant Ships with Special Reference to the 64th S'. *Mariners Mirror* 1959
Lynman J. 'The Scottish Maid as the World's First Clipper'. *Mariners Mirror* 1946
MacGregor D R. *Merchant Sailing Ships 1775-1815*. Conway Maritime Press 1985
Merchant Sailing Ships 1815-1850. Conway Maritime Press 1984
Merchant Sailing Ships 1850-1875. Conway Maritime Press 1984
Fast Sailing Ships. Conway Maritime Press 1988
Salisbury W. 'Hollow Waterlines in Early Clippers'. *Maritime Mirror*. 1946
Simper R. *Scottish Sail*. David & Charles 1974
Steven H M. *The Native Pinewoods of Scotland*. Oliver & Boyd. 1959

General

Census Records Speymouth 1841, 1851, 1861, 1881
Lloyds Register of Shipping 1785-1890
New Statistical Account of Scotland 1845 (NSA) Banff, Moray, Nairn, Inverness, Ross & Cromarty
Statistical Account of Scotland 1791-1799 (OSA) Banff, Moray, Nairn, Inverness, Ross & Cromarty

Scottish Records Office

Collectors Quarterly Account E504 1801-1830 Banff and Inverness
Court of Session Records C596/236/94141 Sedurant Records of Alec Duncan
Registers of Shipping CE 64 111-10 1801-1901
Seafield Muniments GD248

National Library for Scotland

Select Committee appointed to inquire into the state of Agriculture. Third Report PP1836 VIII
Select Committee appointed to inquire into the system of Branding Herring 1881 IX

H.M. Customs

Registers of Shipping - Inverness 1801-1890

Newspapers

Banffshire Journal; Banffshire Advertiser; Elgin Courier; Inverness Courier; Moray & Nairn Express; Northern Times; Aberdeen Journal

APPENDIX A 1

The Burghead Harbour Act, 1858: Harbour dues
Rates on Goods.

ARTICLES OF EXPORT AND IMPORT.

		£	s.	d.
Animals (see Cattle).				
Ballast - - - - - -	per Ton	0	0	1
Bark, all Kinds - - - - -	per Ton	0	1	0
Barrels, Herring and Cod (empty) - -	each	0	0	0½
Beef or Pork - - - -	- per Barrel Bulk	0	0	3
Beer of all Kinds - - - -	- per Barrel Bulk	0	0	3
Bones of Cattle, &c. - - - -	per Ton	0	1	0
Bones (crushed) - - - - -	per Quarter	0	0	2
Blubber - - - - - -	per Ton	0	2	0
Bottles (empty) - - - -	per Gross	0	0	3
Do. (full) - - - -	- per Barrel Bulk	0	0	3
Bran - - - - - -	per Sack	0	0	1
Brass - - - - - -	per Ton	0	2	0
Bricks - - - - -	per Thousand	0	1	0
Butter - - - - - - -	per Cwt.	0	0	2
Candles - - - - -	- per Barrel Bulk	0	0	3
Carboys - - - - - -	each	0	0	3
Carriages, Four-wheeled, viz. :				
Coaches and Chaises - - -	each	0	3	0
Dog-Cart or Phaeton - - -	each	0	1	6
Two-wheeled Gig or Dog-cart -	each	0	1	0
Carts and other Two-wheeled Carriages -	each	0	1	0
Carrots - - - - - -	per Ton	0	0	6
Casks (empty), Puncheons - -	each	0	0	4
Hogsheads - - -	each	0	0	2
Half Hogsheads - - -	each	0	0	1
Cattle, &c. :				
Bulls - - - - -	each	0	2	6
Cows, Oxen, or Queys, fat - -	each	0	2	0
Do. do. lean - -	each	0	1	0
Calves - - - - -	each	0	0	6
Cattle from Orkney and Shetland -	each	0	0	6
Horses - - - - -	each	0	3	0
Ponies under 13 Hands - -	each	0	1	0
Ponies from Shetland - - -	each	0	0	6
Asses - - - - -	each	0	1	0
Pigs - - - - -	each	0	0	3
Sheep - - - - -	each	0	0	2
Lambs - - - - -	each	0	0	2
Chemical Manures - - - -	per Ton	0	1	6
Cinders and Coke - - - -	per Ton	0	1	0
Clay,—China or Stone - - - -	per Ton	0	0	6
Do. Pipe - - - - -	per Ton	0	0	6
Clay and Loam - - - - -	per Ton	0	0	2
Coals of all Kinds - - - -	per Ton	0	0	9
Copper - - - - - -	per Cwt.	0	0	1½
Cork - - - - -	per Barrel Bulk of 70 lbs.	0	0	3
Clothiery and Haberdashery Goods -	- per Barrel Bulk	0	0	3

[*Local.*]   6 *L*

			£	s.	d.
Corn, &c. :					
Wheat and Malt - - - -	per Quarter		0	0	4
Barley, Bigg, Rye, and Buckwheat -	per Quarter		0	0	3
Oats - - - - -	per Quarter		0	0	2
Beans, Pease, and Tares -	per Quarter		0	0	3
Indian Corn - -	per Quarter		0	0	3
Meal of all Kinds - -	per Boll of 8 Stones		0	0	1
Flour - - - - -	per Sack		0	0	2
Cotton Wool - - - -	per 80 Lbs.		0	0	3
Dogs - - - - -	each		0	0	6
Do. (Shepherds') - - - -	each		0	0	3
Dung - - - - -	per Ton		0	0	6
Eggs - - - - - per Barrel Bulk			0	0	3
Fish salted or smoked - - -	per Barrel		0	0	3
Do. (dry) - - - -	per Cwt.		0	0	2
Do. of all Kinds (fresh) - - -	per Cwt.		0	0	1
Flax - - - - -	per Ton		0	2	0
Fruit of all Kinds - - - - per Barrel Bulk			0	0	3
Guano - - - - -	per Ton		0	1	6
Groceries of all Kinds - - - per Barrel Bulk			0	0	3
Grease - - - - -	per Ton		0	2	0
Hares and Rabbits - - -	per Dozen		0	0	2
Do. any smaller Quantity -	per Dozen		0	0	1
Hemp - - - - -	per Ton		0	2	0
Hair - - - - -	per Ton		0	2	0
Hay - - - - -	per Ton		0	1	0
Hoops (Wood) - - - per Bundle of 6 Score			0	0	1
Herrings - - - - -	per Barrel		0	0	3
Do. (fresh) - - - -	per Cran		0	0	2
Iron (Bar, Bolt, and Rod) - - -	per Ton		0	1	6
Do. (made Work) including Rails - -	per Ton		0	2	0
Do. (Pig) - - - - -	per Ton		0	1	0
Do. (Cast Goods) - - - -	per Ton		0	2	0
Lead - - - - -	per Ton		0	2	0
Do. (Shot) - - - -	per Ton		0	2	6
Lard - - - - - per Barrel Bulk			0	0	3
Leather of all Kinds - - -	per Cwt.		0	0	2
Lime - - - -	per Quarter		0	0	1
Oakum - - - - -	per Ton		0	2	0
Oil Cake - - - -	per Ton		0	1	6
Oil of all Kinds - - - - per Barrel Bulk			0	0	3
Ores,—Copper, Iron, Lead, and other Ores -	per Ton		0	1	0
Paper - - - - per Barrel Bulk			0	0	3
Pitch - - - - -	per Barrel		0	0	2
Pelts - - - - -	per Ton		0	1	6
Plaster of Paris - - - -	per Ton		0	2	0
Porter - - - - per Barrel Bulk.			0	0	3
Potatoes - - - - -	per Ton		0	1	0

		£	s.	d.
Ropes and Cordage - - -	- per Barrel Bulk	0	0	3
Rags - - -	- per Ton	0	1	0
Salt - - - -	- per Ton	0	1	0
Salmon - - -	- per Box of 112 lbs.	0	0	3
Slates - - - -	- per Thousand	0	2	0
Seed - - - -	- per Barrel Bulk	0	0	3
Straw - - - -	- per Ton	0	1	0
Spades or Shovels -	- per Two Dozen	0	0	3
Spirits, Foreign and British -	- per Barrel Bulk	0	0	3
Steel - - - -	- per Ton	0	2	0
Stones, Rubble - -	- per Ton	0	0	2
Do. Pavement - -	- per Ton	0	0	6
Do. Ashlar, rough -	- per Ton	0	0	3
Do. Ashlar, hewn -	- per Ton	0	0	4
Millstones -	- each	0	1	0
Gravestones - -	- each	0	1	0
Scythe-stones -	- per Hundred	0	0	1
Grindstones -	- each	0	0	6
All Kinds not mentioned	- per Ton	0	0	6
Sugar of all Kinds -	- per Barrel Bulk	0	0	3
Stucco - - -	- per Ton	0	2	0
Tanners Waste - -	- per Ton	0	1	0
Tar - - -	- per Barrel	0	0	2
Tallow - -	- per Ton	0	2	0
Tiles, Drain and Roofing -	- per Ton	0	1	0
Teas - -	- per Barrel Bulk	0	0	3
Tobacco - -	- per Barrel Bulk	0	0	3
Turnips - -	- per Ton	0	0	6
Tow - -	- per Ton	0	2	0
Tin - - -	- per Ton	0	2	0
Wheels, Carriage or Cart -	- per Pair	0	0	6
Whitening - -	- per Ton	0	1	0
Whalebone - -	- per Ton	0	2	0
Wood:				
Mahogany, Rosewood, and all fancy Woods	per Ton	0	3	0
Foreign, not manufactured -	per Load of 50 Feet	0	2	0
Home-grown Timber, not manufactured, per Load of 50 Feet		0	1	0
Deals, Staves, and all manufactured Woods not otherwise stated - -	per Pound Value at the Port	0	0	6
Railway Sleepers -	- per Hundred	0	2	6
Pit Props, Crown -	- per Dozen	0	0	1½
Do. common -	- per Dozen	0	0	1
Wool of all Kinds - -	per Stone of 24 lbs.	0	0	0½
Wine - - -	- per Barrel Bulk	0	0	3
Yarn - - -	- per Barrel Bulk	0	0	3
For all Articles, Merchandise, Goods, Wares, or Commodities not enumerated - - -	- per Ton	0	2	0
	or per Barrel Bulk	0	0	3

Small Packages under 56 lbs. to be reckoned One Fourth of a Barrel Bulk. The Barrel Bulk of all Articles not otherwise rated to be 5 Cubic Feet, excepting when the said Measure shall exceed 2½ Cwt., in which Case 2½ Cwt. is to be rated a Barrel Bulk.

APPENDIX A 2

Analysis of Imports Banff (B) and Inverness (I) 1805-1829

Port	Birch	Oak	Fir	Beech	Deals	Battens	Staves	Wainscotting	Clap board	Treenails	Oak bark	Birch bark	Masts	Spars	Oars	Hemp	Flax	Clover seed	Wine	Barley	Boxes/tubs	Iron bars	Shovels/scoops	Wooden hoops	Linen	Apples/cork	Blubber/whale fins	B	I
Norway																													
Kristiansand	×	×	×		×	×				×	×	×		×			×						×					40	
Mandal	×									×	×	×																32	
Drammen			×		×	×					×		×	×	×						×							10	2
Porsgrunn	×		×		×	×							×	×							×		×					15	
Langesund	×					×							×	×							×		×					1	
Krageroe	×					×							×	×														1	
Germany																													
Danzic		×					×							×														1	
Stettin	×	×					×							×				×		×								12	12
Hamburg			×	×		×			×	×			×									×		×	×	×		20	
Rostock											×					×	×						×					1	
Russia																													
Riga			×		×			×					×	×	×	×	×											6	24
St Petersburg					×	×							×	×		×												4	59
Kronstadt																													
Memel		×			×			×									×											3	23
Odessa																		×										5	
Sweden																													
Gothenburg			×		×	×				×			×	×	×							×						7	18
Canada																													
Quebec					×		×						×		×													24	
Richebucto			×				×							×														16	
St Johns							×																					2	
Miramichi	×		×																									2	3
Other ports																													
Antwerp											×						×											6	
Rotterdam					×	×		×			×							×						×		×		29	2
Portugal																			×										
Greenland																			×								×	5	
																												239	144

APPENDIX A 3
ANALYSIS OF EXPORTS AND IMPORTS 1850-1880

DESTINATIONS *EXPORTS*		1850	1860	1870	1880
SCOTLAND					
Moray Firth Sundry Ports		21	58	25	2
West Coast Glasgow		10	1	–	–
Greenock		8	–	–	–
Cambelton		5	1	–	–
Islay		1	7	1	–
Sundry Ports		19	13	17	4
East Coast Peterhead & Fraserburgh		8	9	1	–
Sundry Ports		5	3	2	–
Forth Estuary Leith & Grangemouth		28	18	16	7
Stirling		6	11	2	–
Boness		1	5	2	–
Alloa		–	2	10	–
Sundry Ports		1	12	6	–
		129	**161**	**88**	**15**
ENGLAND & WALES					
East Coast Newcastle, Sunderland, South Shields & Middlesburgh		43	169	140	23
Hartlepool		25	21	26	7
Sundry Ports		–	5	3	–
West Coast Liverpool		16	12	3	–
Sundry Ports		1	1	2	–
South Coast London		19	43	13	–
Portsmouth		–	4	4	–
Plymouth		–	–	4	–
Sundry Ports		1	7	4	–
Wales		–	4	1	–
		105	**266**	**200**	**30**
FOREIGN					
Russia		2	–	1	–
Germany		4	15	6	7
Ireland		30	18	1	–
Sundry		2	3	2	2
		38	**36**	**10**	**9**

CARGOES		1850	1860	1870	1880
SCOTLAND					
Grain		63	67	45	11
Flour		3	15	2	–
Timber		15	46	16	1
Herring		18	2	1	–
Sundry Cargoes		30	31	24	3
		129	**161**	**88**	**15**
ENGLAND & WALES					
Grain		6	48	45	20
Potatoes		12	54	28	–
Timber		78	162	122	6
Sundry Cargoes		9	2	5	4
		105	**266**	**200**	**30**
FOREIGN					
Grain		11	9	1	–
Potatoes		18	9	–	–
Herring		8	18	9	9
Coal		1	–	–	–
		38	**36**	**10**	**9**

IMPORTS

PORTS OF ORIGIN

SCOTLAND		1850	1860	1870	1880
Moray Firth	Sundry Ports	33	50	12	1
West Coast	Glasgow	5	4	2	1
	Balachulish	14	9	17	–
	Sundry Ports	2	4	–	–
East Coast	Aberdeen	10	–	–	–
	Sundry Ports	3	9	5	–
Forth Estuary	Leith	36	13	3	4
	Alloa	7	14	3	–
	Boness	–	4	2	2
	Charlestown	12	–	1	–
	Grangemouth	–	5	1	1
	Sundry Ports	10	3	5	–
Fife	Wemyss	43	36	42	26
	Dysart	–	9	24	1
	Burntisland	–	3	1	–
North Coast	Thurso & Castlehill	13	10	13	2
	Lerwick & Kirkwall	1	3	4	–
	Wick	5	2	5	–
	Sundry Ports	2	4	4	–
		196	**182**	**144**	**38**

ENGLAND & WALES					
East Coast	Newcastle, Sunderland, South Shields & Middlesborough	104	158	328	116
	Hartlepool	32	23	14	2
West Coast	Liverpool	21	9	25	9
South Coast	London	20	19ı	20	3
	Southampton	4	2	4	–
	Ipswich	–	–	5	2
Wales		3	11	11	7
		184	**222**	**407**	**139**

FOREIGN		1805-29				
Russia						
	Riga	30	1	2	4	–
	St Petersburg	59	–	16	27	8
	Memel	25	–	1	–	–
	Konigsberg	–	–	3	2	–
	Archangel	6	3	–	–	1
Norway						
	Krageroe	9	8	15	29	9
	Mandal	32	4	4	–	–
	Drammen	12	–	4	2	–
	Christiansand	40	–	2	1	–
	Pursgrunn	15	–	1	–	–
	Brevig	–	–	3	15	1
	Arendal	1	5	2	6	–
	Landsund & Larvig Lillesland	1	–	1	3	1
Germany						
	Stettin	24	1	5	5	1
	Danzig	1	–	3	1	1
	Cuxhaven	–	–	3	–	–
	Hamburg	20	–	4	2	1
	Sundry Ports	2	3	5	2	1

continued over...

IMPORTS

PORTS OF ORIGIN						
Sweden		**1805-29**	**1850**	**1860**	**1870**	**1880**
	Kalmar	–	–	1	7	–
	Gothenburg	26	–	–	–	3
	Sundsval	–	–	2	9	5
Portugal		2	–	1	3	–
Denmark		–	4	2	4	5
Holland		36	4	6	2	1
Belgium		6	–	1	2	1
Canada		46	2	3	–	–
Greenland		5	–	–	–	–
Peru		–	2	–	–	–
North Africa		–	–	–	2	3
Black Sea		5	–	–	1	–
Estonia		–	–	–	–	2
		403	**37**	**90**	**129**	**44**

GOODS IMPORTED					
SCOTLAND		**1850**	**1860**	**1870**	**1880**
	Coal	76	85	78	34
	Manure/Bones	2	7	4	1
	Slates	14	13	18	–
	Grain	14	25	5	1
	Flour	10	2	–	–
	Pavements	15	8	14	2
	Freestone	1	17	1	–
	Timber	8	8	3	–
	Herring	2	7	13	–
	Cattle	1	3	4	–
	Goods	53	7	4	–
		196	**182**	**144**	**38**
ENGLAND & WALES					
	Coal	97	169	303	108
	Lime	29	11	21	4
	Salt	17	5	19	9
	Manure/Bone	15	14	36	5
	Bark	3	2	4	–
	Slates	–	7	10	7
	Goods	16	7	1	–
	Sundry	7	7	13	6
		184	**222**	**407**	**139**
FOREIGN					
	Timber	18	44	77	20
	Grain	2	6	5	5
	Bones	6	35	39	16
	Tar	3	–	–	–
	Sundry	8	5	8	3
		37	**90**	**129**	**44**

An analysis of imports 1805-29 is given in Appendix 2

APPENDIX A 4

Moray Firth Steamship Services 1840-63

North of Scotland Steam Packet Coy

1849 - 1852	*Isabell Napier*
1852 - 1857	*Martello*
1858 - unknown	*Lyra*
1857 - 1860	*Brilliant*
1860 - 1863	*Dundalk* and *Times*

(The last 2 ships may have been in service later than 1863)

Aberdeen Steam Navigation Coy

1844 - 1859	*North Star*
1844 - 1858	*Duke of Rothesay*
1845 - 1857	*Queen*
1857 - 1858	*Commodore*

Aberdeen Leith Clyde Steam Ship Coy

1844 - 1859	*Duke of Richmond* (lost 1859)
1845 - 1847	*Queen* (lost 1857)
1853 - 1856	*Queen* (lost 1856)
1828 - 1839	*Brilliant* (lost 1839)

A Dunn & Co

1857 -	*La Platta*
1858 - 1859	*Kangaroo*

Grant Gilchrist MacKilligan

1860	*Ben My Chree*

OTHER SHIPPING SERVICES OPERATED FROM MORAY FIRTH PORTS

Burghead to Littleferry, Brora & Helmsdale

1809 - 1840	Regular weekly service by small sailing ships one of which was the *Maid of Morven*

Inverness, Burghead, Cromarty, Invergordon & Littleferry

1848 - 1850	*Rothesay Castle*

Burghead to Littleferry

1832 - 1850	*The Burghead Packet* (14 tons)
1851 - 1855	SS *Curlew*
1852	SS *Dunrobin*
1860 - 1863	SS *Heatherbell*
1864	SS *Xantho*

Burghead to Scottish and English Ports

1844	London	*London*
	Aberdeen	*Jean* 64 tons
	Aberdeen	*Elizabeth* 80 tons

Banff & London Shipping Coy (Company dissolved in 1851)

1850	*Royal Consort*	Schooner
	Sovreign	Schooner

Findhorn to Scottish and English Ports

1844	London	*Maid of Moray* 80 tons
		Caledonia 58 tons
1852	London	*Swift* 124 tons
		Kinloss 117 tons
	Newcastle	*Hope*
	Aberdeen	*Hero* 25 tons

SHIPS OPERATING BETWEEN EDINBURGH AND INVERNESS AND BETWEEN
BURGHEAD AND LITTLEFERRY 1840-1880

Steamships

Ben My Chree	Paddle steamer, 589 tons, Barrow 1875
Brilliant	Paddle steamer, 159 tons, Greenock 1821
Commodore	Paddle steamer, 760 tons, 80hp, 1840
Curlew	Screw steamer, 86hp, Dumbarton, 1853
Duke of Richmond	Paddle steamer, 497 tons, 1838
Duke of Rothesay	Screw steamer, 578 tons, 130hp, Dumbarton 1857
Heather Bell	Paddle steamer, 95 tons, 60hp, Glasgow, 1858
Isabella Napier	Paddle steamer, 424 tons, Port Glasgow, 1835
Kangaroo	Screw barque, 1144 tons, 160hp, Port Glasgow
Queen	Paddle steamer, 328 tons, A Hall & Sons, Aberdeen, 1844
Times	Screw steamer, 303 tons, 70hp, Glasgow, 1851
Xantho	Paddle steamer 97 tons, Dumbarton 1848

Sailing Ships

Royal Consort	Schooner 121 tons, Sunderland, 1846
Sovreign	Schooner, 156 tons, Dundee, 1835
??? *Burghead Packet*	Smack 140 tons, Burghead, 1832

APPENDIX A 5

ORIENT
Record of Voyages and Cargoes 1855-1867

	From	To	Cargo
1855			
Aug-Sep	Spey	Sunderland	sleepers
	Sunderland	Lossiemouth	coal
Sep-Dec	Cromarty	Stettin	herring
	Sunderland	Lossiemouth	coal
Dec-Jan	Lossiemouth	Sunderland	sleepers
1856			
Feb-Apr	Scrabster	London	pavement
	London	Wick Castlehill	guano & hoops
Apr-Jul	Castlehill	Leith	pavement
	–	Copenhagen	coal
	Riga	Dundee	flax
Jul-Sep	Boness	Copenhagen	pig iron
	Malmo	Leith	wheat
Sep-Nov	Peterhead	Malmo	herring
	Memel	London	oats
	Sunderland	Lossiemouth	coal
1857			
Feb-Apr	Lossiemouth	Sunderland	props
	Sunderland	Aberdeen	coal
	Aberdeen	Danzig	coal
	Danzig	Aberdeen	wheat
Apr-Sep	Boness	Stettin	pig iron
	Stettin	Newcastle	wheat
	Newcastle	Stettin	coal
	Riga	London	oats
	London	Wick	hoops
	Wick	Stettin	herring
	Stettin	Konigsberg	stone
	Konigsberg	London	wheat seed
	Sunderland	Lossiemouth	coal
1858			
Jan-Feb	Lossiemouth	Sunderland	props
	Sunderland	Lossiemouth	coal
Jun-Jul	Spey	Sunderland	props
	Sunderland	Lossiemouth	coal
Jul-Sep	Lossiemouth	Hartlepool	props
	Hartlepool	Grangemouth	coal
	Bridgeness	Lossiemouth	coal
Sep-Jan	Lossiemouth	Sunderland	props
	Sunderland	Wick	coal
	Lerwick	Stettin	herring
	Copenhagen	Newcastle	barley
	Newcastle	Grangemouth	coal
	Wemyss	Lossiemouth	coal

continued over

	From	To	Cargo
1859			
Jan-Feb	Lossiemouth	Sunderland	props
	Sunderland	Lossiemouth	coal
Feb-Apr	Lossiemouth	Findhorn	barley
	Grimsby	Newcastle	salt
	Newcastle	Lossiemouth	coal & manure
Apr-Jun	Spey	Hartlepool	props
	Hartlepool	Grangemouth	coal
	Charlestown	Lossiemouth	coal
Jun-Sep	Spey	Hartlepool	props
	Hartlepool	Danzig	coal
	Danzig	London	wheat
Sep-Nov	London	Wick	hoops
	Scrabster	London	pavement
	London	Spey	guano
1860			
Dec-Jan	Spey	Sunderland	barley
	Sunderland	Leven	coal
	Spey	Newcastle	props
	Newcastle	–	coal
Feb-Mar	–	Sunderland	props
	Sunderland	Lossiemouth	coal
	Spey	Newcastle	props
	Newcastle	Malmo	coal
	Malmo	Hull	oats
May-Sep	Hull	–	salt
	Newcastle	Danzig	wheat
	Sunderland	Lossiemouth	coal
Sep-Dec	Lossiemouth	Buckie	herring
	Danzig	London	wheat
	London	Inverness	guano
1861			
Apr-May	Leith	Konigsberg	pig iron
	Konigsberg	London	oats
– Sep	Newcastle	Konigsberg	coal
	Konigsberg	Leith	peas
	Charlestown	Lossiemouth	coal
Sep-Nov	Hopeman	Stettin	herring
	Stettin	Leith	wheat
Nov-Feb	Wemyss	Malmo	coal
	Nysted	London	barley
1862			
Feb-May	London	Kirkcaldy	manure
	Dysart	Greifswald	coal
	Konigsberg	Fareham	wheat
Jun-Jul	–	Danzig	coal
	Danzig	Newcastle	wheat
Jul-Sep	Newcastle	Danzig	coal
	Danzig	Leith	wheat
	Wemyss	Lossiemouth	coal
Oct-Dec	Cullen	Stettin	herring
	Stettin	Kirkcaldy	barley
	Wemyss	Lossiemouth	coal

continued over

	From	**To**	**Cargo**
1863			
Feb-May	Wick	Stettin	herring
	Stettin	Grangemouth	wheat
May-Jun	Grangemouth	Stettin	pig iron
	Stettin	Exeter	wheat
Aug-Sep	Newcastle	Stettin	coal
	Stettin	Dundee	timber
	Bridgeness	Lossiemouth	coal
1863/64			
Sep-Feb	Lossiemouth	Burghead	herring
	Stettin	Grangemouth	wheat
	Wemyss	Lossiemouth	coal
Apr-May	Helmsdale	Stettin	herring
	Stettin	Grangemouth	wheat
	Grangemouth	Lubeck	coal
	Danzig	London	wheat
Aug-Oct	Gillingham	Copenhagen	clay
	Danzig	Hartlepool	wheat
	Sunderland	Burghead	coal
1864/65			
Nov-Feb	Grangemouth	Stettin	coal
	Stettin	Leith	wheat
May	Clackmannan	Danzig	coal
	Danzig	Dundee	wheat
Jun-Dec	Dundee	Stettin	coal
1866			
Feb	Danzig	Grimsby	sleepers
	Sunderland	Lossiemouth	coal
	Hopeman	Danzig	herring
	Danzig	Grangemouth	staves
	Bridgeness	Lossiemouth	coal
	Lossiemouth	Sunderland	sleepers
	Sunderland	Burghead	coal
	Burghead	Hartlepool	sleepers
	Hartlepool	Aberdeen	coal
	Sunderland	Lossiemouth	coal
Mar-May	Lossiemouth	Sunderland	props
	Sunderland	Danzig	coal
	Danzig	Hartlepool	peas
	Hartlepool	Danzig	coal
	Danzig	Weymouth	wheat
Oct-Dec	Teignmouth	Dundee	clay
	Sunderland	Lossiemouth	coal
	Portmahomack	Stettin	herring
	Stettin	Fraserburgh	oak
	Sunderland	Lossiemouth	coal
1867			
Mar-Apr	Lossiemouth	Newcastle	wood
	Newcastle	Inverness & Beauly	guano
Apr-Sep	Inverness	Newcastle	staves
	Newcastle	Figueira	coal
	Figueira	Tilbury	salt
	Sunderland	Lossiemouth	coal
Oct-Nov	Helmsdale	Danzig	herring
	Danzig	Hartlepool	staves
	Shields	Lossiemouth	coal

Vessel Sold

APPENDIX A 6

EXPRESS
Record of Voyages and Cargoes 1863-68

	From	To	Cargo	Intermediate Port
1863				
Jul-Sep	Archangel	London	oats	Burntisland
Nov-Dec	London	Marseilles		
1864				
Jan	Marseilles	Yarmouth	oil cake	
Feb	Yarmouth	Sunderland		
Apr	Sunderland	Algiers	coal	
	Algiers	Oran		
May	Oran	Hull	cottonseed	
Jun-Jul	Hull	Malaga	coal	
Aug	Malaga	Hull	oil	
Sep	Hull	Danzig	coal	Elsinore
Nov	Danzig	Newcastle	wheat	
1865				
Jan	Newcastle	Gibraltar	coal & fireclay	Villa Nova & Portimoid
Mar	Villa Nova	Hull	locust beans	
	Hull	Newcastle	salt & beans	
Apr	Newcastle	Danzig	charter	
Jun	Danzig	Jersey	wheat & lathe wood	
	Jersey	London	stones	
Jul	London	Archangel		
Nov	Archangel	London	oats	Lerwick
1866				
Jan	Newcastle	Gibraltar	coal	Mazigan
	Mazigan	London	locust beans	Queenstown
Mar	Burntisland	Stettin	coal	Danzig & Jersey
May	Stettin	Leith	wheat	Burntisland
Jul	Burntisland	Danzig	coal	
Aug	Danzig	Belfast	sleepers	Workington
Oct	Workington	Stettin	iron & coal	
Dec	Stettin	Leith	barley	
1867				
Mar	Leith	Genoa	coal	Lowestoft & Brixham
Aug	Girgenti	Glasgow	sulphur	Girgenti & Gibraltar
Oct	Glasgow	Newport	pig iron	
	Newport	Riga	iron	Elsinore
1868				
Jan	Riga	Belfast	seed	Stornaway
Apr	Ardrossan	Savorna	iron & coal	Milford
	Genoa	Glasgow	lump iron	
Sep	Glasgow	Palermo	coal	Catania & Gibraltar

Vessel sunk off Gibraltar in December 1868 with no loss of life

Lloyd's timber requirements and regulations

Third.—When completed, and, if possible, before the plank be painted or payed.

36. A full statement, agreeably to Form No. 4, of the dimensions, scantlings, &c., of all new ships, verified by the builder, is to be transmitted by the Surveyor, and to be kept as a record in the office of the Society.

RULES TO BE OBSERVED IN BUILDING SHIPS.

TIMBERING.

37. The whole of the timber to be of good quality, of the descriptions hereinafter shewn in a Tabular Form, No. 1, as applicable to the several terms of years for which ships so constructed may respectively be appointed to remain on the List of the First Description of the First Class : the stem, stern post, beams, transoms, apron, knightheads, hawse timbers, and kelson of ships claiming to stand *twelve years*, to be entirely free from *all defects*; the frame to be well squared from the first foothook heads upwards and free from sap, and likewise below, unless the timber be proportionably larger than the scantling hereafter described; every alternate set of timbers to be framed and bolted together to the gunwale. The butts of the timbers to be close, and not to be less in thickness than one-third of the entire moulding at that place, and to be well chocked with a butt at each end of the chock. In all cases in which the heads and heels of the timbers shall be *square*, in vessels intended for the twelve years' grade, a dowel must be introduced into the ends of such timbers in order to connect them together.

I.—The Scantlings to be not less than as follows :

	For Ships	Tons. 150	Tons. 500
Room and space to be	...	20 in.	30 in.
Floors sided, if square, and free from sap, to be at the kelson	8 in.	13 in.
First foothooks sided, if square, at floor heads	...	7 in.	11 in.
Second foothooks sided, if square, at the heads	...	6½ in.	10 in.
Third foothooks sided; and top timbers, if square	...	6 in.	9 in.
The frame to be moulded at kelson	...	8 in.	13 in.
The frame to be moulded at floor heads	...	7 in.	11 in.
Top timbers to be moulded at their heads at the sheerstrake	...	4 in	5 in.

38. The intermediate dimensions for the scantling of timbers between the floor heads and the gunwale to be regulated in proportion to the distance from the two points. Should the room and space be increased, the siding of the timbers to be increased in proportion. Whenever ships are built with *double floors*, some thick planks, not less than three, must be worked inside on the upper and lower floor heads, and be well bolted through and clenched. The plank outside from the wales to the lower floor heads, in vessels of 500 tons, must not be less than four inches thick, and of a proportionate thickness for vessels of other tonnage.

II.—*Deck Beams.*

	For Ships	Tons. 150	Tons. 500
To be moulded in the middle	...	7 in.	9 in.
To be moulded at the ends	...	5 in.	6¼ in.
And to be sided	...	7 in.	10 in.

39. Those at the after-end of the ship to be reduced in proportion to their length.

III.—*Hold Beams.*

	For Ships	Tons. 150	Tons. 500
To be moulded in the middle	...	9 in.	13 in.
To be moulded at the ends	...	7 in.	10 in.
And to be sided	...	9 in.	13 in.

40. Those at the after-end of the ship to be reduced in proportion to their length.

41. The deck and hold beams to be sufficient in number,* and securely fastened to the sides either with lodging knees of iron or wood, or with shelf pieces ; or with a shelf piece and knees : or with some other security equal thereto, so as sufficiently to connect the ends of the beams to the sides of the ship: and, in addition, all vessels of 200 tons shall have at least six *vertical* knees on each side to the DECK beams ; and for every additional 50 tons measurement above 200 tons they shall have one more hanging knee on each side. And ships of 400 tons shall likewise have to their HOLD beams at least eight vertical knees, either as standards or hanging knees (the latter being preferred), and for every additional 100 tons burthen, they shall have one more to each side.† Ships having a depth of hold, measured from the limber-strake to the under side of the lower deck beam, *above* thirteen feet but not exceeding fifteen feet, must be secured with iron riders, in number and description such as are prescribed by the Rules, section 62, or by orlop beams, sufficient in number and properly secured. Ships *exceeding* fifteen feet depth of hold, will be required to have orlop beams; the number to

* As regards the spacing of Beams, it appears to the Committee that the following scale would in general meet the convenience of stowage in all trades, as well as secure the requisite transverse strength, so essential to be attended to according to the tonnage of the vessel.

The spaces between the beams (hatchways excepted) not to exceed the following distances.

	Deck Beams.	Hold Beams.
Vessels under 200 Tons ...	8 feet	4 feet.
200 and under 400 Tons ...	8 feet and 4 feet alternately,	One over every Hold Beam, and one in all double spaces
400 Tons and above ...	4 feet 6 inches.	or in that proportion

† The number of knees required for vessels according to their tonnage will be found more fully described on page 26.

be in no case less than one-half of the number of lower deck beams in the space between the fore-mast and the mizen-mast. The application of this rule to colonial and fir built ships will not exempt them from the full operation of the Rules, section 62. Every ship exceeding 150 tons to have at least one crutch for the security of the heels of the after-timbers of the frame; one pair of pointers in addition to a knee at each end of the wing transom to connect the stern frame with the after-body of the ship; and a transom over the heels of the stern timbers properly kneed. The heels of the cant timbers forward and aft to be stepped into or on the deadwood, and bolted through.

IV.—*Keel and Kelsons.*

For Ships	Tons. 150	Tons. 500
Keel, sided and moulded...	9 in.	13 in.
Main Kelson to be sided...	10 in.	14 in.
— moulded	10 in.	14 in.
The scarphs of Kelson, where only one Kelson, to be...	5 ft.	7 ft.
But where rider Kelsons are added, then they may be	4½ ft.	6 ft.

42. Shifts of timber in ships of 200 tons and upwards, to be not less than one-seventh of the main breadth; and in ships under 200 tons, to be not less than one-sixth of the main breadth.

PLANK.

43. The outside planking to be of good quality, of the description prescribed in the Tabular Form, No. 2, hereinafter shewn, and to be clear of all defects.

44. The inside planking to be of the description shewn in the Tabular Form, No. 3, and free from all foxy, druxy, or decayed planks. The whole to be properly shifted and fastened.

45. No butts to be nearer than five feet to each other, unless there be a strake wrought between them, and then a distance of four feet will be allowed; and no butts to be on the same timber, unless there be three strakes between, as more particularly shewn in the diagram annexed (*see Plate No.* 3); but vessels under 200 tons will be exempted from the full operation of this rule; and in ships of larger tonnage a literal compliance with it will be dispensed with in cases wherein it may be satisfactorily proved that the departure from the rule is only partial, being confined to the ends of the ship, or the thin planking of the topside, and does not injuriously affect the ship's general strength; but such relaxation will not be sanctioned unless an accurate description of the shifting of the plank be transmitted by the Surveyors, to enable the Committee to form a proper judgment on the case.

Thickness of Plank to be not less than as under:

	Tons. 150	Tons. 500
I.—*Outside.* For Ships ...		
Bilge to wales ...	2¼ in.	4 in.
Short hoods ...	2¼ in.	3 in.
Bilge plank ...	3 in.	4 in.
Bilge to keel ...	2¼ in.	3 in.
Wales (average) ...	4 in.	5 in.
Topsides ...	2 in.	3 in.
Sheerstrake ...	3 in.	4 in.
Planksheer ...	2½ in.	4 in.
II.—*Inside.*		
Ceiling below the hold beams ...	2 in.	3 in.
Bilge planks ...	3 in.	5 in.
Clamps and Limber strakes ...	2½ in.	4 in.
Upper-deck Clamps and Spirkettings ...	2¼ in.	3 in.
'Twixt deck-ceiling ...	2 in.	2½ in.
III.—*Deck.*		
Upper deck ...	2¾ in.	3 in.
Waterways, if of hard wood ...	4 in.	5 in.
Do. if of Baltic Fir, Pitch Pine, or Red Pine ...	5 in.	8 in.

In regard to vessels built with *double floors*, see section 38, page 10.

FASTENINGS.

46. The treenails to be of good quality, and of a description of wood *equal to the best material* through which they are to pass. They are to be circular, being either engine-turned, compressed, or planed. All planks above nine inches in width are to be treenailed double and single, except bolts intervene; and if less than that width, then to be treenailed single, and at least one-half of the treenails must go through the ceiling. All ships to be fastened with at least one bolt in every butt, and from the wales to the lower part of the bilges the bolt to be through and clenched. The bilges to have at least one bolt through and clenched in each foothook. The limber strakes to be bolted down to the floors, and one bolt in every floor to be through and clenched. Ships otherwise entitled to stand *higher* than the TEN YEARS grade, in which the whole of the outside fastenings above the floor heads shall consist of copper or mixed metal to the entire exclusion of iron bolts and treenails, and in which no iron bolts are used below the floor heads, shall be allowed an additional period of Two Years.

And Ships otherwise entitled to stand *higher* than the TEN YEARS grade, in which treenails may be used in fastening the plank, but in which *all* the *Bolts* shall be of copper or mixed metal, to the entire exclusion of iron, shall be allowed an additional period of One Year. In all such cases of substitution, the number of bolts must be the same as is already prescribed as above for treenails; the proportion * of *through* and short bolts must be one of the former and two of the latter alternately, so that the *through* bolts may be placed in succession on each edge of the plank, and all the through bolts must be of malleable metal, and clenched on rings (of the same metal) inside. The sizes of the copper or mixed metal bolts must be as under, *viz.*

For vessels of 150 tons and under 200 tons	... ...	$\frac{5}{8}$ in.
200 ditto 500	... ...	$\frac{3}{4}$ in.
500 and above ...	... ...	$\frac{7}{8}$ in.

and the lengths of the short bolts not less than as follows, *viz.*—

When used in plank of $2\frac{1}{2}$ inches,	to be 7 inches long	
— 3 "	8 "	
— 4 "	10 "	
— 5 "	12 "	

and so on in proportion for plank of other thicknesses. The sizes of the bolts required in the several parts hereinafter described, to be not less than as against the same expressed, *viz.*—

For Ships		Tons. 150		Tons. 500
Heel-knee, and dead wood abaft		1 in.		$1\frac{1}{4}$ in.
Scarph of the keel	(In No. 6 Bolts of)	$\frac{3}{4}$ in.	(In No. 8 Bolts of)	1 in.
Kelson bolts, one through each floor		$\frac{7}{8}$ in.		$1\frac{1}{8}$ in.
Bolts through the bilge and limber strakes ...		$\frac{5}{8}$ in.		$\frac{7}{8}$ in.
Butt bolts		$\frac{5}{8}$ in.		$\frac{3}{4}$ in.
Hold beam bolts		$\frac{7}{8}$ in.		$1\frac{1}{8}$ in.
Deck beam bolts		$\frac{3}{4}$ in.		$\frac{7}{8}$ in.
Hooks forward at throat		$\frac{7}{8}$ in.		$1\frac{1}{8}$ in.
———— arms		$\frac{3}{4}$ in.		1 in.
Transoms		$\frac{7}{8}$ in.		$1\frac{1}{8}$ in.
The lower pintle of the rudder		$2\frac{1}{2}$ in.		$3\frac{1}{2}$ in.

The sizes of bolts for vessels of other tonnage will be found more fully described, page 25, and also *Plate No.* 4.

* Whenever *metal fastenings* are used in lieu of treenails this proportion must be observed.

47. In every case where the butt and bilge bolts are not through and clenched, One Year will be deducted from the period which would otherwise be assigned in the classification of the vessel; but this Rule will not be applied to ships built previously to the 1st January, 1835.

48. The scantlings and dimensions for all intermediate sized vessels to be proportionately regulated, agreeably to a scale adopted by the Society, a copy of which is in the hands of each of the Surveyors. *See Plates Nos.* 1 & 2.

49. Ships surveyed while building, in which *all the materials required for a Twelve Years' Ship shall have been used,* and most of the other requisites for that class fulfilled, but which, from partial deficiencies, may not appear to be in all respects entitled to the highest class, although superior to the description of a Ten Years' ship, may be marked in the Book thus, 11 A; thereby denoting that they are to remain in the First Description of the First Class *Eleven Years*, provided they be kept in a state of efficient repair.

50. Ships surveyed while building, in which the scantling and shifts of the timbers, the thickness and shifts of the planks, and size of fastenings may be the same as are required by the preceding rules, and in which the description of materials prescribed in the annexed Tables shall also have been used, but in which the *alternate* sets of timbers shall not have been framed, nor the chocks wrought with a butt at each end, nor the frame so well squared as is required for Twelve Years' ships, but which shall be *in other respects* equal thereto, shall be marked "10 A;" thereby denoting that they are to remain on the List of Ships of the First Description of the First Class *Ten Years*, provided they be kept in a state of efficient repair.

51. In all other cases, ships surveyed while building, and constructed of the materials of good quality, hereinafter shewn in the Tables Nos. 1, 2, and 3, will be classed for the several terms of years respectively appointed for their remaining on the List of Ships of the First Description of the First Class.—All ships, *not built under Survey*, whether in the United Kingdom or abroad for which a class may be claimed, shall be required to have *their timbers completely exposed for examination, by a listing or plank being taken out* (if not originally left open) all fore and aft at the foothook heads, and another between decks; *and a few treenails must likewise be driven out,* so that the Surveyors, from actual inspection, may be satisfied whether or not they are of the quality and make prescribed by the Rules, and the material of the frame and the quality of the treenails being thus ascertained, the same shall be reported to the Committee, and a class assigned accordingly.

52. Ships built in the United Kingdom under a roof, and which shall have

occupied a period of not less than twelve months in their construction, will have One Year added to the period prescribed for their continuing on the List of Ships of the First Description of the First Class.

53. Ships built in the United Kingdom since the year 1834, and *not surveyed while building* by the Surveyors to this Society, or where the owners or builders may have refused to permit them to survey and examine the same at the several periods prescribed by the Rules, will be subjected to the minutest possible examination previously to assigning the class in which they may be placed according to the regulations; but in all such cases One Year will be deducted from the period which would otherwise be allowed, in consequence of their not having been submitted to such survey during their construction. In no case, however, will a higher grade than 10 A be assigned to ships built in the United Kingdom, which shall not have been surveyed while building.

CONTINUATION OF SHIPS IN THE FIRST DESCRIPTION OF THE FIRST CLASS.

54. If, on the termination of the period of original designation, or if at any subsequent period within the limitation hereafter mentioned, a Ship-Owner should wish to have his ship remain, or be replaced on the letter A, he is to send a written notice thereof to the Committee, who shall then direct a Special Survey as follows to be held, consisting of not less than *two* competent persons to be appointed by the Committee, one of whom shall be a Surveyor the exclusive servant of the Society, namely,

SURVEY.

For the purpose of facilitating such survey, the ship shall be either placed in dry dock or laid on the ways, *and the upper works from the lower part of the wales to the upper part of the sheerstrakes, shall be scraped so as to expose the surface of the plank to view.* The attention of the Surveyors shall then be particularly directed to the state of the *upper or main deck* and comings, the upper and lower deck bolts, and the outside planks through which they pass, the *planksheers*, waterways, and beams, so far as they can be examined; the hawse timbers, knightheads, breasthooks, and transoms; the floors and kelsons; the planking outside, *and the treenails passing through* from the light water mark upwards; the ceiling inside, and the frame and inner surface of the outside planking where it may be seen; and the sheer and general form of the ship: *and should any suspicious treenails or bolts appear, the same are to be driven out for inspection.* The Surveyors on these points shall transmit to the Committee a detailed report, accompanied by such observations as may

occur to them, either from inspection of the ship, or from information of the repairs she may have received. If from the report of such special survey the ship shall appear to be in a sound and efficient state, and to have preserved her original form unaltered, the Committee shall continue such ship on the letter A for such further period as they may think fit, not exceeding, however, one-third of the number of years which had been originally assigned. Ships so continued shall be distinguished in the Register Book by the number of years for which the classing is extended, being inserted separately under the number assigned on the original classing, thereby denoting that the ship has been found on survey in such good and efficient order as to entitle her to be continued   years longer on the List of ships of the First Description of the First Class. The period assigned for continuation, will, upon all occasions commence from the time the ship may have gone off the letter A, without regard to the date when the survey for this purpose may have been held.

In cases of the repair of ships for continuation of character under the Rules, section 54, (*but in no other*) materials of an inferior description (but not below those prescribed for the six years' grade) may be permitted to be used in those parts which must of necessity, under the operation of the Rules, section 56, be *entirely removed* on a repair for restoration; subject, however, to the ship-owner, in every instance, making a special application to the Committee for their previous sanction.

RESTORATION OF SHIPS TO THE FIRST DESCRIPTION OF THE FIRST CLASS.

FIRST RULE.

55. If, at any time before the expiration of two-thirds of the number of years *beyond* the period for which ships may have been originally assigned to remain in the First Description of the First Class, an owner be desirous to have his ship restored to the List of Ships of that description, such restoration (on his consenting to the special survey hereinafter described, to be held by two Surveyors, and performing the repairs found requisite) will be granted for a period not exceeding two-thirds of the time originally assigned for her remaining as a ship of the First Description of the First Class, the same to be calculated from the date of such repairs.

Requisites for Restoration.

56. All the bolts in the range of each deck to be driven out, and the planks taken out; the upper deck waterways, and planksheers and spirketting, and the strake next the waterways on the lower deck in the midships to be taken out; the sheathing to be entirely stripped off the

No. 1.—A TABLE exhibiting the different Descriptions of TIMBER, of good quality, to be used in the TIMBERING of SHIPS, as the same will be applicable to the several Terms of Years appointed for Ships to remain on the Character A.

PARTS OF THE FRAME OF A VESSEL	TWELVE YEARS	TEN YEARS	NINE YEARS	EIGHT YEARS	SEVEN YEARS	SIX YEARS	FIVE YEARS	FOUR YEARS	PARTS OF THE FRAME OF A VESSEL
*FLOORS	English } Oak African } Live East-India Teak Morung Saul Greenheart Morra Iron Bark.	The same as in the preceding Class, and admit Live Oak and Red Cedar alternately, Adriatic, Spanish, or French Oak, South American or Australasian } Hard Wood, Mahogany, Cuba Sabicu.	The same as in the preceding Class, and admit Other Foreign White Oak, Red Cedar, Spanish Chesnut.	The same as in the preceding Class.	The same as in the preceding Class, and admit Sound second-hand English or African Oak, or Teak, Hackmatack, Tamarac, Juniper, Larch.	The same as in the preceding Class, and admit Pitch Pine, Hard Gray Elm.	The same as in the preceding Class, and admit Cowdie, Red Pine, Black Birch, Witch Hazel, Elm or Ash [Hy Elm and Wood of good qualia-] English Beech, Spruce.	The same as in the preceding Class.	*FLOORS.
1st FUTTOCKS	English } Oak African } Live East-India Teak Morung Saul Greenheart Morra Iron Bark.	The same as in the preceding Class, and admit Live Oak and Red Cedar alternately, Adriatic, Spanish, or French Oak, South American or Australasian Hard Wood, Cuba Sabicu.	The same as in the preceding Class, and admit Other Foreign Oak below the light water mark, Red Cedar, Spanish Chesnut.	The same as in the preceding Class.	The same as in the preceding Class, and admit Other Foreign White Oak above the light water mark, Sound second-hand English or African Oak, or Teak, Hackmatack—Tamarac, Juniper—Larch.	The same as in the preceding Class, and admit English Ash, Cowdie, Pitch Pine, American Rock Elm, Hard Gray Elm.	The same as in the preceding Class, and admit Baltic Fir, Red Pine, Buck Birch, Witch Hazel, Elm or Ash [Hy Hard Wood of good qualia-] Spruce.	The same as in the preceding Class, and admit English Beech.	1st FUTTOCKS.
2d FUTTOCKS	English } Oak African } Live East-India Teak Morung Saul Greenheart Morra Iron Bark.	The same as in the preceding Class, and admit Live Oak and Red Cedar alternately, Adriatic, Spanish, French } Oak, South American or Australasian Hard Wood, Cuba Sabicu.	The same as in the preceding Class, and admit Adriatic, Spanish, French } Oak, South American or Australasian Hard Wood, Red Cedar.	The same as in the preceding Class.	The same as in the preceding Class, and admit Other Foreign White Oak, Spanish Chesnut, Hackmatack, Tamarac—Juniper, Larch.	The same as in the preceding Class, and admit Cowdie, English or African Oak, or Teak, Pitch Pine.	The same as in the preceding Class, and admit Baltic Fir, English Ash, American Rock Elm, Hard Gray Elm.	The same as in the preceding Class, and admit Elm, Black Birch, Witch Hazel, Spruce.	3d FUTTOCKS.
3d FUTTOCKS and TOP TIMBERS	English } Oak African } Live East-India Teak Morung Saul Greenheart Morra Iron Bark.	The same as in the preceding Class, and admit Red Cedar alternately, Adriatic, Spanish, French Oak, South American or Australasian Hard Wood, Cuba Sabicu.	The same as in the preceding Class, and admit Spanish, French, South American or Australasian Hard Wood, Red Cedar.	The same as in the preceding Class.	The same as in the preceding Class, and admit Other Foreign White Oak, Spanish Chesnut, Hackmatack, Tamarac—Juniper, Larch.	The same as in the preceding Class, and admit Sound second-hand English or African Oak, or Teak, Pitch Pine.	The same as in the preceding Class, and admit English Ash, American Rock Elm, Hard Gray Elm, Red Pine.	The same as in the preceding Class, and admit Yellow Pine, Elm, Black Birch, Spruce.	3d FUTTOCKS and TOP TIMBERS.
STEM STERN POST	English } Oak African } Live East-India Teak Morung Saul.	The same as in the preceding Class, and admit Mahogany, Cuba Sabicu, Greenheart, Morra, Iron Bark.	The same as in the preceding Class, and admit Spanish, French, South American or Australasian Hard Wood, Red Cedar.	The same as in the preceding Class.	The same as in the preceding Class, and admit Other Foreign White Oak, Hackmatack, Tamarac—Juniper, Larch.	The same as in the preceding Class, and admit Cowdie, Pitch Pine.	The same as in the preceding Class, and admit Second-hand English or African Rock Elm, Hard Gray Elm, Red Pine.	The same as in the preceding Class, and admit Yellow Pine, Elm, Black Birch, Witch Hazel, Spruce.	STEM STERN POST.
TRANSOMS KNIGHTHEADS HAWSE TIM-BERS APRON ‡DEADWOOD	English } Oak African } Live East-India Teak Morung Saul.	The same as in the preceding Class, and admit Mahogany, Cuba Sabicu, Morra, Iron Bark.	The same as in the preceding Class, and admit Other Foreign White Oak, Red Cedar.	The same as in the preceding Class, and admit Other Foreign White Oak, Spanish Chesnut, Pitch Pine.	The same as in the preceding Class, and admit Other Foreign White Oak, Hackmatack, Tamarac—Juniper, Larch.	The same as in the preceding Class, and admit English or African Oak, or Teak, Pitch Pine.	The same as in the preceding Class, and admit American Rock Elm, Witch Hazel, Black Birch, English Beech, Spruce.	The same as in the preceding Class, and admit Yellow Pine, Elm, Ash, Black Birch, Witch Hazel, Spruce.	TRANSOMS KNIGHTHEADS HAWSE TIM-BERS APRON ‡DEADWOOD.
MAIN KELSON	English } Oak African } Live East-India Teak Morung Saul.	The same as in the preceding Class, and admit Adriatic, Spanish, French, South American or Australasian Hard Wood, Red Cedar, Australasian ditto, Cuba Sabicu.	The same as in the preceding Class, and admit Other Foreign White Oak, Spanish Chesnut.	The same as in the preceding Class.	The same as in the preceding Class, and admit Pitch Pine, Red Pine, Hackmatack, Tamarac, Juniper, Cowdie.	The same as in the preceding Class, and admit Sound second-hand English or African Oak, or Teak.	The same as in the preceding Class, and admit Elm, Ash.	The same as in the preceding Class, and admit Elm, Ash.	MAIN KELSON.
BEAMS HOOKS and KNEES	English } Oak African } Live East-India Teak Greenheart Morra Mahogany Cuba Sabicu Iron Bark.	The same as in the preceding Class, and admit Adriatic, Spanish, French, South American Hard Wood, Red Cedar, Australasian, Juniper, Cuba Sabicu.	The same as in the preceding Class, and admit Spanish Chesnut.	The same as in the preceding Class, and admit Other Foreign White Oak, Spanish Chesnut, Pitch Pine.	The same as in the preceding Class, and admit Knees of Fir, Pine, or Red Pine, Juniper—Cowdie, Baltic Fir, Red Pine.	The same as in the preceding Class, and admit Second-hand English English or African Oak, or Teak.	The same as in the preceding Class, and admit Yellow Pine, Elm, Ash.	The same as in the preceding Class, and admit Yellow Pine, Black Birch, Witch Hazel, Spruce.	BEAMS HOOKS and KNEES.

but an extent not exceeding one half the entire length of the Keel, in Ships of the Seven Years' Class.

Mem.—For relaxation in favour of Steam Vessels, vide Rules, page 96.

* Black Birch, Witch Hazel, American Rock Elm, Hard Gray Elm, and Cowdie allowed for Floors in Midship.
† Black Birch allowed for First Futtocks amidships, to the same extent in Ships of the Six Years Class.
‡ So far as regards the Material to be used from the height of two feet above the rabbet of the keel.

No. 2.—A TABLE exhibiting the different Descriptions of TIMBER, of good Quality, to be used in the OUTSIDE PLANKING of SHIPS, as the same will be applicable to the several Terms of Years appointed for Ships to remain on the Character A.

PARTS OF THE OUTSIDE OF A VESSEL.	TWELVE YEARS.	TEN YEARS.	NINE YEARS.	EIGHT YEARS.	SEVEN YEARS.	SIX YEARS.	FIVE YEARS.	FOUR YEARS.	PARTS OF THE OUTSIDE OF A VESSEL.
KEEL to the 1st FUTTOCK HEADS.	English, African, or Live Oak / East-India Teak / Red Cedar / Foreign White Oak / Elm / Beech / South American, or any Hard Wood / Mahogany / Spanish Chesnut / Cuba Sabicu.	The same as in the preceding Class, and admit Pitch Pine / Larch / Hackmatack / Tamarac / Juniper / Black Birch / Cowdie.	The same as in the preceding Class, and admit Baltic Fir / Red Pine.	The same as in the preceding Class.	The same as in the preceding Class.	The same as in the preceding Class, and admit Spruce / Yellow Pine.	The same as in the preceding Class, and admit Witch Hazel.	The same as in the preceding Class.	KEEL to the 1st FUTTOCK HEADS.
1st FUTTOCK HEADS to LIGHT WATER MARK.	English, African, or Live Oak / East-India Teak / Red Cedar / Foreign White Oak / South American, } Hard } Wood / or Australian / Spanish Chesnut / Cuba Sabicu / Greenheart / Morra—Iron Bark.	The same as in the preceding Class, and admit Pitch Pine.	The same as in the preceding Class, and admit Baltic Fir / Red Pine / Larch / Hackmatack / Tamarac / Juniper / Cowdie.	The same as in the preceding Class, and admit Elm / English Beech.	The same as in the preceding Class, and admit Ash / Black Birch.	The same as in the preceding Class.	The same as in the preceding Class, and admit Witch Hazel.	The same as in the preceding Class, and admit Black Birch / Ash / Witch Hazel / English Beech.	1st FUTTOCK HEADS to LIGHT WATER MARK.
LIGHT WATER MARK to WALES.	English } Oak / African / Live / East-India Teak / Morung Saul / Red Cedar / Greenheart / Morra / Iron Bark.	The same as in the preceding Class, and admit Adriatic, Spanish, or French Oak / South American, } Hard } Wood / or / Australasian / Mahogany / Cuba Sabicu.	The same as in the preceding Class, and admit Foreign White Oak / Spanish Chesnut.	The same as in the preceding Class, and admit Baltic Fir / Red Pine / Larch / Hackmatack / Tamarac / Juniper / Cowdie.	The same as in the preceding Class.	The same as in the preceding Class, and admit American Rock Elm / Hard Gray Elm.	The same as in the preceding Class, and admit Yellow Pine / Elm, English or French.	The same as in the preceding Class, and admit Black Birch / Ash / Witch Hazel / English Beech.	LIGHT WATER MARK to WALES.
WALES and BLACKSTRAKES.	English } Oak / African / Live / East-India Teak / Red Cedar / Greenheart / Morra / Morung Saul / Iron Bark.	The same as in the preceding Class, and admit Red Cedar / Mahogany / Cuba Sabicu.	The same as in the preceding Class, and admit Adriatic } Oak / Spanish / French / South American, } Hard } Wood / or / Australasian	The same as in the preceding Class, and admit Other Foreign White Oak / Pitch Pine / Spanish Chesnut.	The same as in the preceding Class, and admit Baltic Fir / Red Pine / Larch / Hackmatack / Tamarac / Juniper—Cowdie.	The same as in the preceding Class.	The same as in the preceding Class, and admit Yellow Pine / American Rock Elm / Hard Gray Elm.	The same as in the preceding Class, and admit Black Birch / Witch Hazel.	WALES and BLACKSTRAKES.
TOPSIDES.	English } Oak / African / Live / East-India Teak / Red Cedar / Morung Saul / Morra / Iron Bark.	The same as in the preceding Class, and admit Pitch Pine / Mahogany / Cuba Sabicu.	The same as in the preceding Class, and admit Adriatic } Oak / Spanish / French / South American, } Hard } Wood / or / Australasian	The same as in the preceding Class, and admit Other Foreign White Oak / Spanish Chesnut.	The same as in the preceding Class, and admit Baltic Fir / Red Pine / Larch / Hackmatack / Tamarac / Juniper / Cowdie.	The same as in the preceding Class.	The same as in the preceding Class, and admit Yellow Pine / American Rock Elm / Hard Gray Elm.	The same as in the preceding Class, and admit Black Birch / Witch Hazel.	TOPSIDES.
SHEERSTRAKES and PLANKSHEER.	English } Oak / African / East-India Teak / Greenheart / Morra / Morung Saul / Iron Bark.	The same as in the preceding Class, and admit Red Cedar / Mahogany / Cuba Sabicu.	The same as in the preceding Class, and admit Adriatic } Oak / Spanish / Juniper / South American, } Hard } Wood / or / Australasian	The same as in the preceding Class, and admit Other Foreign White Oak / Spanish Chesnut / Pitch Pine.	The same as in the preceding Class, and admit Larch / Hackmatack / Tamarac / Juniper / Cowdie.	The same as in the preceding Class, and admit Red Pine.	The same as in the preceding Class, and admit Yellow Pine / American Rock Elm / Hard Gray Elm.	The same as in the preceding Class, and admit Spruce / Yellow Pine / Black Birch / Witch Hazel.	SHEERSTRAKES and PLANKSHEER.
WATERWAYS.	English } Oak / African / East-India Teak / Red Cedar / Morung Saul / Mahogany / Cuba Sabicu / Adriatic } Oak / Iron Bark.	The same as in the preceding Class, and admit South American, } Hard } Wood / Red Pine——Pitch Pine / Hackmatack——Tamarac / Juniper——Cowdie. / Adriatic } Oak / Spanish / French	The same as in the preceding Class.	The same as in the preceding Class, and admit Foreign White Oak / Spanish Chesnut.	The same as in the preceding Class, and admit Yellow Pine for the upper deck, provided the beams are well secured independently of the waterways.	The same as in the preceding Class.	The same as in the preceding Class, and admit Yellow Pine / American Rock Elm / Second-hand English or African Oak, or Teak.	The same as in the preceding Class, and admit Spruce / Black Birch / Witch Hazel.	WATERWAYS.

N.B.—For relaxation in favour of Steam Vessels, vide Rules, page 26.

* The use of Elm, in Ships above the EIGHT YEARS grade, to be restricted to a height from the lower part of the main Keel, of one third of the internal depth of the Ship measured, in midships, from the top of the Limber Strake to the top of the Upper Deck Beams.

No. 3.—A TABLE exhibiting the different Descriptions of TIMBER, of good Quality, to be used in the INSIDE PLANKING of SHIPS, as the same will be applicable to the several Terms of Years for Ships to remain on the Character A.

PARTS OF THE INSIDE OF A VESSEL.	TWELVE YEARS.	TEN YEARS.	NINE YEARS.	EIGHT YEARS.	SEVEN YEARS.	SIX YEARS.	FIVE YEARS.	FOUR YEARS.	PARTS OF THE INSIDE OF A VESSEL.
LIMBER STRAKE.	English, African, Spanish, French } Oak; East-India Teak; Morung Saul; Red Cedar; Mahogany; Greenheart; Cuba Sabicu; Iron Bark; South American, or Australian Hard Wood.	The same as in the preceding Class, and admit Other Foreign White Oak; Spanish Chesnut.	The same as in the preceding Class.	The same as in the preceding Class, and admit Pitch Pine.	The same as in the preceding Class, and admit Baltic Fir; Red Pine; Larch; Hackmatack; Tamarac; Juniper; Cowdie.	The same as in the preceding Class, and admit American Rock Elm; Hard Gray Elm.	The same as in the preceding Class, and admit Yellow Pine; Spruce; Second-hand English or African Oak, or Teak; Ash; Elm; Witch Hazel; English Beech.	The same as in the preceding Class.	LIMBER STRAKE.
BILGE PLANKS.	English, African, Spanish, French } Oak; East-India Teak; Morung Saul; Red Cedar; Mahogany; Greenheart; Cuba Sabicu; Iron Bark; South American, or Australian Hard Wood.	The same as in the preceding Class, and admit Other Foreign White Oak; Spanish Chesnut.	The same as in the preceding Class, and admit Pitch Pine.	The same as in the preceding Class, and admit Pitch Pine.	The same as in the preceding Class, and admit Red Pine; Larch; Hackmatack; Tamarac; Juniper; Cowdie.	The same as in the preceding Class, and admit American Rock Elm; Hard Gray Elm.	The same as in the preceding Class, and admit Yellow Pine; Spruce; Black Birch; Second-hand English or African Oak, or Teak; Ash; Elm; Witch Hazel; English Beech.	The same as in the preceding Class.	BILGE PLANKS.
CEILING. — LOWER HOLD.	English, African, Spanish, French } Oak; East-India Teak; Morung Saul; Red Cedar; Mahogany; Greenheart; Cuba Sabicu; Iron Bark; South American, or Australian Hard Wood.	The same as in the preceding Class, and admit Other Foreign White Oak; Spanish Chesnut.	The same as in the preceding Class, and admit Pitch Pine.	The same as in the preceding Class, and admit Baltic Fir; Red Pine; Larch; Hackmatack; Tamarac; Juniper; Cowdie.	The same as in the preceding Class.	The same as in the preceding Class, and admit American Rock Elm; Hard Gray Elm.	The same as in the preceding Class, and admit Spruce; Black Birch; Second-hand English or African Oak, or Teak; Ash; Elm; Witch Hazel; English Beech.	The same as in the preceding Class.	LOWER HOLD.
CEILING. — BETWEEN DECKS.	English, African, Adriatic, Spanish, French } Oak; East-India Teak; Morung Saul; Red Cedar; Mahogany; Greenheart; Cuba Sabicu; Iron Bark; South American, or Australian Hard Wood.	The same as in the preceding Class, and admit Other Foreign White Oak; Pitch Pine; Spanish Chesnut.	The same as in the preceding Class.	The same as in the preceding Class, and admit Baltic Fir; Red Pine; Larch; Hackmatack; Tamarac; Juniper; Cowdie.	The same as in the preceding Class.	The same as in the preceding Class, and admit American Rock Elm; Hard Gray Elm.	The same as in the preceding Class, and admit Spruce; Black Birch; Second-hand English or African Oak, or Teak; Ash; Elm; Witch Hazel; English Beech.	The same as in the preceding Class.	BETWEEN DECKS.
SHELF PIECES and CLAMPS.	English, Adriatic, Spanish } Oak; East-India Teak; Hackmatack; Red Cedar; Greenheart; Morra; Mahogany; Cuba Sabicu; Iron Bark.	The same as in the preceding Class, and admit Foreign White Oak; South American, or Australian Hard Wood; Spanish Chesnut.	The same as in the preceding Class.	The same as in the preceding Class, and admit Pitch Pine; Larch; Hackmatack; Tamarac; Juniper; Cowdie.	The same as in the preceding Class, and admit Baltic Fir; Red Pine.	The same as in the preceding Class, and admit American Rock Elm; Hard Gray Elm.	The same as in the preceding Class, and admit Yellow Pine; Spruce; Black Birch; Second-hand English or African Oak, or Teak; Ash; Elm; Witch Hazel; English Beech.	The same as in the preceding Class, and admit Yellow Pine.	SHELF PIECES and CLAMPS.

American Rock Elm allowed for Inside Planking from Limber Strakes to Bilge Planks, in Midships, to an extent not exceeding two-thirds of the entire length of the keel, in Ships of the seven years' grade.

NOTE.—For relaxation in favour of Steam Vessels, vide Rules, para 56.

APPENDIX A 8a

First Cost of Schooner *Caledonia* of Spey

APPENDIX A 8b -

First Cost of Schooner *Express* of Spey

1863, July 1	Schooner Express of Spey, First cost					
	To J. Geddie Builder Acct	£1010	10	"		
"	Robt Wright Acct chains anchors & blocks	130	10	"		
"	A. Inglis Acct for coulers	3	10	6		
"	Robt Wright Acct extra blocks	"	12	6		
"	Andw Duncan do — do	"	7	10		
"	Fulton & Rind Acct matts sheves	"	7	4		
"	J. Gordon — plumber	1	1	9		
"	A. Carney — sailmaker	290	4	6		
"	Wm McKenzie — blacksmith	51	"	5		
"	Wm Geddie — shipchandler	28	13	4		
"	A. Milne — cooper	9	1	"		
"	A. Leslie — druggist	4	8	"		
"	Chas Strand — painter	18	9	6		
"	Riggers Wages	8	10	8		
"	Mastes do	4	"	"		
"	Aprentice Board	"	11	8		
"	Shipping Masters Acct	1	5	8		
"	Butchers — do	7	8	"		
"	Ballastiny	2	14	"		
"	Railway fair for crew	"	18	3		
		1574	4	11		
"	Discounts	17	16	1	£1556 8 10	

Registrated Owners.

Wm Geddie Kingston	8 Shares
Dr. Geddie —	8 —
Jas. Geddie —	8 —
Alex Geddie —	8 —
Jas. Geddie Garmouth	8 —
John Sutherland Kingston	8 —
John Duncan —	16
	64 Shares

APPENDIX A 9

SHIP CHANDLER'S ACCOUNT RENDERED TO JOHN DUNCAN, SHIPBUILDER, FOR SUPPLY OF GOODS TO SCHOONER *EXPRESS* JULY 1863

	£	s	d		£	s	d
6 gallons Varnish	-	15	6	1 Hand Saw	-	4	8
2¾ gallons Naptha	-	8	3	1 Hand Plane	-	3	-
2 Tar Brushes	-	3	-	2 Caulking Irons	-	1	1
2 Ships Scrapers	-	2	8	1 Log Book	-	3	-
1 Paint Pot	-	1	-	1 Cargo Book	-	1	3
1 Shaver	-	-	4	1 Log Slate	-	2	9
5 lbs Grease	-	2	8½	1 Candlestick	-	1	4
2 Handspikes	-	4	-	1 Fog Horn	-	1	8
1 Oil Feeder	-	1	-	3 Oil Flasks	-	8	6
3 gills Colsa Oil	-	2	8½	2 Cork Fenders	-	7	8
15 x 18" Mast Hoops	1	-	-	1 Wool Mop	-	1	8
1 Padlock	-	1	-	5 Brush Handles	-	1	3
2 Glass Deck Lights	-	5	-	2 Paint Pots	-	2	-
½ lb White Lead	-	-	2½	2 Goblet Pans	-	6	6
3oz Copper Tacks	-	1	4½	1 Beam	-	2	9
4 Bottles Whiskey	-	11	-	1 pair of Scales	-	1	-
4 Ballast Shovels	-	10	2	1 set Weights	-	1	10
Brace Screw Nails	-	-	1½	1 Coffee Mill	-	5	-
1½ lbs Pump Tack	-	2	-	1 Tide Table	-	1	-
1 pair Brass Signal Lamp	2	7	-	Paper, Envelopes, Ink and Pens	-	1	3
2 Brass Padlocks	-	3	-	1 Coffee Pot	-	1	6
1 Iron Padlock	-	1	-	1 Spring Weighing m/c	-	2	9
¾ cwt Salt	-	1	10	4 lb 12 D Nails	-	-	10
½ doz. Knives and Frks	-	4	6	4 lb 22 D Nails	-	-	10
½ doz Table Spoons	-	2	6	6 lb Spike Nails	-	1	3
½ doz Tea Spoons	-	-	9	2 lb Scupper Nails	-	1	4
1 doz Soup Toureen	-	5	-	5 cwt Ship Bread	4	15	-
1 Soup Ladle	-	-	6	2 stone Split Peas	-	4	8
1 Wash Hand Basin	-	1	8	4 stone Barley	-	8	-
1 Tea Pot	-	1	3	1 gallon Seal Oil	-	4	8
½ doz Soup Plates	-	1	6	1 gallon Colsa Oil	-	6	6
½ doz Breakfast Plates	-	1	-	84 lbs Sugar	1	15	-
½ doz Coffee Cups	-	2	9	25 lbs Coffee	1	13	-
1 Cabin Jug	-	-	6	4 lbs Composite Candles	-	4	-
1 Ashet	-	-	6	3 lbs Tea	-	11	9
1 Sugar Basin	-	-	3	2 doz Matches	-	-	10
3 Drain Glasses	-	-	9	1 lb Mustard	-	1	4
3 Tumblers	-	1	3	½ lb Pepper	-	-	8
1 Cooks Soup Ladle	-	1	4	15 lbs Butter	-	15	-
1 Fore Castle Lamp	-	1	4	1 Butter Jar	-	1	6
1 Hand Lead	-	3	9	1 Mustard Pot	-	-	3
1 Deep Sea Lead	-	8	7½	1 Salt Holder	-	-	3
1 Cabin Kettle	-	1	10	6½ lbs White Lead	-	2	8
1 Fore Castle Kettle	-	4	9	6 lbs Black Paint	-	2	3
1 Fry Pan	-	1	8	1 gallon Whiskey	-	16	-
1 Cabin Brush	-	1	3	1 Bath Brick	-	-	3
1 pair of Short Brushes	-	1	-	3 Fishing Lines	-	3	2
2 Deck Scrubbers	-	4	-	Hooks	-	-	3
2 Paint Scrubbers	-	4	6	4 stone Fine Flour	-	9	-
1 Ships Bell	-	19	6	Cost of unidentified items	1	11	4
1 Dipper	-	1	-				
3 Brass Coat Hooks	-	1	6	**Total**	**28**	**13**	**4**
1 Cooks Axe	-	2	10				
3 Gimlets	-	-	11				

APPENDIX A 10

EXTRACTS FROM THE MERCANTILE NAVY LIST 1859

Notice of Examinations of Masters and Mates of 'foreign-going' ships
and of 'home trade Passenger Ships'
Established in pursuance of the Merchant Shipping Act, 1854
and of
Voluntary Examinations in Steam

1. Under the provisions of the Merchant Shipping Act, 1854, no "Foreign-going Ship" * or "Home Trade Passenger Ship" * can obtain a clearance or transire, or legally proceed to sea, from any port in the United Kingdom unless the Master thereof, and in the case of a Foreign-going Ship the First and Second Mates or Only Mate (as the case may be), and in the case of a "Home Trade Passenger Ship" the First or Only Mate (as the case may be), have obtained and possess valid Certificates, either of Competency or Service, appropriate to their several stations in such a ship, or of a higher grade; and no such ship, if of *one hundred tons burden or upwards*, can legally proceed to sea unless *at least one officer besides the Master* has obtained and possesses a valid Certificate, appropriate to the grade of Only Mate therein, or to a higher grade; and every person who, having been engaged to serve as Master or as First, or Second, or Only Mate of any "Foreign-going Ship," or as Master of First or Only Mate of a "Home Trade Passenger Ship," goes to sea as such Master or Mate without being at the time entitled to and possessed of such a Certificate as the Act requires, or who employs any person as Master or First, Second, of Only Mate of any "Foreign-going Ship," or as Master of First or Only Mate of any "Home Trade Passenger Ship," without ascertaining that he is at the time entitled to and possessed of such Certificate, *for each offence incurs a penalty not exceeding fifty pounds.*

2. Every Certificate of *Competency* for a "Foreign-going Ship" is to be deemed to be of a higher grade than the corresponding Certificate for a "Home Trade Passenger Ship," and entitles the lawful holder to go to sea in the corresponding grade in such last mentioned Ship;

* By a "Foreign-going Ship" is meant one which is bound to some place out of the United Kingdom, beyond the limits included between the river Elbe and Brest; and by a "Home Trade Passenger

Ship" is meant any Home Trade Ship employed in carrying passengers; and it is to be observed that *Foreign Steam Ships when employed in carrying passengers between Places in the United Kingdom* are subject to all the Provisions of the Act, as regards certificates of Masters and Mates, to which British Steam Ships are subject (s.291) but, *no Certificate for a "Home Trade Passenger Ship" entitles the holder to go to sea as Master or Mate of a "Foreign-going Ship."*

* * *

A SECOND MATE must be seventeen years of age, and must have been four years at sea.

In NAVIGATION. - He must write a legible hand, and understand the first five rules of arithmetic and the use of logarithms. He must be able to work a day's work complete, including the bearings and distance of the port he is bound to, be Mercator's method; to correct the sun's declination for longitude, and find his latitude by meridian altitude of the sun; and work such other easy problems of a like nature, as may be put to him. He must understand the use of the sextant, and be able to observe with it, and read off the arc.

In SEAMANSHIP.- He must give satisfactory answers as to the rigging and unrigging of ships, stowing of holds, &c; must understand the measurement of the log-line, glass, and lead-line; be conversant with the rule of the road, as regards both steamers and sailing vessels, and the lights and fog signals carried by them.

AN ONLY MATE must be nineteen years of age, and have been five years at sea.

In NAVIGATION. - In addition to the qualification required for a Second Mate, an Only Mate must be able to observe and calculate the amplitude of the sun, and deduce the variation of the compass therefrom, and be able to find longitude by chronometer by the usual methods. He must know how to lay off the place of the ship on the chart, both by bearings of known objects, and by latitude and longitude. He must be able to determine the error of a sextant and adjust it, and find the time of high water from the known time at full and change.

In SEAMANSHIP.- In addition to what is required by a Second Mate, he must know how to moor and unmoor, and to keep a clear anchor; to carry out an anchor; to stow a hold, and make the requisite entries in the ship's log. He will also be questioned as to his knowledge of the use and management of the mortar and rocket lines in the case of the stranding of a vessel, as explained in the official Log-Book.

A **FIRST MATE** must be nineteen years of age, and must have served five years at sea, of which one year must have been as either Second or Only Mate, or as both. *

In NAVIGATION. - In addition to the qualification required for an Only Mate, he must be able to observe azimuths and compute the variation; to compare chronometers and keep their rates, and find the longitude by them form an observation by the sun; to work the latitude by single altitude of the sun off the meridian; and be able to use and adjust the sextant by the sun.

In SEAMANSHIP.- In addition to the qualification necessary for an Only Mate, a more extensive knowledge of seamanship will be required, as to shifting large spars and sails, managing a ship in stormy weather, taking in and making sail, shifting yards and masts, &c., and getting heavy weights, anchors, &c., in and out; casting a ship on a lee-shore; and to secure the masts in the event of an accident to the bowsprit.

A **MASTER** must be twenty-one years of age, and have been six years at sea, of which one year must have been as First or Only Mate, and one year as Second Mate; or two years as First and Only Mate. *

In addition to the qualification for a First Mate, he must be able to find the latitude by a star, &c. He will be asked questions as to the nature of the attraction of the ship's iron upon the compass, and as to the method of determining it. He will be examined in so much of the Laws of the Tides as is necessary to enable him to shape a course, and to compare his soundings with the depths marked on the charts. He will be examined as to his competency to construct rafts, and as to his resources for the preservation of the ship's crew in the event of wreck. He must possess a knowledge of what he is required to do by law; as to entry and discharge, and the management of his crew; and as to penalties and entries to be made in the official log. He will be questioned as to his knowledge of invoices, charterparty, Lloyd's agent, and as to the nature of bottomry; and he must be acquainted with the leading lights of the channel he has been accustomed to navigate, or which he is going to use.

In cases where an applicant for a certificate as Master Ordinary has only served in a fore and aft rigged vessel, and is ignorant of the management of a square rigged vessel, he may obtain a certificate on which the words "*fore and aft rigged vessel*" will be written. This certificate does not entitle him to command a square rigged ship. This is not, however, to apply to Mates, who, being younger men, are expected for the future to learn their business completely.

APPENDIX A 11

Geddie Collection Line Plans

Plan Ref no	Name	Built	Rig	Tons
Group One				
189	*Carpenter*	1832	SR	70
190	*Patriot*	1837	SR ●	124
188	*Reliance*	1838	SR	90
184	*Brutus*	1838	SR ●	135
192	*Arab*	1839	SR	269
195	*Violet*	1839	BK ●	74
197	*Brothers*	1841	SR	100
Group Two				
191	*Vigilant*	1844	SR	78
187	*Isabella Harley*	1846	SR	90
185	*Maria*	1849	SR	68
186	*Laurel/Enterprise*	1850	SR	100/110
210	*Brothers*	1854	BG	190
183	*Alma*	1855	SR	129
218	*New Rambler*	1857	SR	113
209	*Clarissa/St Clair*	1858	BKN/SR	124/122
211	*Lady Ann Duff*	1860	SR	66
207	*Isabella Anderson*	1860	SR	110
215	*Alma*	1861	SR ✧	87
Group Three				
219	*Eident*	1861	SR ✧	174
220	*Chieftain*	1862	BK	192
203	*Champion/Onward*	1865	SR	186/195
206	*Florence Barclay*	1866	BK	343
222	*Union*	1867	SR ■	234
200	*Tollo*	1867	SR	89

●   These vessels were classed by Lloyds as schooners. Spar sizes given in plans are for a brigantine

✧   These vessels were classed by Lloyds as schooners. Spar sizes given in plans are for a barquentine

■   The rigging plan is for a barquentine

Rigging Plans

Plan ref no	Name	Built	Rig	Tons
201	*Union*	1867	BKN	234
202	*Fiery Cross*	1872	BKN	338
204	*Northern Chief*	1873	BK	393
208	*Coronella*	1874	BKN	269
216	*Zephyr*	1869	BKN	256
216	*Alma*	1861	BKN	87

SHIPS BUILT IN MORAY FIRTH PORTS 1780 - 1895

All dimensions are in feet and inches (LxWxD)

The following abbreviations are used:

B	Boat
BG	Brig
BGN	Brigantine
BK	Barque
BKN	Barquentine
DY	Dandy
G	Galliot
K	Ketch
LR	Lugger
SK	Smack
SP	Sloop
SQ	Square Rigged
SR	Schooner
SR(H)	Hermaphrodite Schooner
STM	Steamer
SW	Snow
WY	Wherry

Ships are listed chronologically in alphabetical order
e.g. in the Portsoy listings, *Christian* (1792) comes before *Caledonia* (1856)
but both come before *Flower o' Portsoy*

SPEYMOUTH	Built	Rig	Tons	Dimensions			Builder
Ann	1801	BG	73				
Aid	1802	SP	55	51.6	16.4	8.9	Simpson Geddie
Ann	1802	BG	87				Demster
Ann & Margaret	1804	BG	166				Winchester
Ann	1806	BG	105				Glenmore Coy
Abraham Newlands	1806	SQ	613	125.2	33.0	7.1	Glenmore Coy.
Anna	1807	BG	113				
Aid	1813	SP	59	51.6	16.9	8.5	
Ann	1814	SP	72				
Ann	1814	SP	60				
Ann	1817	SP	68				
Aid	1821	SP	35	42.2	14.6	7.1	Geddie
Alexander	1826	SP	58	52.6	15.8	9.4	
Alexander	1828	SP	75	55.6	18.0	9.7	
Antilles	1834	BK	195				Geddie
Arab	1839	BK	269	90.5	22.6	16.5	Geddie
Antelope	1840	SR	128				
Atholl	1841	SR	63				
Agnes	1842	SR	31	43.4	14.1	7.7	Leslie
Aeriel	1846	SR	59	57.0	15.9	9.0	Hay
Advice	1850	BK	250	91.9	21.7	15.0	Duncan
Aid	1850	SR	40	49.3	14.8	8.3	
Annie Rose	1850	SP	29	43.1	13.9	7.3	Young
Artic	1855	BK	203	100.2	24.9	14.0	Duncan
Arva	1855	SR	133	73.5	20.1	9.7	
Alma	1855	SR	129	74.0	20.0	10.1	Geddie
Arvask	1855	SR	133	73.5	20.1	9.7	
Ajax	1855	STM	175				Duncan
Alex Murray	1857	SR	96	78.9	20.7	10.5	
Active	1857	SR	93	77.0	21.0	10.0	Geddie
Arab	1857	BG	138	95.0	23.4	13.5	
Alert	1858	SR	96	76.6	21.0	10.2	Geddie
Agnes & Jessie	1860	SR	186	102.0	22.9	12.0	Duncan
Ardivalloch	1861	BK	322	115.0	27.0	15.8	Duncan
Alma	1861	BKN	87	76.0	19.8	9.8	Geddie
Annie	1863	SR	98	99.0	21.2	10.4	
Arthur	1864	SR	219	110.0	23.8	14.0	Duncan
Annie Fisher	1865	BG	249	117.0	23.9	14.9	Duncan
Ann Bradshaw	1865	BKN	142	94.0	22.1	12.2	Duncan
Alert	1866	SR	143	90.0	22.0	11.8	Geddie
Amelia Wilson	1867	SR	205	115.0	23.6	11.8	Duncan
Ann	1868	SK	28	46.2	15.1	7.3	
Anna Bella	1869	BK	334	128.0	25.6	15.5	Duncan
Annie Bow	1869	SR	250	112.0	24.9	14.2	Spence
African Belle	1871	BKN	122	84.3	18.6	9.9	Geddie
Abeona	1874	BK	295	125.0	26.2	14.9	Geddie
Advance	1876	SR	100	89.2	21.5	10.4	Geddie
Annie	1877	SR	106	86.8	21.2	10.4	Lee
Agnes	1877	SR	134	96.5	23.2	10.9	Kinloch
Annie Stuart	1878	SR	98	84.6	21.6	10.8	Duncan
Agenoria	1879	SR	168	99.3	23.3	12.0	Duncan
Altmore	1880	BK	349	138.8	26.8	14.8	Geddie
Admiral	1883	DY	81	80.7	22.5	8.5	Duncan
Annie	1883	SR	116	84.0	21.6	10.3	Geddie
Advance	1884	SR	41	64.0	17.4	7.4	Duncan
Afghan Chief	1885	BKN	275	124.4	26.2	12.8	Kinloch
Barbara and Mary	1793	BG	87				
Brittannia	1799	BG	138				

Brittannia	1802	SR	75	56.6	17.1	8.9	Logie
Beufort Castle	1809	BG	109				
Barbara & Ann	1816	SR	72	55.1	17.1	9.0	
Brothers	1823	SP	56	43.1	16.6	8.6	
Banff Packet	1836	SP	35	44.7	13.8	8.1	Geddie
Beatrice	1837	SP	41				Geddie
Benjamin	1838	SR	97	73.8	20.2	11.0	Palmer
Brutus	1838	SR	116	69.6	18.9	11.3	Geddie
Brothers	1839	SR(H)	68	56.5	16.7	9.6	Geddie
Billow	1841	SR	111	62.9	17.4	10.2	Geddie
Brothers	1841	SR	82	60.6	17.2	10.1	Duncan
Blossom	1842	SR	78	56.8	15.4	9.1	Geddie
Blossom	1848	SR	53	52.9	16.0	8.8	
Brutus	1848	SR(H)	109	72.2	21.3	11.3	
Brittannia	1849	BG	154	82.2	20.2	11.9	Duncan
Bell & Mary	1849	SR	68				
Billow	1851	SR	55				
Brothers	1854	BG	159	81.6	20.5	12.4	Geddie
Brothers	1854	BG	190	84.0	22.0	12.5	Geddie
Barbara Innes	1857	BN	119	83.0	22.0	13.2	
Barrogil Castle	1858	BR	93	70.2	19.3	9.1	Duncan
Ballindalloch	1859	SR	85	75.5	20.0	10.0	Young
Billow	1863	SR	96	96.0	21.6	10.0	Geddie
Britannia	1866	SR	217	107.0	23.9	13.9	Kinloch
Bella Rose	1868	SR	197	103.0	28.3	13.5	Spence
Billow	1870	SR	72	71.0	20.0	8.5	Geddie
Beautiful Star	1873	SR	221	111.3	21.9	13.3	Geddie
Blue & White	1875	BKN	163	102.6	21.3	12.2	Kinloch
Billow	1876	SR	68	71.0	20.0	8.6	Geddie
Ben Aigen	1882	SR	96	84.9	21.3	10.0	Geddie
Blue & White	1887	SR	99	98.0	21.6	10.8	Kinloch
Collingwood	1785-91	SQ	300				Glenmore Coy.
Cotsford	1799	SQ	349				
Caroline	1805	SP	18	32.0	11.0	5.4	
Content	1806	BG	187	84.0	23.0	14.0	Glenmore Coy
Cornelia	1814	BG	137				
Caledonia	1818	BG	110				
Craigellachie	1819	BG	109	64.0	21.1	10.6	Proctor
Caledonia	1820	SP	59				
Craigellachie	1827	SK	76	50.6	18.2	9.7	Winchester
Chance	1832	SP	29	40.2	13.6	6.8	
Carpenter	1832	SR	70	55.2	17.5	9.4	Geddie
Catherine Ann	1834	SR	78	59.2	17.8	10.7	
Cheerful	1841	SR	71				
Caledonia	1845	SR	111	71.9	17.0	10.7	Duncan
Catherine	1846	SR	102	66.4	18.0	11.0	Duncan
Cheerful	1847	SR	97	70.3	18.1	10.6	Duncan
Commerce	1848	SR	76	70.0	18.3	10.2	
Ceres	1849	SR	133	75.8	19.7	11.7	Duncan
Christian	1850	SR	110	75.4	18.5	10.7	
Caberfeigh	1853	SR	88	70.3	17.9	9.7	Young
Challenger	1854	BG	180	83.0	23.4	11.5	
Comet	1854	SR	80	77.3	19.7	9.4	Geddie
Countess of Caithness	1854	BG	175	81.0	22.0	11.0	
Countess of Seafield	1854	BG	126	82.0	21.8	11.1	Duncan
Catherine Anderson	1855	BG	174	79.0	23.6	11.6	
Countess of Caithness	1856	SR	71	67.2	18.8	9.0	
Countess of Fife	1857	SR	57	82.0	20.9	10.5	
Clarissa	1858	BKN	124	83.0	22.0	11.4	Geddie
Caberfeigh	1859	BG	151	89.0	22.7	12.0	Duncan

Catherine McIver	1862	SR	92	82.0	21.3	9.7	Duncan
Chieftain	1862	SR	192	103.3	23.6	12.5	Geddie
Caledonia	1864	SR	191	102.0	23.8	13.2	Geddie
Charlotte	1864	SR	146	93.0	22.7	11.7	Geddie
Champion	1865	SR	186	103.2	23.2	13.0	Geddie
Clara	1866	BKN	269	127.0	25.5	14.9	Duncan
Chieftain	1868	BK	339	134.6	27.3	15.8	Kinloch
Clansman	1870	BKN	382	134.5	26.6	16.3	Kinloch
Cavalier	1871	SR	80	82.0	20.5	9.8	Kinloch
Coronella	1874	BKN	269	127.0	25.5	14.9	Duncan
Cock o' the North	1877	BKN	235	116.3	24.1	13.4	Geddie
Dispatch	1785-91	SR	34				Glenmore Coy.
Duke of Gordon	1785-91	SQ	500				Glenmore Coy.
Duchess of Gordon	1787	SQ	324				Glenmore Coy.
Duke of York	1798	SQ	449				
Diana	1805	BG	133				
Dabrachie	1811	SP	76	56.0	18.1	10.0	Geddie
Dunrobin Castle	1819	SP	42	45.2	15.0	6.1	Geddie
Dispatch	1827	SR	53	53.10	17.5	9.6	Geddie
Diana	1835	SP	56	49.7	11.0	9.0	Anderson
Dart	1849	SP	27	42.2	13.0	7.5	Duncan
Driver	1850	SR	64	65.4	16.8	8.8	Geddie
Diadem	1859	BK	307	109.0	25.5	15.5	Duncan
Dove	1866	SR	79	77.1	20.0	8.4	Duncan
Duke of Richmond	1868	SR	294	128.0	25.4	14.9	Duncan
Diana	1868	SR	125	86.0	22.0	11.0	Duncan
Dagmar	1870	BK	348	131.0	26.6	15.4	Kinloch
David & Kate	1872	SR	80	72.0	19.0	8.6	Lee
Dispatch	1888	SR	100	90.1	21.5	10.3	Geddie
Elizabeth	1780	SP	60				
Euphan	1784	SP	56				
Elgin Star	1786	SP	56				
Essay	1787	SQ	297				Glenmore Coy.
Ellis	1792	BG	81				
Elizabeth Anderson	1793	SP	33				
Elizabeth	1796	SP	48	46.0	16.3	6.1	
Eliza	1798	SP	50				
Elizabeth	1798	BG	200				
Expidition	1803	SQ	291				Glenmore Coy.
Eliza	1806	SP	65				
Eliza	1807	BG	131	68.0	21.0	12.0	Glenmore Coy
Eliza	1813	SP	82	57.6	19.1	9.4	
Eliza	1819	SR	93	59.1	19.1	9.0	
Elizabeth	1823	SP	33	41.9	13.1	6.1	Anderson
Elizabeth	1827	SP	60	50.0	17.1	9.2	
Enterprise	1838	SR	88	57.0	16.5	10.2	
Elspet	1838	SR(H)	62	55.0	16.0	9.2	Leslie
Elizabeth	1840	SR	70	57.5	16.6	9.5	Leslie
Earl of March	1841	SR	84	54.8	15.9	9.5	Leslie
Earl of Aberdeen	1841	SR	124				Duncan
Enterprise	1841	SR	106				
Eagle	1842	SR	89	58.4	16.4	9.2	Duncan
Equity	1843	SR	63	60.4	16.7	9.1	Geddie
Echo	1848	SR	77	64.1	17.4	9.5	Geddie
Enterprise	1850	SR	110	76.7	21.1	10.9	Duncan
Empress	1852	SR	135	96.2	21.2	10.2	
Earl of Clarendon	1856	SR	83	73.1	19.7	9.7	Duncan
Elizabeth Scott	1856	SR	86	76.8	20.6	9.5	
Eident	1861	SR	174	100.0	23.3	12.5	Geddie
Express	1861	SR	88	79.0	20.0	9.1	Duncan

Enterprise	1862	SR	87	80.0	21.2	9.5	Duncan
Express	1863	SR	135	95.0	21.8	11.8	Geddie
Enterprise	1863	BK	314	131.0	26.6	14.5	Duncan
Elisa	1869	SR	240	111.6	24.1	14.1	Kinloch
Earl of Moray	1872	SR	100	86.5	26.1	10.9	
Erasima	1875	SR	150	102.6	21.3	12.2	Kinloch
Emulator	1878	SR	155	98.8	23.3	11.6	Kinloch
Ensign	1883	SR	116	87.0	21.3	10.2	Anderson
Friendship	1786	BG	80				Leslie
Friendship	1789	SP	65				
Friendship	1790	SP	54	50.9	16.4	7.7	Glenmore Coy.
Flaxton	1794	SQ	329				Glenmore Coy.
Freemason	1797	SP	72	52.3	19.0	9.0	
Friends	1799	BG	75				
Friendship	1801	SP	40				
Findlay	1810	BG	180	81.8	24.9	13.8	
Five Friends	1814	SP	63	53.7	17.0	8.4	Geddie
Friendship	1818	SP	35	41.0	14.8	6.8	
Flora	1826	SP	46	45.6	15.8	7.9	Winchester
Farmer	1828	SP	54	49.1	16.1	8.2	Proctor
Fancy	1833	SP	54	49.1	16.3	8.7	Geddie
Francis William	1834	SK	58	50.8	16.9	8.9	Geddie
Fear Not	1837	SK	83	66.3	17.6	6.3	Duncan
Favourite	1840	SR	50	50.1	15.7	9.4	Hay
Fidelity	1845	SR	87	67.4	17.6	10.0	Geddie
Findhorn	1849	BG	151	82.0	20.0	12.4	Duncan
Flower of Moray	1852	SR	118	75.0	19.0	11.0	Duncan
Flower of Enzie	1858	SR	74				
Fantasy	1858	SR	77	74.0	20.5	9.0	Duncan
Furness Abbey	1866	SR	70	76.0	20.0	8.8	Spence
Florence Barclay	1866	BK	343	137.0	25.9	15.3	Geddie
Flower of Moray	1869	SR	240	111.6	24.4	14.1	Kinloch
Fiery Cross	1872	BKN	338	133.2	24.3	15.3	Geddie
Freuchny	1875	BK	324	128.3	26.3	15.0	Geddie
Fede	1875	SR	150	99.5	23.1	12.4	Kinloch
Finlaccan	1877	SR	115	88.6	21.6	10.6	Duncan
Flying Fish	1885	STM	44	70.0	18.2	6.8	
Flora Emily	1885	SR	92	87.8	21.1	10.3	Anderson
Good Intent	1785	SR	35				Glenmore Coy.
Glenmore	1786	BG	76				Glenmore Coy.
Good Intent	1791	BG	107				
Good Intent	1798	BG	100				
George	1800	SQ	573				Glenmore Coy.
Garmouth	1801	SP	55				
Glenmore	1806	SQ	298				Glenmore Coy.
George & Alexander	1818	SR	36				Geddie
George Canning	1825	BKN	134				
Good Design	1830	SP	33	46.4	15.4	8.4	Winchester
Gardner	1841	BK	304				Geddie
Guardian	1844	SR	61	61.0	15.8	9.6	Leslie
Garland	1849	SR	98	73.8	18.1	10.3	Geddie
Glen Grant	1853	SR	64	58.1	16.8	9.0	Hay
George	1853	SR	120	67.5	20.5	10.0	
Gleaner	1854	SR	102	71.0	24.3	10.7	
Grace	1855	SR	155	80.0	21.0	10.4	
Glenmore	1858	BK	254	106.0	24.6	14.2	Duncan
Good Hope	1861	BG	162	93.0	23.0	12.5	Stewart
Gipsy	1861	SR	96	76.0	20.8	10.3	Geddie
Grace Rome	1867	SR	85	75.0	21.2	9.9	Young
Gipsy	1868	SR	194	103.0	24.0	13.2	Geddie

Glengyle	1868	SK	35	52.0	16.3	7.9	Kinloch
Garmouth	1870	SR	209	108.8	23.7	13.5	Geddie
Guiding Star	1870	SR	103	83.0	19.6	10.6	Geddie
Glendonwyn	1872	SR	150	95.7	20.5	12.2	Kinloch
Glance	1873	SR	162	102.0	23.5	12.2	Spence
Glide	1873	SR	97	85.0	21.4	10.3	Geddie
Gaya	1877	BKN	240	116.3	24.1	13.4	Geddie
Glenfield	1881	SK	29	57.0	17.3	6.3	
Harriot	1785	SP	25				Glenmore Coy
Henry	1797	BG	94				Glenmore Coy.
Helen	1805	SP	69	52.0	17.9	6.1	
Harriot	1806	BG	130				Glenmore Coy.
Hero	1811	SP	83				
Hope	1811	SR	95				Demster
Helen & Katty	1822	SP	22	39.0	12.5	5.6	Geddie
Hope	1826	BKN	95	60.4	19.4	10.9	Geddie
Helen	1826	SP	66	53.4	17.2	9.2	Winchester
Hero	1835	SR	76	58.4	17.8	9.7	Geddie
Helen	1837	BG	91				Leslie
Highlander	1840	SR	74	53.0	15.7	9.2	Duncan
Harmony	1841	SR	73	54.0	15.1	8.9	Hustwick
Heroine	1846	SP	21	40.8	17.5	6.8	Young
Henrietta	1847	SR	68	61.9	17.0	9.3	Leslie
Helen Brown	1847	SK	32	46.9	12.9	7.4	Geddie
Hope	1857	SR	85	67.0	20.3	10.0	Young Bros
Heather Bell	1858	SR	73	68.5	19.5	9.2	
Hero	1868	SR	98	80.0	21.2	10.1	Duncan
Harmony	1868	SR	160	96.0	23.0	12.8	Duncan
Industry	1787	BG	127				Leslie
Industry	1799	SP	38	43.7	14.1	7.4	
Isabella	1799	SP	73				
Isabella	1803	SP	46	48.4	15.4	8.0	Falconer
Isabella	1828	SR	65				
Imperial	1838	SK	44	47.0	15.0	8.4	Geddie
Isla	1840	BG	119				Geddie
Intellect	1841	SR	110	63.1	17.9	10.4	
Isabella Harley	1846	SR	90				Geddie
Industry	1852	SR	90	69.5	18.0	9.5	
Isabella Anderson	1856	SR	41	54.4	16.0	8.0	
Isabella Anderson	1860	SR	110	77.0	21.0	11.0	Geddie
Industry	1863	SR	131	90.0	22.7	11.3	Geddie
Industry	1865	SR	90	78.0	21.4	10.1	Young
Iona	1865	SR	116	84.0	21.1	10.6	Geddie
Isabella Wilson	1865	SR	178	102.0	23.1	13.0	Kinloch
Isa Reid	1876	SR	99	88.7	21.3	10.4	Geddie
Indian Chief	1878	BKN	339	125.7	26.2	14.7	Kinloch
Jane	1785	SP	70				Glenmore Coy.
Jean	1799	SQ	182				Leslie
James	1800	SR	104				
John	1802	SR	69				
Jean	1804	BG	78				
John & Isabella	1806	BG	90				
John	1807	BG	70				
James	1808	SP	70				
Jessie	1811	SP	78				
Jessie	1814	BG	147				
Jane	1815	BG	170				
Janet	1816	SP	55	49.3	16.9	8.8	Logie
Jeans of Spey	1817	SP	69	50.9	16.1	8.0	Anderson
John Alexander	1820	SR	51	52.6	15.6	9.3	Geddie

James of Banff	1823	SP	26	37.3	13.4	5.0	Winchester
James	1824	SP	47	48.2	15.5	7.1	Geddie
Johns	1825	SP	45	46.9	15.4	7.1	Proctor
James & Isabella	1825	SR	68	55.0	16.2	9.2	
Johns	1830	SR	55	48.0	16.8	8.1	
John Black	1830	SW	168				
John Barrie	1835	SP	52	52.3	17.1	8.2	Leslie
Jack Tar	1836	BKN	79	54.2	16.0	9.5	Leslie
Janet Henderson	1836	SP	52				Leslie
Jane	1838	SR	130				
Janet & Isabella	1838	SR	55	51.2	15.5	9.6	Geddie
James Duff	1838	SR	82	61.4	17.3	10.1	Leslie
Janet	1842	SR(H)	92	55.3	16.8	9.3	Duncan
Joseph	1842	SR	75	54.0	15.8	9.0	Geddie
Jessie	1843	SR	107				Leslie
Johns	1846	SR	91	70.7	17.8	10.1	
John Walker	1847	BG	118	75.3	19.6	10.8	Duncan
Jane & Mary	1848	SR	77	63.0	16.5	9.4	
Jane McDonald	1855	BKN	116	80.0	22.5	11.2	Duncan
Johns	1855	SR	107	78.5	21.1	11.0	Badenoch/Young
James	1857	SR	56	61.0	19.5	9.3	
James & Margaret	1857	SR	65	66.0	19.2	9.1	
Jane	1862	SR	58	63.0	18.3	9.4	Young
John Henry	1864	BG	253	116.0	24.2	14.7	Duncan
John Duncan	1866	SR	87	77.0	20.7	9.9	Duncan
James	1867	SR	85	73.0	20.4	9.3	Duncan
Jeanie Loutit	1869	BK	493	148.9	27.9	17.2	Kinloch
James Holt	1870	BK	338	131.0	26.8	15.4	Kinloch
Jane Stewart	1872	BKN	196	106.1	23.7	13.6	Geddie
Jessie	1873	SR	79	79.1	20.4	9.3	Lee
John Pearn	1874	SR	69	80.4	19.3	9.6	Lee
James W. Fisher	1874	SR	173	106.5	23.0	12.3	Duncan
Jacinth	1877	SR	100	86.3	21.1	10.5	Duncan
Janet Henderson	1877	SR	52	50.7	15.3	8.8	Leslie
Jessie	1878	SR	99	85.8	21.4	10.6	Spence
Janet Storm	1890	SR	113	90.7	21.3	10.6	Geddie
Kingston	1788	BG	143				Glenmore Coy.
Kitty & Jessie	1790	SP	58				
Kingston	1832	SP	34	41.9	14.2	7.2	
Konigsberg	1877	SR	99	87.4	21.0	10.5	Duncan
Kaffir Chief	1878	BK	382	140.0	27.2	14.9	Kinloch
Lord Alexander Gordon	1785/9	SQ	350				Glenmore Coy.
Lady Charlotte Gordon	1785/91	SQ	180				Glenmore Coy.
Lady Charlotte Hope	1803	SP	67				
Lady Madeline Sinclair	1804	SQ	610	123.1	33.3	11.0	Glenmore Coy.
Latona	1810	SR	78				Skelton
Lord Nelson	1818	SR	66				
Lady Jane of Spey	1822	SP	58	51.0	16.6	8.2	Winchester
Lerwick	1825	SP	95				
Lady Jane	1835	SP	44				Geddie
Lilias	1835	SP	61	52.2	16.8	8.9	Geddie
Lady Fyffe	1836	SK	48	50.7	15.4	8.2	Leslie
Lord Melbourne	1836	SR	66	54.7	16.0	9.5	
Lady Lovat	1837	SR	81	60.3	17.2	10.3	Geddie
Leslie	1841	BG	123	65.5	18.0	10.6	Leslie
Lookout	1846	SR	98	71.6	17.9	10.4	Geddie
Laurel	1849	SR	66	59.5	16.4	9.3	
Laurel	1849	SR	100	76.8	20.1	10.4	Geddie
Louisa	1851	SR	100	77.0	21.0	10.5	
Lochnagar	1853	SR	120	67.5	20.5	9.9	

Lady Emma	1854	SR	183	95.0	23.5	11.0	
Lass o Doune	1856	SR	99	81.0	21.5	10.4	Geddie
Lilias	1856	SR	99	78.3	20.6	10.5	Geddie
Louisa	1857	SR	113	75.1	20.8	10.2	Duncan
Lady Ann Duff	1860	SR	66	66.5	18.6	9.2	Geddie
Lord Clyde	1861	SR	98	78.0	21.1	10.3	Geddie
Laurel	1862	SR	91	78.8	21.3	10.3	Stewart
Look Out	1863	BKN	139	93.3	21.8	12.0	Duncan
Leader	1866	SR	200	106.0	23.5	13.5	Kinloch
Linnet	1867	SR	105	81.0	22.6	10.0	Geddie
Lady of the Lake	1867		37	50.0	16.1	7.3	Young
Lord Napier	1868	SR	169	98.0	23.3	12.5	Duncan
Laurel	1870	SR	89	82.2	18.3	9.8	Geddie
Lark	1871	SR	83	80.8	18.7	8.9	Geddie
Louisa	1873	SR	100	77.0	21.0	10.5	
Lord Macduff	1875	BK	505	157.5	30.1	17.6	Kinloch
Lord Reidhaven	1875	SR	146	96.1	22.7	11.7	Duncan
Lord March	1876	SR	161	98.9	23.3	12.1	Duncan
Leading Chief	1876	BKN	315	124.0	26.0	14.6	Kinloch
Letterfourie	1876	BKN	339	134.3	26.3	14.3	Duncan
Lord Duffus	1877	SR	141	98.0	23.0	11.5	Duncan
Leader	1881	SR	100	84.2	21.6	10.3	Duncan
Marquis of Huntly	1790	SQ	380				Glenmore Coy.
May	1794	BG	77				
Mary	1795	BG	86				
Mary	1799	BG	86				
Mariann & Ann	1803	G	72				
Mariner	1813	SR	97	93.9	19.0	8.1	Simpson/Geddie
Mariner	1813	SP	77	55.6	18.1	9.9	Simpson/Geddie
Mary	1814	BG	153				
Margaret	1814	BG	94				Demster
Marys	1817	SP	28	42.7	13.0	5.5	
Marchioness of Huntly	1825	SP	57	49.0	16.1	8.6	Winchester
Marshall	1827	SR	84	64.6	17.0	10.1	Winchester
MacAllan	1827	SK	50	48.4	15.8	7.0	Proctor
Mary Ann	1827	SK	79	57.3	18.3	9.8	Winchester
Matilda	1827	SR	69				
Margaret	1836	SR	62	55.6	16.0	9.2	Geddie
MacIntosh	1838	SR	97	58.7	17.1	10.1	Leslie
Malcolm	1839	SK	30	38.0	13.0	8.0	Hay
Martha	1839	SR	56				
Main	1841	SR	81	58.9	17.2	10.1	Leslie
Margaret	1842	SR	75	55.6	15.7	9.0	Geddie
Mary Ann	1842	SR	83	58.3	15.9	9.5	Leslie
Margaret Young	1842	SR	47	45.6	13.6	8.2	Young
Maid	1843	SK	33	40.0	12.0	6.9	Geddie
Margaret	1844	SR	23	38.9	12.5	6.8	
Mormond Maid	1845	SR	98	71.3	18.6	10.6	Leslie
Maid	1847	SP	22	41.7	12.5	6.4	
Myrtle	1848	SR	88	69.0	17.8	10.0	Geddie
Maria	1849	SR	68	60.7	17.1	9.3	Geddie
Mary Ann	1849	SR	55	54.2	15.9	8.9	
Maria	1851	BG	130	78.0	19.8	11.0	
Margaret	1853	SR	62	66.5	18.0	10.0	Duncan
Myrtle	1853	SR	62	66.5	18.0	10.0	Duncan
Margaret Ann	1856	SR	84	75.0	19.5	10.0	Duncan
Margaret Jane	1856	SR	99				Hay
Margaret Edward	1856	BK	281	141.0	26.9	16.5	Geddie
Mary McLauchlan	1856	SR	101				
Meg Merrilees	1856	SR	79	80.0	20.0	10.1	Duncan

Mary Stewart	1857	SR	116	82.2	21.3	10.7	
Meteor	1858	BKN	161	99.0	22.1	11.7	
Marie	1858	SR	137	83.8	22.1	11.5	
Moir	1859	SR	67	68.1	19.3	9.0	Duncan
Mary & Jane	1859	SK	32	49.5	16.0	7.5	
Matchless	1860	BKN	143	86.5	23.2	11.5	Duncan
Maid of Foyers	1862	SR	72	72.2	19.8	9.6	Duncan
Margaret	1862	SR	96	80.0	21.8	10.2	Geddie
Margaret Jane	1866	SR	145	96.0	22.1	12.1	Duncan
Margaret	1867	BKN	96	80.0	21.0	10.4	Geddie
May Queen	1870	SR	277	117.2	25.0	14.7	Spence
Mariner	1871	BG	284	119.3	26.6	15.0	Hay
Mary	1873	SR	100	85.8	21.5	10.4	Geddie
Mountblairy	1874	SR	138	95.1	22.3	11.6	Geddie
Maggie	1875	SR	100	90.2	21.3	10.5	Geddie
Mountaineer	1876	BK	312	130.3	26.0	14.9	Geddie
Morning Star	1877	BKN	258	113.0	24.9	14.7	Spence
Morning Star	1878	SR	99	86.6	21.3	10.4	Duncan
Mary Ann	1879	SR	157	99.0	23.6	12.1	Spence
Mabel	1882	SR	99	88.4	21.4	10.3	Duncan
Maggie Low	1883	SR	100	88.7	21.2	10.1	Kinloch
Moray Chief	1888	BKN	314	137.7	26.3	12.9	Kinloch
Neptune	1785	SR	70				Glenmore Coy.
Neptune	1814	SP	67	54.5	18.1	9.6	
Neptune	1815	SP	70	54.6	17.6	9.7	Geddie
Neptune	1825	SP	64	51.8	17.4	9.2	Geddie
Nymph	1854	SR	150	77.0	22.0	11.0	
New Rambler	1857	SR	113	80.0	21.3	11.1	Geddie
Northern Chief	1873	BK	393	143.5	28.2	16.0	Geddie
Nyanza	1876	BKN	232	109.8	24.3	14.2	Spence
Nile	1876	BK	333	124.1	26.3	14.6	Spence
Northern Belle	1877	SR	215	114.6	25.0	13.0	Geddie
Overton	1792	SQ	318				Glenmore Coy.
Orion	1797	BG	141				
Orion	1797	BG	141				
Osbourne	1798	SQ	475				Glenmore Coy.
Olivia	1826	SR	96	56.4	17.6	10.3	
Olive	1850	SP	37	48.0	17.8	8.0	
Ocean Child	1854	SR	149	78.0	21.0	10.5	
Orient	1855	SR	103	77.5	20.5	10.5	Geddie
Ocean Gem	1857	SR	79	71.6	20.4	9.6	
Olive	1860	SR	87	71.0	20.4	10.0	Young
Onward	1865	SR	195	105.0	23.8	13.2	Geddie
Ocean Chief	1872	BK	386	136.6	23.8	16.1	Kinloch
Ocean Racer	1875	BKN	192	109.0	23.8	13.1	Spence
Olive Branch	1878	SR	80	78.3	19.5	9.4	Duncan
Princess of Wales	1795	SQ	384				Glenmore Coy.
Pelham	1802	BG	121				Glenmore Coy.
Pilgrim	1802	BG	121				Glenmore Coy.
Phoenix	1802	SP	78				
Princess of Orange	1824	BK	184				
Paradise	1824	SR	115				
Ploughman	1833	SR	71	56.1	17.4	9.4	Geddie
Patriot	1837	SR	124				Leslie
Patrick	1837	SR(H)	95	63.8	19.2	10.8	Geddie
Pearl	1840	SR	75	56.4	16.9	9.9	Leslie
Perserverance	1840	SR(H)	98	63.6	18.3	10.7	Duncan
Peggy	1844	SR	52	44.2	15.1	8.2	Duncan
Primrose	1850	SR	79	62.3	17.5	9.6	Young
Peter Brown	1854	SR	94	97.0	21.3	10.5	Hay

Perserverance	1857	SR	123	83.0	22.1	10.6	
Pelham	1859	BG	254	113.9	25.8	14.0	Hay
Prince of Wales	1861	SR	99	80.0	21.2	10.5	Duncan
Paragon	1864	SK	26	45.5	15.1	6.7	
Petrel	1865	SR	74	77.0	20.6	8.5	Duncan
Progress	1866	SR	177	100.0	23.8	12.8	Geddie
Press Home	1867	SR	99	80.0	21.8	10.3	Geddie
Progress	1875	SR	99	88.4	21.7	10.2	
Pearl	1876	SK	47	64.0	18.2	9.7	Duncan
Pet	1876	SR	161	96.8	21.4	12.5	Geddie
Pscyhe	1880	BKN	335	131.5	26.0	14.7	Kinloch
Recovery	1789	SP	60				
Rothiemurcus	1812	SQ	322				
Ruby	1826	SR	88				
Ranger	1836	SK	124	84.4	19.8	11.7	Badenoch/Young
Ruby	1837	SK	42	47.0	14.9	8.4	Geddie
Reliance	1838	SR	90	62.8	17.6	10.3	Geddie
Runcina	1840	SR	93	59.0	16.8	9.7	Geddie
Rambler	1847	SR	96				
Rose	1852	SR	120	70.4	18.0	10.2	Geddie
Roman	1857	BG	136	87.6	22.4	11.0	
Royal Charlie	1861	BG	192	112.5	23.3	12.7	Duncan
Reaper	1864	SR	146	93.0	22.5	12.0	Kinloch
Rapid	1865	SR	242	113.0	23.3	14.5	Duncan
Rival	1866	SR	139	91.0	22.8	12.0	Spence
Racer	1867	SR	149	94.0	23.3	12.3	Spence
Right O Way	1867	SR	84	75.0	20.0	9.9	Duncan
Ranger	1871	SR	94	84.5	18.5	10.1	Kinloch
Rob O The Ranter	1874	SR	147	96.7	22.5	11.8	Geddie
Ruby	1884	SR	117	91.0	21.1	10.3	Kinloch
Racer	1889	SR	109	90.0	21.4	10.2	Anderson
Speedwell	1785	BG	120				Glenmore Coy.
Success	1785	SP	54				Glenmore Coy
Sally & Ann	1789	SQ	240				Glenmore Coy
Sykes	1790	SQ	241				
Sally	1793	SP	50				
Sarah	1801	SQ	572				Glenmore Coy
Spey	1808	SP	48	47.2	15.1	7.6	
Star	1817	SP	54				
Success	1817	SP	60	52.2	17.1	8.7	
Spey	1820	SP	48	47.2	15.1	7.6	
Speedwell	1823	SR	67	53.6	16.0	9.4	Proctor
Sir Edward Banks	1825	SR	105				
Spey	1825	BG	139				
Sally	1832	SP	63	52.1	16.1	8.6	Geddie
Scotia	1834	SR	75	57.3	17.8	9.4	
Star	1840	SK	24	38.3	12.4	5.9	Hay
Sir James Gordon	1841	SR	79	59.0	17.6	9.4	Hay
Stranger	1846	BK	220	96.3	24.3	15.0	
Susan	1848	SR	61	57.3	15.4	9.0	
Scotia	1849	SR	122	77.8	21.5	11.2	
Spitzbergen	1851	SR	313	104.5	23.7	15.9	Duncan
Soho	1853	SR	48	56.1	15.9	8.4	
Sir George Brown	1855	BG	134	87.6	21.6	11.8	Badenoch/Young
Spey	1857	BG	167	93.0	25.5	12.6	Geddie
St Clair	1859	SR	122	83.0	22.2	11.1	Geddie
Sarah	1859	SR	91	77.5	21.1	9.9	
Strathisla	1860	SR	71	70.0	20.5	9.5	Duncan
Strathspey	1860	SR	126	89.0	22.4	11.3	Stewart
St Devenick	1864	SR	257	114.8	24.8	14.5	Geddie

Surprize	1866	SR	87	79.7	21.8	9.9	Young
Standard	1867	SR	98	80.0	21.8	10.3	Geddie
Satellite	1867	SR	275	120.0	25.0	14.8	Geddie
Successor	1868	SR	93	81.6	21.0	10.6	Geddie
St Athens	1871	SR	100	86.1	19.3	10.9	Geddie
Sutherland	1873	SR	100	84.8	21.5	10.6	Spence
Scotia	1873	BK	321	129.1	26.2	15.3	Kinloch
Sapphire	1875	SR	75	76.2	12.6	6.9	Duncan
St Duthus	1875	SR	80	81.0	20.8	9.6	Duncan
Spinaway	1875	BK	437	148.5	28.7	16.6	Geddie
Scottish Chief	1877	BKN	328	124.0	26.1	11.4	Kinloch
Speedwell	1878	BKN	245	118.2	24.8	12.9	Spence
Swiftsure	1878	BKN	333	132.3	26.6	14.9	Geddie
Tyningham	1798	SP	49				
Two Sisters	1803	SP	42	46.9	15.1	7.9	Robertson
Thomas & Nancy	1820	SP	47				
Traffic	1849	SR	91	76.3	18.3	10.4	
Tarool	1857	SR	101	77.0	21.2	11.0	
Trade Wind	1857	SR	81	68.0	20.0	9.7	
Tullochgorum	1867	SR	165	94.0	22.0	12.3	Duncan
Tollo	1867	SR	89	82.0	20.5	9.6	Geddie
Triumph	1868	SR	302	131.0	25.4	14.1	Geddie
Union	1841	SR	47	43.4	13.9	7.8	Leslie
Unity	1847	SR	88				
Unity	1848	SR	53	68.5	17.9	10.0	Geddie
Union	1867	BKN	234	113.4	25.4	14.3	Geddie
Vigilant	1819	SK	19	38.0	12.0	6.5	
Violet	1839	SR	74	61.8	19.3	9.7	Geddie
Vigilant	1844	SR	78	65.0	17.4	8.0	Geddie
Vine	1846	SR	94	71.4	20.2	10.1	Geddie
Victor	1848	SR	91	61.0	16.4	9.6	
Vesta	1850	SR	96	70.2	18.6	10.5	
Venture	1855	SR	94	73.0	20.0	10.4	Young
Vesper	1859	SR	98	80.4	21.3	10.0	Hay
Vindex	1862	BK	290	120.3	26.3	14.8	Hay
Vine	1863	SR	94	76.0	21.0	10.3	Kinloch
Victor	1864	SR	215	107.0	24.0	13.9	Kinloch
Velocity	1865	SR	182	100.0	23.0	13.0	Kinloch
Vinco	1867	SR	222	111.0	23.8	14.0	Kinloch
Vigil	1867	SR	102	77.0	21.3	10.2	Duncan
Vigilant	1867	BK	303	125.4	25.4	14.9	Geddie
Vision	1867	SR	99	80.6	21.0	10.2	Duncan
Victory	1868	SR	252	113.4	24.9	14.6	Kinloch
Vigilant	1871	BKN	303	125.4	25.4	14.9	Geddie
Voyager	1873	BKN	242	119.0	22.9	13.5	Kinloch
Volunteer	1873	SR	147	99.7	23.8	11.0	Duncan
Viscount MacDuff	1874	SR	290	123.7	25.8	15.2	Spence
Venture	1878	BKN	249	119.3	25.1	12.9	Geddie
Vigo	1878	SR	96	85.3	21.5	9.5	Geddie
Viking	1878	SR	92	85.5	21.5	9.5	Geddie
William & Jean	1793	SP	55				
William	1803	SP	60	53.9	16.7	7.1	Robertson
Waterloo	1819	SR	77				Proctor
William	1831	SR	42				
Williams	1831	SK	64	52.1	17.0	9.2	Geddie
Woodman	1837	SR	67	57.5	17.3	10.6	
Williams	1838	SK	64	57.2	16.3	9.3	Geddie
Wave	1839	SR	75	58.0	17.0	9.9	Leslie
Western	1840	SR	98	60.0	18.3	10.2	Geddie
Waterwitch	1851	SR	62	59.0	16.9	9.1	Hay

Wave	1856	SR	99	79.0	21.0	10.5	
Waverley	1863	BG	215	111.0	23.7	13.8	Duncan
Wanderers	1863	SR	235	111.5	24.0	13.5	Geddie
Welkin	1864	SR	99	78.8	21.5	10.0	Geddie
William & Sarah	1865	SR	145	93.0	21.6	12.0	Duncan
Wanderer	1874	SR	256	121.3	25.0	13.9	Kinloch
Wandering Chief	1876	BK	447	147.0	27.7	17.0	Kinloch
Yucatan	1791	SQ	214				Osbourne
Young Alexander	1840	SK	18	34.0	10.7	6.4	
Ythan	1854	SR	162	82.0	21.0	10.6	
Yacht	1874	SR	72	74.0	19.7	9.5	Spence
Ythan	1876	SR	86	83.7	21.3	9.0	Geddie
Zephyr	1857	SR	115	80.5	21.6	11.2	Geddie
Zephyr	1869	BKN	256	118.0	24.5	14.2	Geddie
Zone	1874	SR	100	87.7	21.7	10.0	Duncan

BANFF	Built	Rig	Tons	Dimensions			Builder
Alexander	1801	SP	36	43.6	14.1	7.6	
Alexander	1816	SR	67				
Ann	1817	SR	90	58.8	19.2	10.0	
Alexander Ross	1830	SP	29	38.3	14.2	5.7	
Active	1855	SR	55	65.0	18.0	8.8	J Watson
Amy	1870	SR	126	88.4	27.7	11.6	J Watson
Agnes M Gordon	1870	BG	128	88.0	22.5	11.2	J Watson
Alice	1873	SR	99	83.9	21.7	10.3	J Watson
Andrew Longmore	1874	SR	125	93.4	23.0	11.4	J Watson
Barbara	1796	SP	63				
Brothers Increase	1799	SP	36	43.9	14.7	7.6	
Brittannia	1805	SP	64				
Brilliant	1805	SP	64	52.6	17.6	8.8	
Betsy	1807	SP	40				
Black Nib	1819	SP	25	40.7	13.4	6.7	J Harper
Bubona	1833	BN	106	58.9	18.8	10.8	
Boyne	1836	SR	104	63.5	18.2	11.0	F Dockar
Brothers Increase	1836	SK	18	35.5	12.2	6.4	
Blossom	1840	SR	99	78.9	20.5	11.0	J Dick
Banffshire	1855	SR	86	77.3	19.5	10.4	
Boyn	1865	SR	98	78.0	21.0	10.1	Geddie
Banff	1870	SR	85	77.2	20.8	10.0	
Bella	1872	SR	88	82.3	21.7	10.3	J Watson
Baron Skene	1874	SR	99	84.0	21.2	10.6	Geddie
Ban Righ	1879	SR	94	87.0	21.7	10.4	J & W Geddie
Barbara	1884	SR	98	85.2	21.8	10.4	J & W Geddie
Courier	1805	SP	47				
Courier	1806	SP	63	52.1	17.8	8.9	
Chance	1841	SR	101	63.8	17.9	10.8	J Dick
Clunie	1841	SR	97	63.8	17.7	10.7	J Dick
Countess of Seafield	1856	BG	150	95.5	23.0	12.9	J Watson
Cecilia	1865	SR	68	69.7	19.4	9.1	Geddie
Constance	1868	SR	99	81.0	21.5	10.3	J & W Geddie
Chase	1872	SR	99	82.0	22.0	10.6	Geddie
Cairnrankie	1872	SR	79	77.3	20.0	9.4	J Watson
Craig Gowan	1873	SR	85	75.6	21.9	10.9	J Watson
Dispatch	1795	SP	45				
Duchess of Bedford	1804	SP	90	59.8	19.4	10.0	Wm Walker
Duchess of Gordon	1809	SP	65	52.8	17.7	8.8	Wm Walker
Dubona	1833	SR	91	58.9	18.8	10.8	
Deveronside	1864	SR	233	109.5	25.0	13.9	J Watson
Deveron	1871	BG	133	89.0	22.1	11.3	J & W Geddie
Dantzic	1871	SR	98	81.2	21.5	10.5	J & W Geddie
Earl of Fife	1863	SR	232	104.0	25.0	14.0	J Watson
Eliza	1866	SR	86	76.0	20.4	9.8	Foot
Eliza Ann	1876	SR	127	88.6	27.6	11.2	Geddie
Elizabeth	1877	SR	80	79.0	20.0	9.2	J Watson
Emporer	1882	SR	99	83.8	21.8	10.6	J & W Geddie
Fortitude	1794	SP	70				
Findlater & Seafield	1797	SP	57				
Friendship	1805	SP	60				
Fair Wind	1866	SR	96	82.5	21.5	10.0	J Watson
Forrissian	1868	SR	194	108.2	23.6	12.7	J Watson
Forward	1869	SR	131	94.6	22.6	11.0	J Watson
Flower of Banff	1871	SR	127	88.5	22.6	11.7	J Watson
Fleetwing	1874	SR	95	85.2	21.7	10.3	J Watson
Fair Wind	1876	SR	135	98.3	23.8	11.1	J Watson
George	1798	SW	146				

Gardenstown	1799	SP	50				
George	1804	SP	56	50.3	16.2	8.0	W Walker
George	1811	SP	75	57.1	18.3	9.6	
Guiding Star	1870	BKN	249	117.0	25.5	13.4	J Watson
Gladstone	1873	SR	131	95.6	22.7	11.7	J & W Geddie
Gowan	1878	SR	119	95.0	22.7	11.1	J & W Geddie
Glen Boyn	1879	BK	197	111.5	24.7	12.4	J Watson
Happy Return	1800	SP	76	56.3	18.3	9.4	Wm Walker
Hope	1803	SR	77				
Hero	1816	BG	153				
Hope	1836	SK	20	35.4	12.4	6.5	F Dockar
Hope	1844	SR	77				
Helen West	1878	SR	100	87.0	21.6	10.6	J Watson
Industry	1788	BG	100				
Isa	1861	SP	87	76.0	20.0	10.2	J Watson
Isabella	1865	SR	147	94.0	23.3	11.0	J Watson
Jane	1799	SP	66				
Jean	1802	SR	78	56.2	18.8	9.8	
Jean	1803	SP	75	56.1	18.3	9.2	Wm Walker
Jean	1804	BG	87				
John	1807	BG	83	58.2	19.0	9.1	Wm Walker
Jane	1814	BG	86				
Jane Sinclair	1841	SR	83	61.9	17.3	10.1	J Sinclair
Jane Simpson	1867	SR	94	81.4	21.6	9.8	J Watson
Jessie Ann	1877	SR	130	92.3	22.6	11.1	J & W Geddie
Katty	1795	SP	36	39.6	15.3	7.5	
Lord Fife	1789	SP	76				
Lord Gardin	1799	SP	50				
London Packet	1800	SP	78				
Lively	1802	SP	36	41.5	15.0	7.7	
Laurel	1815	BG	151				
Lark	1821	SP	62	51.8	17.3	8.8	Wm Walker
Lady Duff	1841	SR	93	72.3	17.7	10.9	J Dick
Lady Gray	1854	SW	136	80.6	20.1	11.9	
Lady Abercrombie	1857	SR	56	67.8	18.0	8.9	
Lady Gordon Cumming	1858	SR	58	90.0	21.2	11.0	J Watson
Lady Ida Duff	1866	SR	91	78.5	20.5	10.0	J W Geddie
Lass o Doon	1867	SR	95	81.1	21.3	10.2	Wm Geddie
Lochnagar	1867	SR	96	78.2	21.6	10.2	Wm Geddie
Lady of the Lake	1867	SR	75	72.0	19.9	9.4	J Watson
Lord Clyde	1869	SR	99	86.5	22.3	11.0	J & W Geddie
Lothair	1870	SR	87	78.0	20.9	9.9	Geddie
Lady of the Lake	1878	SR	85	78.5	20.6	9.4	J Watson
Molly	1781	SP	66				
Mayflower	1799	SP	62				
Molly	1800	SP	65				
Magnet	1805	SR	110	67.1	20.1	11.1	
Margaret	1806	BG	112				
Margaret	1807	SP	58	52.3	17.1	8.9	
Mary	1821	SP	21	39.6	17.1	5.5	P Petrie
Margaret	1828	SK	34	43.6	13.2	7.1	
Mary	1839	SK	23	38.0	12.0	6.5	J Dick
Matilda	1854	SR	91	70.4	18.9	10.0	J Watson
Matilda	1854	SR	87	72.7	20.2	9.0	
Mary	1859	SK	21	40.2	13.2	6.3	J Dick
Matilda Calder	1864	SR	160	101.0	23.8	11.5	J Watson
Mayflower	1866	SR	184	104.0	23.8	12.3	J Watson
Maggie	1867	SR	100	82.0	21.6	10.3	J Watson
Mary	1875	SR	99	86.7	21.5	10.3	J Watson

Name	Year	Rig	Tonnage	L	B	D	Builder
Mary Nish	1888	SR	88	86.7	21.8	10.3	Geddie
Nancy	1803	SP	68	52.2	17.1	8.1	Wm Walker
Northern Maid	1844	SR	98				
Norseman	1873	SR	119	87.7	21.9	10.9	J Watson
Ocean	1812		191				
Ocean	1842	SR	95	62.5	18.9	10.3	
Olivia	1865	SR	76	71.8	20.0	9.5	
Olivia	1875	SR	74	74.0	19.2	9.3	J Watson
Perserverance	1860	BG	194	103.7	23.1	13.2	J Watson
Paragon	1866	SR	99	80.0	21.5	10.2	J Watson
Pioneer	1868	SR	74	76.9	20.5	9.6	Watson
Queen	1801	BG	104	63.1	20.1	11.3	
Regent	1811		115				
Stettin	1802	BG	105				
Sisters	1814	SP	55	49.0	16.7	8.6	Wm Walker
Stag	1815	SP	48	47.6	15.1	8.0	Wm Walker
Sprightly	1817	SP	58				
Swift	1818	SP	52				
Swift	1828	SP	52	48.6	16.2	8.2	Wm Walker
Smart	1841	SR	86	62.8	16.8	10.4	J Dick
Sir Alec Duff	1842	SR	66	66.5	16.6	9.6	J Dick
Sovereign	1842	SR	123	78.4	20.4	10.7	J Dick
Sir Robert Calder	1862	SR	160	82.6	23.5	11.7	J Watson
Sovereign	1872	SR	78	79.6	20.5	9.0	J Watson
St Helena	1876	SR	122	91.2	27.4	10.8	Geddie
Swift	1895	SR	71	73.4	20.2	9.0	Geddie
Thetis	1805	SK	107				
Thames	1813	SP	62				
Thomas	1813	SP	62				
Thames	1819	SP	61	52.2	17.3	9.6	
Tom Duff	1839	SR	85	60.0	18.0	10.4	J Dick
Tarlair	1870	SR	85	77.2	20.8	10.0	J Watson
Union	1787	BG	124				
Vine	1802	SW	100				
Victory	1857	SK	57	51.5	15.4	7.2	
Vistula	1870	SR	125	88.0	22.1	11.2	J & W Geddie
Volant	1875	SR	99	86.8	21.7	10.3	J & W Geddie
Victoria	1876	SR	108	86.5	21.7	10.3	J Watson
Victor	1877	SR	111	90.0	22.4	10.6	J Watson
William	1801	SP	44	47.7	15.1	8.0	
Watsons	1855	SK	29	45.3	12.9	7.2	J Watson
Woodbine	1857	BK	252	113.4	25.1	15.2	
Watson	1875	SR	209	112.9	25.3	12.8	J Watson
Waterlily	1876	SR	99	86.4	21.6	10.3	J Watson
Zephyr	1850	SR	108	69.7	19.9	10.3	J Watson

BUCKIE	Built	Rig	Tons	Dimensions			Builder
Andrew	1801	SP	17	34.0	11.8	3.1	
Ann	1801	B	16	32.9	11.9	4.3	
Auchindoon	1865	SK	42	54.0	17.4	8.6	Young
Alexandrina	1866	SR	90	81.8	21.9	9.9	Young Bros
Active	1866	SR	72	74.3	20.7	9.7	Young Bros
Brothers Increase	1804	SP	71	36.0	17.9	4.0	A Sinclair
Bonny Lass	1826	LR	23	38.3	12.9	5.5	A Gunn
Catharine	1824	LR	18	37.0	11.6	4.1	W Slater
Charlie	1826	LR	25	39.6	12.1	5.6	A Sutherland
Elspet	1801	B	19	34.6	12.3	4.4	
Fairlie	1865	SR	173	101.1	23.7	12.8	Young
Freedom	1868	SK	21	41.0	15.9	6.3	G Smith
Hound	1823	LR	21	38.2	12.1	5.2	
Industry	1801	SP	21	34.6	13.0	4.0	
Janet	1822	LR	21	39.0	12.0	5.0	W Slater
Jean	1822	LR	19	36.8	11.8	4.1	A Skakel
Janet	1823	LR	23	40.0	12.4	5.0	W Slater
Jean	1826	LR	23	39.1	12.1	5.6	A Skakel
Kitty	1822	LR	21	39.0	12.2	5.0	A Sutherland
Lookout	1824	LR	20	39.8	12.5	5.2	A Skakel
Margaret	1795	B	16	33.1	11.8	4.1	
Margaret	1799	B	17	34.0	11.1	4.1	
Margaret	1801	B	16	34.6	11.8	4.3	
Margaret	1823	LR	23	40.2	12.4	5.1	A Skakel
Morning Star	1864	SR	82	74.5	21.1	9.8	Young
Mary Ann	1864	SR	162	96.9	23.7	12.2	Young
Peggy	1800	SP	16	32.1	11.9	2.8	
Peggy	1824	LR	24	40.1	12.8	5.3	A Skakel
Rose	1824	LR	23	38.6	12.0	5.4	J Sinclair
Swallow	1801	B	17	34.6	11.8	4.3	
Snow	1822	SP	25	41.0	12.6	6.0	
Star of Peace	1867	SR	87	78.0	21.0	9.6	Young
Union	1805	B	29	37.8	14.6	5.1	W Slater
Warwick	1795	B	15	32.9	11.4	3.1	A Sinclair

BURGHEAD	Built	Rig	Tons	Dimensions			Builder
Active	1802	SP	53	48.3	17.0	8.2	
Active	1825	SP	55	48.2	17.0	8.0	
Betsey	1802	SW	109	60.6	21.5	10.1	
Betsy	1826	SR	83	57.6	18.6	9.6	
Burghead	1832	SK	14	39.9	11.6	4.1	J Hendry
Barr	1841	BK	128	72.0	19.0	12.0	J Femister
Dolphin	1837	SP	45	46.4	15.8	9.0	J Femister
Desparandum	1884	SP	48	53.8	16.1	4.5	
Essex	1800	B	15	32.7	11.6	4.3	
Elsie & Isie	1840	SP	27	40.7	13.0	6.8	J Femister
Elizabeth	1842	SR	81	64.0	17.3	10.0	J Smith
Friendship	1812	SP	34	42.1	14.2	6.0	
Georgina	1811	SP	51	50.0	16.4	7.7	Hendry
Georgina	1825	SP	53	50.4	16.6	7.8	
Jean	1802	SP	60	50.8	17.7	9.11	
John & Isobel	1806	BG	89	52.8	20.2	10.4	J Hendry
Jean	1818	SP	64	50.8	17.9	9.7	
Lord Nelson	1809	SP	73				
Maggy Jappy	1792	B	17	33.5	11.4	3.11	
Margaret	1793	SP	16	31.4	11.1	3.6	
Murray of Caithness	1805	SP	47	48.0	15.1	7.8	
Mary Hill	1837	SP	25	38.0	12.4	7.9	
Nelly & Jean	1806	SP	58	49.7	17.7	8.5	
Three Sisters	1801	SP	33	39.9	14.7	6.7	
William	1795	B	17	33.0	11.1	4.2	

CLACHNAHARRY							
Betsy	1832		16	38.0	13.3	5.2	G McIntosh
Brothers	1837	SP	15	38.7	11.5	6.5	J McDonald
Charlotte	1835		54	45.1	17.4	9.0	D McDonald
Inverness	1842	SP	19	37.0	12.7	6.2	J McDonald
Invernesshire	1848	SR	77	69.1	16.8	9.2	R Wright
Jean	1832	SP	22	39.9	12.6	4.10	W Allan
Lyon	1820	SP	31	44.7	14.0	6.6	A Patience
Lady of the Lake	1835		63	52.4	17.2	8.0	J Jones
Mary Ann	1821	SK	26	39.8	13.2	6.1	H Allan
May	1833		25	38.9	13.5	4.8	H McIntosh
Mary Ann	1839	SP	20	42.0	13.9	7.1	J McDonald
Peggy	1815	SP	35	46.6	16.1	8.1	
Peggy	1824	SP	35	43.3	13.6	6.0	
Perserverance	1833		27	42.1	13.4	6.3	J McDonald
Swift	1816	SP	22	37.1	12.8	4.8	
Success	1834	SP	18	38.0	12.4	6.1	D McDonald
Tamerlane	1843	SP	90	39.8	12.4	4.4	D McKenzie
Telegraph	1848	SR	97	71.5	18.0	10.6	R Wright

CROMARTY	Built	Rig	Tons	Dimensions			Builder
Ann	1819	SP	21	39.0	12.4	5.0	A Bain
Alma	1855	SP	15	43.7	15.5	4.3	
Betsy	1815	SP	66	53.4	17.1	9.2	H Allen
Catharine	1811	SP	36	42.0	14.9	7.8	Hall
Dolphin	1850	SR	38	46.7	15.4	8.2	J Allan
Freemason	1811	SP	36	40.0	15.6	3.1	A Bain
Jane	1813	SP	31	40.0	13.8	6.9	
Mary & Ann	1826	SP	27	40.0	13.2	5.1	
Peggy	1822	SP	14	36.0	10.3	5.3	H Ross
Peggy	1825	SP	70	38.5	17.6	5.3	
Perserverance	1825	SR	71	54.0	16.4	10.0	
Rose	1814	BG	160	72.1	21.8	12.0	
Sutors of Cromarty	1830	SR(H)	105	64.7	19.8	11.8	H Allan
Tain	1813	SP	20	35.0	13.6	5.1	H Ross

CULLEN	Built	Rig	Tons	Dimensions			Builder
Active	1823	SP	31	39.7	14.1	5.1	J Ross
Agnes	1824	LR	18	37.3	11.4	5.0	
Active	1825	LR	19	38.0	11.7	4.8	
Ann	1826	LR	19	37.1	11.1	4.1	
Argo	1894	LR	17	43.0	14.3	6.5	
Brothers	1814	SP	23	35.6	13.4	4.1	J Ross
Berwick	1823	LR	23	39.1	12.6	5.4	J Ross
Bore Away	1824	LR	17	35.6	11.5	4.1	J Sinclair
Blood Hound	1824	LR	23	39.3	12.8	5.3	G Campbell
Brave	1826	LR	20	38.2	12.2	5.4	J Sinclair
Brothers	1830	SP	24	39.0	13.0	5.1	
Brothers	1842	SK	29	41.6	13.4	7.6	J Ross
Balaclava	1848	SK	16	43.1	13.9	5.2	
Boyne	1857	SP	19	41.6	15.0	5.6	
Christian	1806	B	18	36.0	11.1	4.4	J Sinclair
Christian	1822	LR	23	41.3	13.0	5.6	J Ross
Catherine	1823	LR	16	35.9	11.0	5.0	J Sinclair
Canary	1824	LR	25	41.3	13.0	5.6	
Catherine	1826	LR	17	36.7	11.6	5.4	A Skakel
Essex	1805	B	18	34.9	12.0	2.9	J Sinclair
Elspet	1807	B	20	36.6	12.7	4.9	J Sinclair
Earl of Seafield	1855	SK	33	45.3	13.9	7.7	J Sinclair
Findlater	1803	B	19	34.2	12.3	4.3	J Sinclair
Friendship	1806	B	17	34.6	12.0	4.6	J Sinclair
Findlater Seafield	1809	B	18	35.8	12.0	4.2	J Ross
Fame	1811	SP	24	37.5	13.1	5.7	J Ross
Friendship	1819	SP	23	38.1	12.8	5.6	
Friendship	1824	LR	24	39.9	12.8	5.4	J Ross
Friendship	1828	SP	23	38.0	12.8	5.6	
Frolic	1855	SP	22	50.1	14.1	6.0	
Fancy	1867	SK	26	48.0	14.9	6.8	Harthill
Galloper	1823	LR	19	36.6	11.1	4.1	J Sinclair
George	1827	SR	19	41.0	11.8	5.4	J Smith
Hawke	1825	LR	25	40.9	12.1	5.3	J Sinclair

Cullen (cont)

Heckler	1865	SK	19	45.2	13.3	5.8	Findlay
Isabella	1813	LR	21				
Industry	1822	LR	17	35.1	11.3	5.2	J Ross
Industry	1823	LR	23	39.4	12.7	5.4	J Sinclair
Jean	1819	SP	23	39.9	12.9	5.8	
Jane & Margaret	1823	LR	17	36.3	11.4	4.1	J Sinclair
Jumper	1824	LR	25	40.0	13.2	5.3	J Sinclair
Jumper	1824	LR	17	37.2	11.4	4.9	J Sinclair
John & Alexander	1829	SP	34	40.9	14.3	5.6	
James	1838	SK	38	44.0	14.1	8.3	J Smith
Jeans	1840	SR	82	61.4	17.2	10.2	J Smith
Jane Sinclair	1841	SR	108				
James Grant	1848	SK	17	48.5	14.5	5.4	
Jane	1883	K	40	64.5	19.7	7.3	Gardner
Lochineal	1823	LR	23	40.0	12.6	5.7	J Sinclair
Lion	1824	LR	25	40.4	13.3	5.5	J Sinclair
Lookout	1824	LR	17	37.3	11.0	4.1	J Sinclair
Lady Grant	1825	LR	18	38.6	11.4	5.6	J Sinclair
Margaret	1808	B	18	34.0	12.1	4.3	J Ross
Margaret	1820	LR	17	36.5	11.3	4.6	
Margaret & Jane	1823	LR	22	39.0	12.1	5.2	J Sinclair
Maggy Lauder	1823	LR	15	35.0	11.0	4.6	J Sinclair
Mary	1824	LR	17	35.5	11.7	5.1	J Sinclair
Margaret	1824	LR	21	39.7	12.2	4.6	J Ross
Margaret	1825	LR	16	35.6	11.3	5.2	A Skakel
Margaret	1826	SP	20	41.4	11.9	6.2	J Wilson
Margaret	1828	SK	39	43.7	15.1	8.2	J Sinclair
Mary Ann	1832	SP	30	38.4	14.5	6.6	
Rose	1822	LR	21	40.0	12.2	5.3	A Skakel
Rambler	1825	LR	24	39.6	12.6	5.6	A Skakel
Ranger	1825	LR	16	35.4	11.2	5.5	J Ross
Speedwell	1824	LR	17	37.6	11.0	5.2	J Sinclair
Swan	1845	SR	57	54.6	16.0	8.1	J Ross
Unity	1824	LR	27	39.6	12.3	5.3	
Williams	1844	SP	20	41.4	12.3	5.6	J Sinclair

FINDHORN

Name	Built	Rig	Tons	Dimensions			Builder
Ann	1793	SR	45	44.0	15.8	7.9	
Amelia	1827	SR	110	64.3	20.1	10.1	
Ann	1827	SP	35	42.8	14.1	8.2	
Ann Maria	1828	SR	73	98.6	23.5	11.2	
Ann	1855	SR	82	68.0	17.4	9.6	A Anderson
Amaranth	1873	SR	73	98.6	23.5	11.2	
Betsy	1831	SP	67	52.0	16.7	10.2	
Ceres	1839	SR	119	70.0	17.4	10.0	A Linton
Caledonia	1841	SR(H)	68	61.1	16.0	9.5	J Cook
Cornucopia	1865	SR	188	107.1	24.5	17.7	A Anderson
Diana	1817	SP	68	55.3	18.1	10.0	
Delight	1829	SR	91	60.4	19.0	10.9	
Earl of Moray	1839	SR	85	64.0	16.2	10.8	T Munro
Exile	1864	SR	200	105.4	24.5	13.4	A Anderson
Favourite	1807	SP	36	43.7	14.7	7.2	
Friendship	1814	SK	15				
Findhorn	1826	SW	150	77.6	21.2	4.6	
Forrest	1836	SP	39	44.0	14.4	9.3	
Forrester	1841	SR	57	53.4	14.9	9.2	A Linton
Gleaner	1844	DY	18	45.4	13.6	5.3	A Linton
Grace Milne	1846	SR	101	82.0	17.9	11.1	A Linton
Hero	1849	SP	25	44.0	12.3	7.3	R Allan
Isobel	1795	B	17	33.6	11.7	4.5	
Industry	1815	SP	52	48.1	16.9	8.10	K Femister
Janet	1801	SP	48	48.7	16.1	8.4	
Janet	1816	SP	49	48.2	16.2	8.0	
Johns	1827	SP	40	44.4	15.7	8.2	
James & Jessie	1833	SP	58	51.0	17.0	9.6	
James Ferguson	1856	SR	104	78.9	21.4	10.5	
Kinloss	1835	SR	117	73.3	18.4	11.1	Alex Linton
Margaret	1805	SP	65				
Margaret	1825	SP	34	43.0	14.0	6.5	
Mary Hill	1837	SP	25	38.0	12.4	9.0	R Robertson
Morayshire	1841	SR	72	60.0	16.7	9.9	A Linton
Maid of Moray	1842	SR	80	63.0	17.0	10.0	A Linton
Minnie of Mayfield	1866	BK	270	118.3	25.3	14.8	A Anderson
Novar	1828	SR	87	64.0	16.6	10.9	
Nomad	1867	SR	149	94.3	23.6	11.8	A Anderson
Princess	1841	SR	66	59.0	15.8	10.2	T Munro
Rose	1837	SP	34	43.0	14.4	8.3	
Rooftree	1860	SR	82	79.9	20.6	9.1	
Speedwell	1812	SP	35	44.0	14.3	5.11	J Hendry
Sir Wm Cumming	1824	SP	39	46.6	16.6	7.9	
Swift	1842	SR	124	88.0	18.9	11.3	A Linton
Snowflake	1866	SR	98	82.7	21.7	10.4	A Anderson
Thistle	1839	SP	37	47.0	13.6	8.4	T Munro
Tryst	1857	SR	61	65.9	18.6	8.8	
Violet	1893	SK	16	27.7	8.7	4.3	

INVERNESS	Built	Rig	Tons	Dimensions			Builder
Ann	1806	SK	77				
Ann & Margaret	1821	SP	43	41.7	15.6	8.2	
Adventure	1825	SP	27	36.6	14.0	5.9	
Alexander	1827	SP	50	46.0	15.1	8.7	
Ann	1831	SP	18	50.9	12.3	6.0	
Agnes & Barbara	1833	BG	67	52.9	16.1	10.1	
Ann McKay	1840	SR	47	49.4	15.8	8.8	A Munro
Augusta	1846	SR	88	66.0	17.3	10.4	J Cook
Aid	1852	SR	36	48.7	14.1	7.0	R Wright
Aeolus	1857	SR	112	84.0	20.9	10.6	
Africa	1859	SM	14	47.8	13.3	4.3	
Ardross	1864	SR	184	100.6	22.9	12.9	R Stewart
Altdownie	1867	BG	216	104.5	24.3	13.3	R Stewart
Borham	1818	SP	21	37.1	12.2	4.7	J Carstairs
Bonny Lass	1821	SP	28	42.0	14.8	7.3	
Bell Rock	1830	SP	37	47.0	15.3	7.6	
Bell Rock	1830	SP	25	38.0	12.4	9.0	R Robertson
Bonny Lass	1831	SP	37	40.3	14.5	7.7	
Barbara	1837	SK	30	42.8	14.0	7.8	A Munro
British Queen	1839	SR	95	65.8	18.2	11.2	A Munro
Belle	1840	SR	105				
Banff	1867	SR	234	109.1	24.4	13.9	Stewart Bros
Culloden	1797	SP	76				
Clachnacuddin	1826	SP	57	48.6	17.4	8.6	R Stewart
Caledonia	1827	SK	104	64.0	19.6	11.4	
Christian	1829	SR	19	42.3	12.1	6.1	
Catherine	1830	SP	37	47.6	14.1	7.0	
Christian	1831	SR	72	37.0	13.0	9.3	
Constitution	1837	SR	83	58.6	17.7	10.6	T Munro
Christian	1838	SR	90	63.6	18.0	10.3	
Christian	1841	SR	90	63.6	18.0	10.3	
Caledonia	1841	SR(H)	68	61.1	16.0	9.5	A Munro
Caroline	1844	SR	44	41.9	14.9	8.0	K Forbes
Czar	1860	SK	16	45.5	14.2	5.2	
Cantray	1863	SR	101	81.6	21.2	10.3	R Stewart
Clachnacuddin	1871	SR	224	173.2	25.3	13.6	R Stewart
Citadel	1879	SR	246	109.8	25.2	13.8	R Stewart
Delight	1829	SR	91				
Dunrobin	1838	SR	84	61.4	17.4	10.6	
David	1838	SR	77	59.6	16.7	10.1	J Cook
Edward & Jane	1825	SR	26	38.7	13.4	6.9	J Carstairs
Eleanor	1825	SP	17	32.9	11.1	7.0	
Elizabeth	1826	SR	85	59.0	18.6	10.9	
Eagle	1829	BG	112	62.3	20.1	11.4	A Munro
Enterprise	1842	SR(H)	115	75.2	19.4	11.0	J Cook
Favourite	1828	SP	25	41.5	14.2	7.2	J Cook
Fairly	1832	SP	33	43.0	15.1	8.1	J Cook
Farmer	1841	BG	80	60.0	17.7	9.8	A Munro
Favourite	1843	SR	73	54.1	18.1	9.1	
Fox	1848	SP	19	39.5	12.5	5.7	J Cook
Glenmoriston	1820	SR	83				
George	1836	SP	43	47.0	14.4	8.7	
Grace	1864	SR	99	78.7	21.2	10.4	R Stewart
Glenalbyn	1868	SR	208	104.0	24.0	13.4	R Stewart
George Reed	1878	SR	99	89.8	21.7	10.4	R Stewart
Hope	1806	SP	34				
Hope	1821	SP	32	43.0	14.0	5.4	

Inverness (cont)

Highland Chief	1849	SR	91	73.4	16.5	10.2	
Hilda	1879	SR	91	79.6	22.0	9.9	R Stewart
Inverness	1824	SR	81	59.9	18.0	10.2	
Isabella	1826	SR	82	56.7	18.1	10.4	
Industry	1846	SP	21	42.7	12.9	6.7	J Cook
Janet	1811	SP	22	37.0	12.6	4.6	J Patience
James	1826	SP	33	40.6	14.6	7.1	
Jean Geddes	1830	SP	28	39.0	13.9	6.1	A Munro
John Alexander	1834	SR	42	46.5	15.3	8.6	J Cook
Jane	1834	SR	25	42.3	12.4	7.0	
Jane	1838	SR	50	51.6	15.3	9.0	A Munro
Jessie Stephen	1839	SR	52				
Janet & Ann	1844	SR	19	40.0	12.3	5.7	
Janes	1847	SR	60	61.0	15.4	10.0	J Cook
James	1850	SR	110	73.1	18.6	11.0	R Wright
Kandy	1838	SP	15	34.6	12.1	5.0	J Cook
Lady Jane	1803	SP	25	38.4	12.8	7.2	
Lively	1817	SP	32	41.8	14.1	7.6	
Lively	1825	SP	32	42.8	14.1	7.6	
Lord Glenelg	1835	BG	161	74.0	23.0	13.0	
Leslie Cook	1837	SK	22	42.8	13.3	8.1	
Louisa	1852	SR	68				
Lochlee	1865	SR	247	115.0	24.0	14.0	R Stewart
Lochawe	1866	BK	264	125.2	25.4	12.7	R Stewart
Lochalsh	1873	SR	99	87.0	20.9	10.6	R Stewart
Mary Ann	1821	SP	51	46.0	16.8	7.3	
Mary Ann	1825	SP	35	43.2	15.7	7.7	
Mary Ann	1825	SP	26	40.0	13.2	5.1	H Allan
Margaret	1838	SK	15	39.2	12.0	6.0	D McLeod
Matilda	1842	SR	89				
Mermaid	1842	SP	17	42.4	9.7	6.4	
Margaret & Sarah	1843	SP	25	39.8	13.4	7.3	D Paterson
Maid	1843	SR	48	54.1	15.0	8.6	A Munro
Mary	1844	SR	13	34.4	12.3	4.6	R Fraser
Margaret	1851	SK	16	39.1	11.6	5.0	W Sutherland
Margaret	1853	SP	14	39.2	11.8	5.1	J Stephen
Moray	1866	BG	145	91.2	22.5	11.7	R Stewart
Nancy	1814	SP	52				
Ness	1819	SP	44	44.3	16.1	7.8	
Ness	1828	SK	58	51.4	16.3	9.2	
Nairnshire	1875	SR	99	85.2	21.0	10.4	R Stewart
Peace & Plenty	1807	SP	66	54.2	17.9	9.0	
Prince Albert	1840	SR	99	69.0	17.6	11.3	A Munro
Peace & Plenty	1840	SP	41	48.0	14.0	8.8	J Cook
Portland	1848	SR	76	60.2	17.1	10.0	J Cook
Penelope	1853	SK	13	40.8	17.1	4.3	J Cook
Recovery	1827	SP	21	39.7	13.1	6.0	
Reform	1832	SP	42	48.4	14.4	9.2	J Cook
Rose Hall	1840	SP	20	44.0	15.4	5.4	J Cook
Royal Tar	1842	SR(H)	60	60.6	16.9	10.0	A Munro
Rose Bud	1842	SR	71	67.5	18.0	10.4	A Munro
Rover Bride	1842	SK	17	34.4	14.4	6.5	J McDonald
Royal Burgh	1847	SK	15	34.7	12.9	4.4	J Cook
Rose Hall	1850	SK	19	53.2	14.1	4.2	W Bayne
Ranger	1863	WY	20	44.8	16.6	5.0	
Sophie & Isabella	1825	SP	63	54.1	17.1	8.1	
Stirling Castle	1838	SR	78	60.0	16.8	10.0	

Inverness (cont)

Sally Ann	1849	SR	58	62.1	16.1	9.2	R Wright
Snowdrop	1849	SR	34	52.0	19.8	6.9	J Cook
Stephens	1854	SP	36	48.5	15.8	7.4	J Stephen
Senator	1857	SR	99	69.1	18.2	10.2	R Wright
Sovereign	1877	SR	109	90.0	22.0	10.5	MacGregor
Two Sisters	1813	SP	22	38.0	12.6	4.6	J Patience
Thomas	1831	SP	40	42.0	15.6	7.0	
Trusty	1846	SP	21	42.7	12.9	6.11	
True Blue	1847	SK	16	45.3	15.1	4.2	
Thornbush	1859	SK	15	34.8	13.9	5.9	
Unaminity	1839	SR	132				
Vine	1831	SP	22	41.5	13.1	5.2	
Victoria	1834	SR	80	56.0	17.1	10.6	
Village Maid	1864	SR	139	87.7	22.3	11.8	R Stewart
Watson	1835		42	47.0	14.6	9.0	J Cook
Weasel	1841	SR	41	48.7	14.1	7.8	J McDonald
Wick Lassies	1865	SR	128	86.7	22.4	11.3	R Stewart

LOSSIEMOUTH

Ann Garrow	1856	SP	17	41.7	14.4	5.6	
Agnes	1859	SK	14	47.8	13.3	4.3	
Agnes	1859	SR	40	52.2	16.5	8.5	J Smith
Braes of Moray	1854	SR	99	75.5	18.5	5.6	Geddie
Barbara	1855	SP	35	52.3	15.5	7.5	
Betsy	1857	SP	20	42.2	11.8	6.0	W Scott
Brazilian	1869	SR	246	116.4	24.4	14.1	Jack
Beautiful Star	1873	SR	220	112.4	24.2	13.4	
Clansman	1855	SR	77	69.9	19.6	9.9	
Charter	1862	SR	79	74.5	20.1	9.4	
Chieftain	1868	SR	194	106.9	23.2	13.1	Jack
Elsie	1858	SR	76	74.9	19.9	9.3	
Eliza	1867	SR	217	107.4	24.6	13.4	Geddie
Farmers	1848	SP	19	41.1	12.4	5.5	G Campbell
Fidelity	1862	SK	43	56.0	17.2	8.1	
Helen & Mary	1858	SR	71	72.9	19.8	9.0	
Inch Broom	1856	SR	61	63.9	18.0	9.1	
Inverness	1862	SP	29	51.3	15.2	6.6	
Inverugie	1862	SK	30	52.8	14.7	6.6	
Jessie	1857	SR	71	68.8	19.6	9.4	
Jack	1863	SR	185	99.5	23.8	12.4	J Smith
Kate	1858	SR	79	78.3	20.0	9.4	
Louisa	1856	SP	34	51.0	15.5	7.7	
Lossie	1867	SR	87	77.0	20.9	10.0	Geddie
Murray	1855	SR	57	61.0	18.1	8.9	
Margaret Reid	1857	SR	100	79.0	21.4	10.5	
Margaret West	1862	SR	96	82.6	20.6	10.1	Wm Geddie
Ruby	1862	SR	86	78.8	20.2	9.7	Geddie
Robert Anderson	1867	SR	80	81.1	20.6	10.0	Jack
Pitcavney	1837	SP	41	48.0	14.0	8.0	J Bremner
Sailor	1860	SR	49	63.7	18.0	8.5	J Smith
Telegraph	1864	SP	17	40.6	13.5	5.4	

MACDUFF	Built	Rig	Tons	Dimensions			Builder
Anne	1804	SP	50	40.2	16.1	8.2	
Alexander	1816	SP	67	53.0	17.1	9.3	G Wilson
Abeona	1818	SR	68	55.4	16.4	10.2	J Hutcheon
Alpha	1826	SP	37	41.1	14.1	8.0	W Anderson
Albion	1849	SR	64	54.0	14.4	9.1	
Charming Betsy	1800	SP	59	52.3	16.1	8.4	
Caledonia	1805	SP	72	54.3	18.1	9.7	Anderson
Deveron	1840	SR	108	65.6	18.8	11.0	W Anderson
Flora	1801	SP	80	58.0	18.7	9.6	
Hope	1803	SP	49	47.2	16.2	7.1	Wm Wilson
Highlander	1860	SK	18	39.6	15.3	5.8	
Harvest Home	1885	LR	104	62.5	19.1	6.0	
Jean	1802	SP	73	56.1	18.1	9.8	
Jean	1803	BG	86	59.6	19.1	10.1	Wm Anderson
John & Mary	1823	SP	16	36.0	10.8	4.1	Wm Anderson
Katty	1786	SP	63	52.1	17.8	8.9	
Lady Abercrombie	1807	SP	52	49.5	16.6	7.4	W Anderson
MacDuff	1802	SP	102	64.9	19.1	9.1	
Minerva	1803	SP	75	56.4	18.5	9.3	W Anderson
MacDuff	1814	SR	102	65.0	19.1	9.1	
MacDuff	1821	SP	52	50.1	16.0	8.6	J Hutcheon
Mary	1829	SR	38	44.8	14.5	8.2	
Sisters	1848	SK	30	44.4	13.2	7.0	
Scotia	1849	SR	99	69.3	18.2	10.5	
Star of Hope	1883	LR	21	48.2	17.5	16.1	Duncan
Thetis	1801	SP	107	65.1	20.2	10.0	
Thomas	1815	SP	33	41.0	14.6	6.5	
Thistle	1828	SP	24	37.1	12.7	7.4	Wm Steel
Victoria	1839	SR	50	51.8	15.2	8.5	J Smith
Welcome Messenger	1824	SK	19	35.5	11.7	5.0	Wm Ross

NAIRN

	Built	Rig	Tons	Dimensions			Builder
Countess of Cawdor	1850	BG	125	83.3	21.0	11.2	Wm Anderson
George & Alexander	1842	SR	62	59.6	16.0	9.4	R McKenzie
Hope	1811	SR	94	60.8	19.9	10.6	W Logie
Henrietta	1819	SP	25	39.6	13.9	5.4	J Forbes
Haidee	1852	SR	27	46.0	12.4	6.7	
John & Margaret	1841	SP	28	40.5	14.3	7.0	J Main
Lady Louisa Stewart	1850	SR	90	68.6	18.2	9.7	W Anderson
Mary	1854	SP	21	43.8	13.1	5.5	G Fraser
Margaret & Elizabeth	1856	SR	107	80.2	20.1	10.4	H & A Mann
Nairnshire	1840	SR	63	48.0	15.8	9.6	J Wilson

	Built	Rig	Tons	Dimen sions			Builder
PORTSOY							
Agenora	1814	SR	57				
Agnes Smith	1859	SR	64	63.3	18.8	9.6	
Adelaide Moir	1876	SR	92	80.7	20.9	10.0	Smith & Ritchie
Brittania	1855	SR	57	59.5	19.0	9.5	J Smith
Blossom	1862	SR	112	66.7	18.7	11.7	J Smith
Christian	1792	SP	74	36.2	13.1	4.2	
Caledonia	1856	SR	70	65.8	18.8	9.7	J Smith
Camilia	1877	SR	91	76.4	21.2	10.0	Smith & Ritchie
Colonel Moir	1884	DY	30	56.0	16.8	7.2	Wood
Flower o' Portsoy	1875	SR	75	72.1	19.7	9.6	Smith
James & Alexander	1838	SP	33	42.5	13.8	7.7	J Smith
Jane Rose	1877	SR	77	73.1	19.6	9.7	Smith & Ritchie
Kitty	1815	SR	105				
Lily	1878	SR	74	76.6	21.0	9.6	Smith & Ritchie
Penelope	1793	SP	36	33.0	14.8	6.6	Walter Logie
Patriot	1839	BG	99	63.6	12.4	11.0	J Smith
Renown	1866	SR	167	97.2	24.0	17.2	J Smith
Reliance	1871	SR	83	73.6	22.3	10.5	H Milne
Scotia	1854	SR	67	63.0	16.3	9.3	J Smith
Sweet Home	1861	SR	77	76.4	19.1	10.2	
Scottish Maid	1864	SR	98	81.3	21.0	10.2	J Smith
Union Grove	1858	BG	141	89.0	24.0	11.4	J Smith
ROSEHEARTY							
Barbara	1785	SP	20	36.4	17.1	4.4	
Christian	1786	B	18	34.1	11.7	4.1	
Elizabeth	1801	SP	25	37.4	13.1	4.1	
Friendship	1804	SP	25	36.0	13.6	4.2	Wm Gordon
Isobel	1802	SP	53	50.1	16.6	8.1	
Jean	1801	SP	25	37.2	14.5	4.1	
John	1803	SP	65	53.6	17.6	'8.8	Wm Gordon
Katty Ann	1798	SP	18	34.7	11.8	3.8	
Margaret	1786	SP	36	42.4	14.9	7.3	Wm Gordon
Rose Hall	1823	LR	23	38.9	12.1	5.3	
Saltoun	1801	SP	18	30.1	11.9	3.8	
Three Brothers	1807	SP	26	38.9	13.3	5.0	Wm Gordon
SANDEND							
Bondie	1841	SR	55	57.8	15.0	9.8	J Smith
Bloom	1844	SR	42	49.3	14.1	8.0	J Smith
Boyne Castle	1847	SK	23	41.0	12.3	6.6	J Smith
Betsy	1848	SR	91	66.3	17.8	10.5	J Smith
Binn	1872	SK	22	49.4	16.8	5.9	H Milne
Earl of Seafield	1833	SP	40	40.8	14.9	7.1	
Eliza Forbes	1856	BG	162	84.5	22.2	13.1	J Smith
Friendship	1827	B	27	36.0	14.5	5.0	A Johnston
Fidelity	1856	SR	71	64.0	19.3	9.6	J Smith
Forbeses	1879	DY	24	55.1	17.0	5.9	
Hero	1849	SR	54	53.4	16.1	8.2	
Industry	1786	B	25	35.1	16.7	5.0	
Industry	1842	SK	22	36.5	12.1	6.8	
Jane Smith	1846	SR	99	67.0	18.0	10.3	J Smith
Lord Reidhaven	1843	SR	50	57.3	14.3	8.3	
Margaret Woods	1854	SP	39	47.0	13.8	8.3	J Smith
Portsoy	1828	SP	38	47.2	14.0	8.1	
Rose	1850	SR	43	51.6	14.5	8.2	

SMALL PORTS	Built	Rig	Tons	Dimensions			Builder
Avoch							
Gracie	1810	SP	31	41.8	17.2	5.5	
Rosehaugh	1841	SR	80	58.6	15.6	10.9	D Davidson
Beauly							
Sarah	1839	SP	25	46.5	13.0	7.6	D McKay
Industry	1844	SR	83	65.4	7.2	10.3	
Muirton	1844	SP	19	40.2	12.4	6.4	J McLennan
Lady Lovat	1845	SR	89	67.5	16.5	10.6	W Drake
Industry	1847	SP	19	44.5	13.0	5.1	J McLennan
Belleport							
Minerva	1841	SR	89	63.1	17.2	11.1	J Hall
Lady Ross	1842	SR	79	62.0	17.6	10.1	J Hall
Ann	1843	SR	66	57.2	17.0	9.7	J Hall
Dingwall							
Friendship	1827	SP	24	37.6	12.6	6.6	
Seaforth	1834	SR(H)	94	62.3	18.6	10.4	
Elizabeth McKenzie	1842	SP	23	33.3	12.9	6.6	H McKenzie
Findochty							
Findlater	1801	B	15	30.1	11.4	4.5	
Friendship	1814	SK	15				
Union	1848	SK	15	38.9	17.0	5.3	
Fortrose							
Osprey	1862	SP	16	43.4	13.5	5.0	
Fowles							
Industry	1832	SP	23	39.7	11.6	6.7	J Cook
Fowles	1833	BG	109	64.6	20.2	11.4	J Cook
Fochabers							
Marchioness of Huntly	1817	SK	27				
Gardenstown							
Peggy	1786	B	16	33.6	11.7	4.2	W Stephen
Rose	1786	SP	53	47.9	16.5	8.4	
Brothers	1799	SP	76	54.2	18.7	9.5	
Mayflower	1801	SP	25	37.0	13.3	6.4	
Lady Abercrombie	1809		52				
Friendship	1812	SP	29				
Black Boar	1823	SK	17	33.9	11.8	4.8	
George	1823	SP	58	50.9	17.1	7.1	Dockar
Hopeman							
Drunman	1841	SR	71	64.8	17.2	9.9	J Hendry
Findhorn	1843	SP	14	40.0	12.2	4.6	R Allan
Dalvey	1852	SP	23	42.0	12.0	6.6	A Anderson
Isabella Anderson	1852	SP	28	45.0	12.9	6.7	A Anderson
John William	1864	SK	22	42.6	14.8	6.3	
Brothers	1877	SK	36	49.0	18.2	6.9	
Invergordon							
Catharine	1840	SR	83	60.8	16.4	10.4	J Hall
Woodman	1855	SP	15	41.0	13.4	4.8	
Kessock							
Lady Jean	1803	SP	30	39.4	14.4	6.1	
Alex McKenzie	1850	SK	14	40.5	12.0	5.1	
Lady McKenzie	1850	SK	14	40.5	12.0	5.1	A McKenzie
James	1857	SP	18	40.7	14.5	5.6	
Meikle Ferry							
Catharine	1830	SP	25	38.6	13.6	5.5	
Jane Arnott	1843	SP	14	38.7	12.0	5.4	D McKenzie

Munlochy								
	Mary	1821	SP	23	37.0	13.0	5.4	
Portgordon								
	Hero	1844	SK	18	39.6	11.8	6.1	J Geddes
	Sister	1846	SK	27	44.7	12.4	7.1	J Gordon
	Fortune	1853	SK	17	37.5	11.9	6.0	
	Brave	1856	SK	17	40.0	13.2	5.8	
	Braes of Enzie	1857	SR	66	62.8	20.1	9.1	
	Pedestrian	1857	SR	75	69.8	20.4	9.6	
	Catharine & Charles	1859	SK	24	43.6	15.5	6.9	
	Ocean Star	1859	SR	56	66.0	20.1	8.8	J Geddes
Portessie								
	Friendship	1803	B	19	34.4	12.3	4.6	
	Heather Bloom	1823	LR	18	36.5	11.6	4.1	G Campbell
	Janet	1824	LR	18	35.1	11.6	5.2	G Campbell
	Fairly	1825	LR	19	38.0	12.0	4.1	
	James & Margaret	1856	SK	14	42.2	13.3	6.0	
Portlick								
	Mary	1820	SR	22	38.0	12.1	3.1	
Portnocky								
	Hope	1825	LR	17	36.7	11.5	5.2	
Ross-shire								
	Henry	1782	BG	51				
	Thomas & Mary	1790	SP	40				Sanderson
Rosemarkie								
	Salmon	1830	SP	26	43.0	13.2	5.1	
	Gnarl	1832	SP	22	41.0	14.7	5.2	J Munro
	Michael Miller	1834	SP	27	42.0	14.1	6.7	J Munro
	Louisa	1852	SR	69	59.8	16.3	9.7	J Cook
Whitehills								
	Northern Maid	1844	SR	84	63.3	17.0	10.1	J Watson
	Friends	1848	SR	44	58.0	15.8	7.8	

INDEX